D1002798

UNSETTLED
EXPECTATIONS

UNSETTLED EXPECTATIONS
Uncertainty, Land and Settler Decolonization

EVA MACKEY

FERNWOOD PUBLISHING
HALIFAX & WINNIPEG

Copyright © 2016 Eva Mackey

All rights reserved. No part of this book may be reproduced or transmitted in
any form by any means without permission in writing from the publisher,
except by a reviewer, who may quote brief passages in a review.

Editing: Penelope Jackson
Cover image: "Generations" used with permission of artist, Jane Ash Poitras
Cover design: John van der Woude
The poem "Even after Everything" by Robin Kimmerer
is reprinted with permission of the author.
Printed and bound in Canada

Published by Fernwood Publishing
32 Oceanvista Lane, Black Point, Nova Scotia, B0J 1B0
and 748 Broadway Avenue, Winnipeg, Manitoba, R3G 0X3
www.fernwoodpublishing.ca

This book has been published with the help of a grant from the Federation for the
Humanities and Social Sciences, through the Awards to Scholarly Publications Program,
using funds provided by the Social Sciences and Humanities Research Council of Canada.

Fernwood Publishing Company Limited gratefully acknowledges the financial support of
the Government of Canada through the Canada Book Fund, the Manitoba Department
of Culture, Heritage and Tourism under the Manitoba Publishers Marketing Assistance
Program and the Province of Manitoba, through the Book Publishing Tax Credit, for
our publishing program. We are pleased to work in partnership with the Province of
Nova Scotia to develop and promote our creative industries for the benefit of all Nova
Scotians. We acknowledge the support of the Canada Council for the Arts, which last
year invested $153 million to bring the arts to Canadians throughout the country.

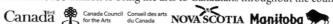

Library and Archives Canada Cataloguing in Publication

Mackey, Eva, 1956-, author
Unsettled expectations : uncertainty, land and settler
decolonization / Eva Mackey.

Includes bibliographical references and index.
Issued in print and electronic formats.
ISBN 978-1-55266-889-4 (paperback).--ISBN 978-1-55266-898-6
(epub).--ISBN 978-1-55266-899-3 (kindle)

1. Indians of North America--Land tenure. 2. Indians of
North America--Claims. 3. Indians of North America--Legal status,
laws, etc. 4. Decolonization--Canada. 5. Decolonization--United
States. I. Title.

E98.L3M32 2016   333.2   C2016-903189-6
                   C2016-903190-X

CONTENTS

Dedicated to Eleanor Mackey,
who always embraced life with creative uncertainty.
1932 – 2014

ACKNOWLEDGEMENTS

This book took many years to research and write, and on that journey I have grown indebted to many, many people. I would like to start by thanking all the people who spoke with me and whom I interviewed while doing research for this book. I especially thank Brooke Hansen, Bernadette (Birdie) Hill, Frieda Jacques, Ada Jacques, Andy Mager, Ernie Olson, Irving Powless, Jack Rossen, Julie Uticone, and Jim Uticone. I am also thankful to the many others who wished to remain unnamed.

I want to give special thanks for warm friendship, careful reading, and brilliant comments on early drafts to Jennifer Henderson, Davina Bhandar, Julie Marcus, Allison Mackey, and Samah Sabra. I am deeply thankful to Michael Asch for urging me to think about jurisdiction and other important things. I have been sustained and propped up by friends and family, and am so grateful for your support over the years, no matter how many kilometers have kept us apart: thank you Rahnuma Ahmed, Shahidul Alam, Natasha Ballen, Keith Denny, Jasmin Habib, Sal Houghton, Mike Ma, Robin Peace, Tracy Porteous, Becki Ross, Pat Williams, Judy Millen, Clarke Mackey, Doug Mackey, Elly Mackey, Ariel de Leon-Mackey, Mateo de Leon-Mackey and Gustavo de Leon. I am always thankful to my ever-supportive and inspirational mentors from long ago at Sussex: Susan Wright and Brian Street.

For their energy and passion about these issues, I thank the superb MA and PhD students I have been fortunate to work with over the years: Robyn Green, Kelly Black, Charlotte Hoelke, Diana Cullen, Shaun Stevenson and students in the "Decolonizing Canada" graduate seminar since 2010. I also thank research assistant Nicki Thorne. I so appreciate the support I received from my superb colleagues at McMaster Department of Anthropology (especially Harvey Feit and Matthew Cooper), and my wonderful colleagues at the Carleton School of Indigenous and Canadian Studies, especially my friends Jennifer Adese, Kahente Horn-Miller,

Anne Trépanier and Cathy Schmueck. I am particularly thankful for the unfailing support of the School Director, Peter Hodgins, who ensured I had time and space to finish this book.

For helpful comments on papers I have presented on this research, I'd also like to thank workshop and panel participants at two BRCSS Virtual Seminars at Massey University, New Zealand, in 2011, especially Avril Bell; the "Crabgrass Gang" for feedback at the workshop in Victoria in 2008; participants in the McMaster Centre for Globalization and the Human Condition workshop in 2007; and members of Department of Educational Anthropology, Danish University of Pedagogy, Copenhagen, Denmark, in 2005. I am thankful for the comments from the anonymous reviewers of earlier drafts, most especially for the perceptive and generous commentaries from the Fernwood reviewers. I also want to give special thanks to Robin Wall Kimmerer for permission to include her poem as the epilogue.

I wish to acknowledge the financial support I have received from the Social Sciences and Humanities Research Council of Canada, McMaster University, and the Fulbright Scholarship Commission.

Some of the material in this book was previously published in portions of essays and book chapters, and is reprinted with permission here. Publications include: "Unsettling Expectations: (Un)certainty, Settler States of Feeling, Law, and Decolonization," *Canadian Journal of Law and Society / Revue Canadienne Droit et Société* (2014) 29: 235–252; "Competing or relational autonomies? Globalization, Property and Friction Over Land Rights." In William D. Coleman (ed.) *Property, Territory, Globalization: Struggles over Autonomy* (2011), pp. 148-171, Vancouver: UBC Press; and "'Universal' Rights in National and Local Conflicts: 'Backlash' and 'Benevolent Resistance' to Indigenous Land Rights," *Anthropology Today* (2005) 21, 2:14–20.

Words are not sufficient to communicate my appreciation to Candida Hadley, extraordinary editor, Penelope Jackson, superb copyeditor, and others at Fernwood Publishing. And finally, and as always, to Mary Millen.

Part One

CONTACT ZONES AND THE SETTLER COLONIAL PRESENT

INTRODUCTION

Settler Colonialism
and Contested Homelands

The wave of panic in Chatham-Kent, Ontario, began in December 1998 when the Canadian federal government announced that it had made an "Agreement in Principle" with the Caldwell First Nation to resolve its outstanding land claim near Blenheim, Ontario. If the Caldwell members approved the agreement, the First Nation would receive $23.4 million to purchase 4,500 acres of land over 25 years on the "open market," land that could eventually be designated a reserve. When the government called a public town hall meeting in Blenheim to discuss the agreement with "local citizens," more than 2,500 people came out, and the meeting was volatile and uproarious. Many people attending shouted at the government speakers, claiming that they had not been consulted; others yelled that a reserve would drive up land prices and destroy local farming. Some residents passed around a petition asking Ottawa "not to allow a new reserve in the area," a petition they said "more than two-thirds" of the people at the meeting signed (Crouch 1998). According to one reporter, only two Native people were visible at the meeting, and there was no presentation by the Caldwell Band. However, three Ontario Provincial Police officers were on hand for crowd control (Crouch 1998). Several people told me afterwards that one of the most striking moments of the meeting occurred when a woman from the area, Jackie Gladstone, stood up in the audience in the midst of jeers and yelling. She tearfully apologized to her neighbours for mistakenly selling a piece of land to "the Natives." She said she had not known they were "Natives" or that they were starting a reserve.

Immediately after the meeting, a group called Chatham-Kent Community Network (CKCN) formed to counter the land claim. They printed signs saying "NOT

FOR SALE," organized local meetings, wrote reports and letters to newspapers, sent submissions to government and politicians, hired lawyers and went to court to contest the claim. They also set up a "land development" company to "protect" farmers by preventing land sales to the Caldwell First Nation.

Around the same time, opposition to the Cayuga Nation land claim was reaching a peak in Union Springs and Seneca Falls, in upper New York State. The Cayuga Nation had reclaimed 64,000 acres on the northern edge of Lake Cayuga, on the basis of an illegal treaty made by New York State. The backlash to their land rights case, organized by a group called Upstate Citizens for Equality (UCE), was volatile, and all over the area, handmade signs sprouted against the claim. In 1999, UCE organized a well-attended car rally protesting the land claim. Hundreds of people in decorated cars gathered in a supermarket parking lot. Like a Fourth of July festival, people were dressed in stars and stripes outfits and huge American flags flew everywhere. Vehicles were decorated with handmade signs including: "United we stand—the land of the free," "Equal rights under the law," and "We are native Americans."

When the 20-mile rally route ended in a farmer's field, participants raised an American flag, "pledged allegiance" with hands on hearts and sang the national anthem, all while looking upwards towards the fluttering flag. The Master of Ceremonies then introduced eight marksmen for the "64-shotgun salute." He said: "Of course the highest salute you can get militarily is the 21-gun salute, but this is for our 64,000 acres that are under claim, unjustly! We should be able to own it after residing on it for 204 years." The crowd then cheered as the eight marksmen fired 64 shots into the air.

I use these events to begin this book because, as examples from the sites in which I carried out fieldwork about local conflict about land rights, they exemplify the volatile nature of the images, ideas and emotions that come into play in conflicts about Indigenous[1] land rights in North America. Land rights conflicts in settler nations pivot on the profound and foundational tension between national and settler expectations of entitlement to the land, and the repeated and longstanding assertions by Indigenous peoples that these lands were most often taken without their consent and that they are still their territories.

Images of land rights as dangerous to local people and, more broadly, as a risk to the unity and equality of nations, recur in all of these conflicts. Why do protesters against Indigenous land rights, in Canada and the United States, so often sing the national anthem? How do warlike images of "standing on guard" for the nation (including ritual gunshots in New York) figure in anti–land rights sentiment? Why and how do land rights—which challenge long-standing relationships between Indigenous and non-Indigenous people as well as the "progress" and mythologized history of nation-states—unearth deep-seated desires and brutal angers? What are the shapes this resistance takes? What kinds of self-evident ideas and histories inflect them?

Unsettled Expectations is a critical multi-site ethnography that examines conflict over Indigenous land rights in Canada and the United States as a lens through which to understand historical and ongoing relationships between Indigenous and non-Indigenous peoples in settler colonies. The goal of the research is to try to understand the lived practices and discourses of people defending and countering Indigenous land rights—as a grounded point of departure to examine the limits and possibilities of decolonization. It focuses on struggles over land because in this way attention is directed to foundational conceptual and material dilemmas in settler nations, dilemmas deeply interlaced with historical, cultural and economic issues. It forces confrontation with legacies of colonial pasts and the possibilities and limits of imagining and building decolonized futures. As Cole Harris (2004, 168) points out, the "experienced materiality of colonialism" is grounded in "dispossessions and repossessions of land." Indeed, "the actual geographical possession of land is," according to Said (1994, 78), what "empire in the final analysis is all about." Colonial and national struggles for possession of Indigenous land were, and continue to be, material conflicts that dispossess Indigenous peoples for the benefit of others in settler nation-states. But that process was not only about guns, laws and boundaries. It was also necessarily about ideas and concepts that enabled and legitimized that dispossession: a range of complex and often contradictory ideas about progress, property, entitlement, categories of personhood and relationships between different peoples. My research documents how these ideas and practices cannot be contained in an historical past. As I explore in this book, they live on today in adapted yet strikingly similar form: in law, government policy, the media and in the angry and passionate discourses of people who oppose land rights. They are also, as my research discusses, actively being challenged.

Settler colonialism is a particular form of European colonialism "premised on land acquisition and population *replacement*" (Pasternak 2014, 147). Unlike colonialists in South Asia and most of Africa, settlers in Canada and the U.S. [and Australia and New Zealand] did not go back to live in their colonial metropoles. Rather, "they stayed, seeking eventually to replace Indigenous societies with their own" (Pasternak 2014, 147). Settlers build "self-sustaining" states, nations and legal systems that are "organized around settlers' [ongoing] political domination over the Indigenous population" (Weitzer 1990, in Pasternak 2014) as well as over immigrants who are imported as labour by the settler nation. These immigrants later become encompassed (although they are still racialized) in the ideologies of settler nations during 20th century re-inventions of national identities through ideologies of multiculturalism (Canada and Australia) and the "melting pot" (United States). Despite ideologies of cultural pluralism, struggle over territory is central because, as Simpson (2011, 211) argues: "Settler colonialism is predicated on a territorial possession by some and, thus, a dispossession of others. In this model of colonialism, "the settler never leaves," so the possession of territory requires the disappearance of 'the native'" (Wolfe 1999, 2006).

Conflict over Indigenous land rights indicates that the "Native," however, did not disappear as planned. Land rights conflicts are therefore deeply *embodied, grounded*, and *material* disputes that are also about interpretations of history, justice and identity, because they raise the difficult question of who is entitled to ownership of the national homeland. The conflicts I discuss in this book inspire confrontations with problematic questions about what *home* means in settler colonial societies. Such questions about home, I suggest, may help us to understand more deeply the limits and the possibilities of Indigenous-settler relationships. Indigenous people in settler nations make particular claims for recognition based on "their status as *colonized* people—people dispossessed in their own homelands. Thus the very survival of indigenous cultures depends on their survival as a people 'at *home*'" (Bell 2008, 851), *home* in the lands that settlers now own and call home, in nations built upon the appropriation of those very homelands. Contemporary claims for land and culture cannot be separated from demands for recognition of past injustices, which means colonial and national pasts—how those lands were taken—inevitably live *in* the present. Questions about home, then, raise subsequent, necessary queries about past *and* present injustice and about property, possession and dispossession. The question of who calls settler nations home is, as Moreton-Robinson (2003, 27) writes, "inextricably connected to who has possession, and possession is jealously guarded" by non-Indigenous settlers.

Unsettled Expectations emerges from my repeated observation that, despite differences, there are remarkable similarities in the kind of dissent and conflict about Indigenous land rights that settler nations have experienced over the last 30 to 40 years. I noticed these themes first when I was in Australia, after the momentous "Wik decision," when aboriginal land rights were finally a consideration and some expressed fears that "Aborigines" would invade backyards in Sydney and Melbourne (Mackey 1999a). For Canadians, simply the mention of placenames such as "Oka," "Caledonia," "Burnt Church" and "Ipperwash" evokes familiar images of violence and passionate conflict. *Time Canada* noted in 1999 that across Canada, "flash points of irritation and hostility are erupting as non-natives struggle to come to terms with the most sweeping and comprehensive social adjustment in the country's history: the attempt to bring justice and legal closure to the frustrated claims of Aboriginal people." The media use common-sense language to describe what they often call "roadblocks," "occupations," or "blockades," guarded by "masked warriors," who almost always appear in photographs looking ferocious, waving flags or large sticks. Indigenous peoples and their supporters, on the other hand, often call these actions "reclamations." While they have undertaken high-profile direct actions and negotiations to highlight their historical entitlements, there has been a simultaneous increase in local and national groups protesting that no one should have "special" rights within nations. Increasingly since the attacks to the World Trade Centre in 2001, Indigenous protestors are depicted as "terrorists" whose actions "threaten national unity" and/or "security" (Adese 2012a; Wakeham 2012; Diabo and Pasternak 2011; Monaghan and Walby 2012; Monaghan 2013).

The Canadian government recently passed Bill C-51, an anti-terrorism bill that many Indigenous groups argue will further criminalize Indigenous peoples' activism in defense of their territories against resource extraction. In the United States, until recently many tribes were offered casino deals for their land rights. Indian leaders are often presented as money-hungry capitalists, manipulating their special rights for high financial returns. They are often seen as un-American because they go against the creed of "one nation, under god." Meanwhile, statewide and national coalitions of organizations and pressure groups mobilize against land rights for Indian tribes, in the name of "equality."

Unsettled Expectations emerges from over a decade of ethnographic research on local conflict about Indigenous land rights in Canada and the U.S. I have interviewed government employees responsible for land rights, and engaged in participant observation and interviewed people on all sides of a number of land rights conflicts that often come to blows at local levels.[2] I have carried out several intensive case studies that form the ethnographic core of this book. The case studies and examples become lenses through which I develop a broader yet empirically grounded critical discussion of how colonial ideas and practices influence settler-Indigenous relations, and how they can be challenged.

I started this research because, as a settler-Canadian,[3] I wanted to understand, in a more complex, nuanced and historicized manner, how and why the same events and processes could be experienced and explained so differently by people who inhabit the same territory, and yet who are socially located in very different ways in terms of power, history and space. How and why can so many non-Indigenous people see assertions of Indigenous "rights" as "invasion" of their lands, or even "terrorism"? How do legal frameworks, enacted nationally, regionally and locally actually function in the context of land claims? Who uses law and how? What are the effects? In the context of such conflict over history, colonialism and contemporary Indigenous land rights, how might we imagine de-colonized and just versions of citizenship, belonging and space? Can we really imagine de-colonizing "our home" *on* "Native land"[4] (now seen as property) when property, power and history are so contested? What gets in the way? How might it be possible for diverse peoples, with complex and overlapping histories of injustice and collusion, to live together justly, when history, property and the division of lands, resources and power are so contested? What gets in the way of decolonizing relationships *and* territorial spaces? How is it possible to even imagine a collective project of diverse people living together in a settler colony in a way that does not reproduce the brutal and subtle violence of ongoing colonialism, modernity and capitalism? This question, lately often framed as how to "decolonize" settler nations, has no definitive answer (Tuck and Yang 2012). But can we even begin to imagine what it might entail? This book is an exploratory examination of such issues that builds from ethnographic research on communities experiencing conflict over land rights.

LAND, PROPERTY, HISTORY AND THE EMERGENCE OF "SETTLER STRUCTURES OF FEELING"

My case studies include the conflict over the land rights case of the Caldwell First Nation in Southwestern Ontario, Canada, including members of the group fighting the land agreement, the Chatham-Kent Community Network (CKCN). At the time, the Caldwell Agreement-in-Principle proposed to resolve the specific land claim by buying land for sale on "the open market." The Caldwell could, after purchasing enough land, then apply for reserve status. During fieldwork, signs produced by the CKCN stating "NOT FOR SALE" were ubiquitous, posted on farms, homes and businesses in the area. In New York State I researched the land rights cases of the Cayuga Indian Nation and the Onondaga Nation, including interviews with members of the anti–land rights group "Upstate Citizens for Equality," as well as the solidarity groups SHARE (Strengthening Haudenosaunee-American Relations Through Education) and NOON (Neighbours of the Onondaga Nation).

I conceptualize the ethnographic sites of conflict over land rights as "contact zones" (Pratt 1992, 6) of ongoing practices of settler colonialism within which I could explore structures and practices that maintain and challenge colonialism, as well as the construction of settler subjectivities. For Pratt, a "contact zone" is a space of colonial encounter "in which peoples geographically and historically separated come into contact with each other and establish ongoing relations, usually involving conditions of coercion, radical inequality, and intractable conflict." Contemporary land rights conflict is a conceptual and material continuation of those earlier attempts to "establish ongoing relations." Although settler nations tried to *settle* "ongoing relations" through ideologies and laws that produce Australia, Canada, the U.S. and Aotearoa/New Zealand as settled, secure and legitimate national spaces—and not *un*settled colonial "contact zones"—ongoing conflict over land rights indicates that the process remains "unsettled."

As I carried out interviews and research, I found that people who rejected land rights often defended their own rights to land by mobilizing concepts, frameworks and feelings that were powerfully familiar. Similar to the ideas I heard in Australia during my research there in the 1990s (Mackey 1999a, 1999b), the people I interviewed in North America consistently referred to the threats and dangers of land rights to the nation and to a deep sense of entitlement and a supposedly natural right (even a responsibility) to own and develop property/land, even if it may have been taken from Indigenous people. They felt they had laboured and improved the land and helped build the nation and that they were entitled to their private property. On these grounds, they felt certain of their entitlement to the land and expected it to be ongoing and unchallenged. They also consistently expressed powerful feelings of uncertainty, crisis and anxiety about the future within the context of the land claims. They felt angry about this uncertainty, treating it as unexpected and unfair. The angry uncertainty as a result of Indigenous land rights, I suggest in this book, is a result of having those expectations of ongoing entitlement challenged. The anger implicitly constructs an opposite normative state of affairs in which settlers and the settler nation-state did, or believed it did, have certain and settled entitlement to the land taken from Indigenous peoples. These are what I call the "settled expectations" that have been unsettled as a result of land rights.

The angry sense of ongoing entitlement led me to the question of how, on what grounds, do settlers feel entitled, settled and certain about their right to own and control the territory? How is it possible for the colonizers to claim to have stronger and more legitimate sovereignty over the territory, simply through arriving and asserting the claim, despite the vibrant collectivities of Indigenous people living there who did not consent to the land being taken and owned in this way? Why are Indigenous sovereign nations forced to "claim" land from the nation-state when it was theirs in the first place? Is it a matter of relying on our nations' numerical and/ or state "power to justify our legitimacy" (Asch 2014, 6)? On what grounds can and do settler nations claim such all-encompassing sovereignty? These questions propel this book.

SETTLED AND UNSETTLED EXPECTATIONS

Legal decisions in the U.S. in the last several years have also more explicitly reasserted the logic of the "settledness" of settler entitlement, for example, when the concept of "settled expectations" became central to the landmark decision in the *Sherrill vs. Oneida* case in the Second Circuit Court of Appeals in 2005. It argued that Oneida land rights would disrupt the reasonable "settled expectations" of the other residents of the area. In this book, then, I explore how it is made possible, materially and conceptually, for the legal, political and cultural defence of the "settled expectations" of current inhabitants (descendants of those who deliberately *unsettled* Indigenous nations over centuries), to almost always supersede the just desires of Indigenous nations for recognition of their historic rights to their land. I follow the messy and complex career of some of these ideas, mapping them through their earlier incarnations in the colonial Western philosophical frameworks of Hobbes (1651) and Locke (1690), to their life in legal frameworks such as the "Doctrine of Discovery," *terra nullius* and other more recent versions of settler sovereignty that are now embedded in national legal systems and land claims policies. These ideas were based on a notion of unquestioned European sovereignty over the land at the moment of contact, despite the presence of complex Indigenous societies living on/with that land. I explore aspects of the centuries-long processes that normalized the settled expectations of some subjects and refused the just desires of others. The book is called *Unsettled Expectations* because it explores what happens when settler colonial expectations of entitlement become deeply unsettled, as they have in recent years.

While "settled expectations" is a term used in the legal case mentioned above, here I employ it as a metaphor for the conceptual frameworks that I discuss in the first part of the book. I explore how legal, institutional and cultural processes support the idea that the settler nation is entitled to the land, and examine how non-Indigenous people and governments often unconsciously and unintentionally employ and embody common-sense colonial paradigms and relations. As I track in Part One of this book, Western philosophy, law and land claims policy have all sought, in distinct and flexible ways, to attain certainty in "settled expectations" for settler projects. For example, the Crown and the nation-state's legitimacy are based on the legal assumption (or as I call it, the "fantasy of entitlement") that their sovereignty is necessarily superior, stronger and deeper than any claims of Indigenous people because *underlying title* belongs to the Crown. This is settler law, even if such claims have not been proven or if Indigenous people are not themselves "reconciled" to that interpretation. This is settler certainty, both assumed and defended with philosophy, law, legislation and bureaucratic policy.

FANTASIES OF ENTITLEMENT

In this book I use the term "entitlement" in a particular way. In the present, the term "entitled" is commonly used to describe an individual with a particular attitude or sensibility, communicating that they perceive themselves as deserving of a particular kind of treatment by others, or even in the world. I am using it in a slightly different way, more specifically in terms of a longstanding, structured, collective privilege. In this sense it is more akin to class because it has been socially legitimized as a "right" to land and other privileges, historically and in the present, through colonial and national projects. In terms of entitlement, whether it be the "settlement thesis"[5] that underlies Canada's claim to Native land, Australia's "doctrine of *terra nullius*" or the U.S. "Doctrine of Discovery," a key assumption underlying most laws that address Indigenous rights to land in settler nations is that the sovereignty of the "modern" state will always trump "customary" or "common-law" Indigenous rights.

For example, the Canadian Constitution of 1982 states that "Aboriginal people" have an inherent right to self-government. Yet, as pivotal court decisions since 1982 have interpreted these *inherent* rights, they only exist as long as they can be *"reconciled with"* Crown sovereignty (Borrows 2002, 8). In law, Indigenous people must adapt, adjust and conform to the primacy of state sovereignty. As Michael Asch puts it,

> In the final analysis, Canada still rests its foundational legitimacy on the ideology and legal reasoning of English colonialism. The lynchpin of this ideology and legal regime is the firm conviction that the acquisition of sovereignty, legislative authority, and underlying title by the crown is unproblematic even without the agreement of the Indigenous peoples on whose territories we settled. (Asch 2007, 110)

In other words, the nation-state's legitimacy is based on the legal assumption that its claim to sovereignty is necessarily superior, stronger and deeper than any assertions of Indigenous people because *underlying title*—the real "bedrock" title—belongs to the Crown.

These so-called "logics" of settler national sovereignty over land are what I call the elaborate and illogical (though extensively rationalized) "fantasies of possession" and "fantasies of entitlement" that have built settler certainty. Even though they are "fantasies" they have powerful effects in the world, often through their materialization in law. Although the legal frameworks in Canada and the U.S. are both extremely complex and decidedly different from one another, one clear similarity in both systems is the legal rationale for the sense of entitlement I encountered during my fieldwork. As I show in Part One, laws were developed to recognize some aspects of Indigenous rights and the occupation of their territories, yet such recognized rights are only partial, limited and secondary because the ultimate and higher sovereignty always belongs to the Crown or the state. This ultimate, supposedly superior sovereignty, as I discuss below, is variously "invented," "conjured" like a "spell," assumed, asserted and rarely questioned (Borrows 2002).

Settler fantasies of possession and entitlement are also "more than just fantasies" (Bell 2008, 862). They are embedded, "unconscious expectation[s]" of how the world will work to reaffirm the social locations, perceptions and benefits of privilege. These fantasies are expectations of long-standing, settled expectations that have been legitimated through repeated experiences across lifetimes and generations of being "centered and dominant," an expectation "sedimented into the practices and attitudes" of these settler citizens (Bell 2008, 862).

This longstanding pattern, in which colonizers assume entitlement to claim sovereignty over Indigenous lands, continues to be repeatedly re-enacted *post-facto* in law as well as in the discourses of the people I interviewed. Colonization and settler nation-building have entailed the repetitive embedding and realizing of settler assertions of certainty and entitlement, and the repeated denial of Indigenous personhood and sovereignty, all of which are embedded in the interpretation of early moments of colonial/settler assumptions of sovereignty over territory. This pattern emerges from a set of stories that, as I will discuss, are grounded in delusions of entitlement based on arguments that should make no sense even to those who created them and turned them into laws. At the same time, these rationales have a particular pattern and "logic" that I trace throughout this book. They are socially embedded, unconscious expectations of how the world will work, and are relied upon to reaffirm social locations, perceptions and benefits of privilege that have been legitimated through repeated experiences across lifetimes and generations. Thus, I find the term "settled expectations" a powerful and polysemic metaphor for the taken-for-granted settler frameworks and practices of entitlement and expectation of ongoing privilege that I examine in this book.

In Part One, I examine such settler logics and epistemologies as they emerge and influence nation building, laws and policies over time. In Part Two, I explore the discourses and arguments used by activists against Indigenous land rights, demonstrating that although these discourses are flexible and often contradictory, they are also underpinned by the colonial and national assumptions of settled expectations discussed in Part One.

In Part Three, and in the book as a whole, I suggest that the possibility of finding a way to genuinely share contested geographical, conceptual and legal spaces between Indigenous and settler peoples and governments is profoundly problematic within settler frameworks, which are predicated upon self-evident Western enlightenment ideals and concepts of property, personhood and entitlement. Undoubtedly, legal, political and economic acts of redistribution are necessary, yet as I argue, may not be possible or sufficient without a fundamental shift in settler common-sense frameworks, a shift in concepts for thinking about and experiencing relationships and power within spaces. In other words, it is necessary to unsettle "settled expectations." The change we need, I contend, has to do with how we—and by "we" I mean relatively privileged non-Indigenous citizens of settler nations—think and act when it comes to the dominant and self-evident frameworks that many of us share. These frameworks, as I discuss in the chapters that follow, are so longstanding and self-evident that they are most often invisible (as other than truth and/or "common-sense") to those who share them. Indeed, to even begin to imagine meaningful structural changes in Indigenous-settler relationships may first require the kind of epistemological shifts I discuss here.

In the final section of the book (Part Three), I also explore what such an epistemological shift might look like as I build on ethnographic research I undertook with groups including Indigenous and non-Indigenous people who were working to create alliances in support of Indigenous land rights. I explore these alliances as a lens through which to imagine what it might mean to respond appropriately—as a settler Canadian or U.S. citizen in the 21st century—to the past, present and future of our nations' relationships with the Indigenous peoples who lived here before we did, and who continue to live here. What roles can and should non-Indigenous people play in decolonizing processes? Who is responsible for the hard and necessary work of decolonizing relationships? Colonization and decolonization are about relationships, and therefore the possibility of decolonization depends on *all* parties changing how they relate to one another. For too long, decolonization has been seen as an Indigenous issue. Thus, it makes sense that we, as settler descendants, take responsibility and engage in learning how to participate in this process. In exploring these questions, I build on my case studies by engaging with Indigenous and feminist philosophy in order to explore how we might imagine and theorize the building of such relationships more broadly. I argue that they require settlers to move beyond the sedimented frameworks of settled expectations of certain entitlement to land and control over Indigenous people in their efforts to imagine and build new kinds of relationships to land and with Indigenous peoples.

My discussion here is not, however, offered as a *general model* of decolonial practice. Nor do I suggest that a change in settler viewpoints could ever, on its own, obliterate colonial relations. Clearly, having a few settler people change the way that they think about Indigenous-settler relations will not immediately challenge the centuries of common-sense political, economic and legal oppression that Indigenous peoples have faced, nor the ontologies and epistemologies that have supported it. It could not suddenly solve the many problems Indigenous peoples face in terms of lands and sovereignty, education and health, poverty, racism, or the Indian Act. I suggest that fundamental shifts in settler perspectives must happen not instead of but *in addition to* serious structural, economic and political changes. However, if settlers are ever to fully engage with decolonization, and actually work mindfully on developing solutions to some of the above issues without reproducing the kinds of overt and subtle colonialism discussed in this book, it must begin somewhere. This book is offered as a gesture towards possible ways to imagine some of that necessary work. It is a small first step towards viewing how settlers might begin to deal with the "settler problem." This book, therefore, is an exploratory contribution to the important journey—both imaginative and practical—of learning how to unsettle expectations and move beyond the traps and limitations of ongoing settler colonialism, in order to learn new ways of building relations of *both* autonomy and interconnection with our Indigenous neighbours.

THE "SETTLER PROBLEM," INDIGENOUS
SOVEREIGNTY AND DECOLONIZATION

Although *Unsettled Expectations* addresses the politics of historical and present-day relationships between Indigenous and non-Indigenous peoples, the centrality of the theme of certain entitlement to land and jurisdiction means that it takes the relationships between Indigenous sovereignty and ongoing settler colonialism as its pivotal problem. Such a focus on sovereignty means that material relations (who got the land and how?) stay at the centre of questions about human relations. Examining the grounds upon which settler colonial nation-states feel entitled to, and certain of, sovereign jurisdiction means that instead of conceptualizing Indigenous people as the problem for the settler state, I focus on the "settler problem" (Epp 2003; Regan 2010),[6] critically examining what Andrea Smith (2012) calls the "the logics of settler colonialism." These "logics" are the "social, ideological, and institutional processes through which the authority of the settler state...is enacted" (Rifkin 2011, 343). Keeping Indigenous sovereignty at the centre of my analysis provides a key foundation of my critical project, because I hope to undercut the ubiquitous and self-evident assumption that the settler state was and is entitled to assert sovereignty over Indigenous peoples and territories. Thus, I do not proceed by critically assessing and evaluating Indigenous sovereignty claims, as this is something the state and the anti–land rights activists that I interviewed felt entitled and even responsible for doing consistently (as I discuss in Part Two, Chapters 3 and 4). This self-ascribed and long-standing sense of entitlement to know and assess Indigeneity underpins settler colonialism, and is one of its foundational epistemological logics. As I show throughout this book, the long history of the construction of supposedly authoritative knowledge about Indigenous peoples provides settlers with what has become a self-evident right to assess, control and manage Indigenous lives and sovereignties, thus bolstering the fantasy of uncontestable settler sovereignty. I therefore focus on settler sovereignty, and how entitlement to sovereignty was created and continues to be legitimated through attempts to circumscribe, extinguish and manage Indigenous sovereignty in specific ways (Nicoll 2004b, 19). Based on my ethnographic material, I also explore how settlers' "structures of feeling" and relationships are shaped inevitably by the legacies and ongoing processes of the knowledges, logics and practices of settler colonialism.

My focus on the "settler problem" is also informed by thrusts within feminist, whiteness, settler-colonial, Indigenous and queer theory.[7] In these fields, although bringing silenced and subordinated knowledges and experiences to light was and is important, it also became clear it was and is necessary to examine "unmarked and yet normative" categories (Mackey 2002, 3) in order to understand how "regimes of the normal" and "normalizing logics" (Smith 2010, 41–2) work to create authoritative knowledge about "others," and in this way subtly (and sometimes violently) exclude, encompass, and establish implicit grounds of comparison. The study of such normalizing logics is a vibrant and fruitful field of critical inquiry within the academic disciplines and interdisciplinary fields above, as well as for political thought and activism. Here, I explore the "normalizing logics" of settler colonial entitlement, within which sovereignty is the critical ground.

Non-Indigenous citizens of settler nations might not see sovereignty (either their own or Indigenous sovereignty) as a central concern. Most of us go about our daily lives as if questions of ownership of land and jurisdiction of territory do not need to be asked or answered. We take it for granted that we are citizens of our countries, and that these countries have sovereignty and jurisdiction over these territories we live in (see Asch 2014). If we think about Indigenous people, it may be that we wish to help them become "equal" to other Canadians or Americans, and yet also able to maintain their "cultures," not imagining or understanding that their vision of this land and their place in it and relationship with it is not encompassed or erased by the settler nation-state's jurisdiction. These are the tricks enacted by the "normalizing logics" of settler colonialism that I discuss throughout this book: settler sovereignty and jurisdiction are assumed to be always-already settled, over, complete. Indigenous sovereignty appears to have been silenced, except in moments of "crisis" such as the conflicts that I explore in this book, when settler certainty and "settledness" become deeply disturbed by its vibrant re-emergence. I discuss and define this sense of "settler anxiety" in more detail in the next chapter.

Many Indigenous peoples, however, do not share this sense of the self-evident nature of settler sovereignty and jurisdiction, or a desire to "belong" to settler-nations in the manner permitted. As Audra Simpson argues:

> Indigenous peoples did not lay down and die; they persist, and in so doing, they defy all expectations—working resolutely to assert their nationhood and their sovereignty against a settler political formation that would have them disappear or integrate or assimilate. It is that very desire and that political formation that some may hope will instead die—or, at the very least, be subject to deep revision. Indian sovereignty is real; it is not a moral language game or a matter to be debated in ahistorical terms. It is what they have; it is what, in the case of the United States, they have left; and thus it should be upheld and understood robustly—especially as Indians work within, against, and beyond these existing frameworks. Indians continue to exercise their sovereignty through the moment of empire and within an empire that is of such hyberbolic force and self-definition that it can imagine itself as deterritorialized, global, all the while retrenching its territorial force within borders. They do this within the geopolitical borders

of nation-states that cut through their land and across which they must now ask permission to traverse. (Simpson 2011, 211–212)

Instead, as we see, their own sovereignty is central to their individual and collective lives, identities, spirituality and politics and, as a separate matter, to negotiating nation-to-nation relationships with settlers and the settler state. It is important to point out that in my analysis, when I use the term "sovereignty" with regards to Indigenous peoples, I do not understand sovereign in exactly *the same way* as Western nation-states do. Taiaiake Alfred has made a compelling critique of the ways in which Indigenous assertions of sovereignty may trap aboriginal politics in a Western state paradigm, doomed to fail. He argues that sovereignty is itself a Western concept, implying, most dangerously, a state model. According to him, Indigenous politicians, by making a claim to sovereignty are ("even if they don't really mean it" and are using it as a political "bargaining chip"), "making a choice to accept the state as their model" (Alfred 1999, 80). He says that Indigenous traditional nationhood "stands in sharp contrast to the dominant understanding of 'the state': There is no absolute authority, no coercive enforcement of decisions, no hierarchy, and no separate ruling entity" (1999, 80). Here, accounting for the distinctions made above, I use the term "sovereignty" based on my interpretation of how the Onondaga Nation (discussed in Chapter 6) use the term. I use it to indicate a parallel version of established community and sociality that is as equally valid as, yet distinct from, Western state sovereignty. Such a concept includes autonomous relationships to territory, law, spirituality, ontologies and lifeways, a form of autonomy (and difference) that cannot be encompassed as simply another "minority" within an overarching Western nation-state sovereignty paradigm.

In terms of relations with nation-states, Alfred points out that Indigenous people seek justice, and that means building a "framework of respectful coexistence on the fundamental acknowledgement of the integrity and autonomy of the various elements that make up the relationship" (Alfred 1999, 86). Thus, the grounding of territory, land and the respect for Indigenous sovereign relations to territory is essential to settler processes of decolonization. Sium, Desai and Ritskes (2012, 1) argue that despite the "certainty that decolonization centers Indigenous methods, peoples, and lands, a decolonized future is a 'tangible unknown,'" a site of contestation. Decolonization cannot affirm "settler futurity" (Tuck and Yang 2012, 1–3). Decolonization, however, will require what Taiaiake Alfred calls "radical imagination":

> In order to decolonize, Canadians and Americans have to sever their emotional attachment to their countries and reimagine themselves, not as citizens with the privileges conferred by being descendants of

colonizers or newcomers from other parts of the world benefitting from white imperialism, but as human beings in equal and respectful relation to other human beings and the natural environment. This is what radical imagination could look like. (Alfred 2010, 6)

This book is framed as a study that examines relationships between Indigenous and non-Indigenous peoples in settler nations through the lens of conflict over land rights. Through examining the ethnographic materials and writing this book I have come to the conclusion that if Indigenous sovereignty continues to be dismissed, erased, extinguished and delegitimized there can be (Nicoll 2004a, para 35–6) "no ground for better relationships" between Indigenous peoples and other citizens in settler nations. The "ground of Indigenous sovereignty" must be the starting point for all people who live on these lands to "come into relationship" with each other and Indigenous peoples (Nicoll 2004a, para 35–6).[8] The important question to begin with is not, therefore, Is there Indigenous sovereignty? but instead, What is the relationship of other citizens of Canada and the United States (in whose name those national sovereignties are claimed and defended) to Indigenous sovereignty? (Nicoll 2004a, para 35). As I argue (in Part Three), decolonization and entering "into relationship" will require the kind of "radical imagination" Alfred calls for above, as well as what Nicoll calls an "embodied awareness of 'being in Indigenous sovereignty'" (2004b, 19).

Nicoll argues that "being in Indigenous sovereignty" is a difficult task for settlers because "investment in white sovereignty is compulsory on the basis of our national identity. We are conditioned to exercise our sovereignty against that of Indigenous Australians" (2004b, 19). My ethnographic discussions in Part Two show how the citizens of the United States and Canada fighting land claims whom I interviewed resist "being in Indigenous sovereignty" by drawing on a complex and often contradictory range of settler colonial and nationalist frameworks in order to assess, contain and delegitimize it, at the same time dehumanizing Indigenous personhood and, most importantly, naturalizing settler logics of superior and certain sovereignty. In Part Three, I discuss Indigenous–non-Indigenous alliances, suggesting that, in these specific cases, people engage in epistemological shifts that unsettle their "settled expectations" of certainty, allowing them to experience "being in Indigenous sovereignty" and preparing the ground for new decolonizing relations.

LAND RIGHTS/LAND CLAIMS AND DECOLONIZATION

When I began this project, it seemed that the government land claims process held promise as a site that could potentially promote decolonization. Given the focus on material reparations (land) and autonomy ("self-government"), I thought that "land claims" might indicate the possibility of a more substantial shift in Indigenous-settler relationships than the politics of cultural recognition I had analyzed in *House of Difference* (Mackey 2002). This was a "recognition" that promised, at most, limited symbolic inclusion in the liberal nation-state. However, over time, during fieldwork with the Indigenous groups involved in land claims processes, I began to see the negative effects of engaging in land claims, whether they be what the Canadian government calls "specific claims" or "comprehensive claims."[9] During the same time, the Conservative Government of Canada has increased the push for land claims agreements through their version of "negotiation," instead of "rights-based claims,", in courtrooms, hoping to promote resource development. As part of the same "First Nations Termination Plan" (Diabo 2012), the government has also introduced legislation detrimental to Indigenous rights and governance. In addition, many scholars and activists have now demonstrated that engaging with the state through government-sponsored programs, including land claims, is not a route to autonomy or to decolonization (Alfred 2009, 2001; Alfred and Corntassel 2005; Christie 2007a). These programs are instead, as Coulthard (2007, 438) argues, most often based on an assimilative logic of incorporation into existing power structures that "promises to reproduce ... configurations of colonial power." For this reason, although "land *claims*" cannot promise decolonization, a topic I discuss in more detail in Chapter 2, *struggles over* land *rights* are fruitful sites ("contact zones") for analyzing both the deep tensions and possibilities of change within Indigenous-settler relations. They are also excellent sites for examining the "states of feeling" of the people with whom I did fieldwork.

UNCERTAINTY, ANGER, AND SETTLER STATES OF FEELING

Many of the people I interviewed who opposed land claims were angry and resentful about what they saw as their unexpected and dangerous emergence. As I discuss in more detail in Part Two, they saw the situation as unexpected and unfair. Many made arguments that the economic uncertainty brought on by Indigenous land rights meant they could not carry out business and farming properly; they could not plan or develop their businesses and their communities. They organized protests, arguing that their cultures and communities were "at risk" (Mackey 2005). Others spoke longingly of a time "before," when they *had* been certain and secure in their lives, land and futures. The way that they argued against land rights appeared to be underpinned by the feeling that never before had their faith in their secure ownership of property, and their trust in the territorial integrity of nation, been betrayed in this way.

One goal of this book is to show that the deep feelings that I encountered when interviewing people should not be conceptualized as extreme or abnormal responses. I argue that instead they should be seen as "normal" responses to land rights actions, *if* they are conceptualized within the context of longstanding axiomatic frameworks of settler colonialism. These responses must be taken seriously in any efforts to decolonize, especially because the beliefs that underpin them are also pivotal in jurisprudence and broader dominant culture. Indigenous land rights, I suggest, understandably disrupt their longstanding "settled expectations" of entitlement. Critically examining such feelings helps us to see how ongoing colonialism and processes of settlement become naturalized and self-evident, and how they move from being what I call "fantasies of entitlement" to becoming embedded in law, in material worlds, and in the emotions of citizens.

The passionate anger expressed by the non-Indigenous people that I interviewed should not be surprising. It makes sense that, if people feel that their property and their expectations of a particular life and future might be suddenly and unexpectedly destroyed, they feel endangered, uncertain and angry. We can imagine that generations of settlers have grown up steeped in ubiquitous narratives about how their families (and other families like them) have worked hard on the land to build the nation. Such narratives have never before seemed to be at odds with the national narrative, or with the settled laws of the land. The people I spoke to appeared to feel as though they had been thrown into a state of vertigo: their settled worlds seemed to have been turned upside down.

Saying that such responses are not surprising is not to condone them. Nor is it to blame people, individually or collectively, for experiencing or acting on them. The point here is that no matter how emotionally potent or understandable these emotions may be, they are also not simply individual emotions that occur naturally or spontaneously. In settler nations, one "pernicious aspect of colonial power is that it shapes perceptions of reality," and in doing so creates an illusion of the deep "permanency and inevitability" of existing power relations (Waziyatawin 2012, 72). This is an illusion or fantasy of certainty as the predestined nature of "settler futurity" (Tuck and Yang 2012, 1).

Such feelings undoubtedly reflect numerous intersecting anxieties and contexts. In part, ubiquitous popular interpretations of the dangers of land rights for "equality" and economic prosperity are promoted widely by mainstream media and other sources. In the public imagination, they are often perceived as embodying a myriad of catastrophic and unpredictable risks and dangers to existing relationships and political and economic arrangements. Anger about uncertainty also likely reflects how late modern subjects may experience precarity in this era of flexible accumulation and neo-liberal economics, and should thus be understood within a proliferation of "a broader set of anxieties over economic security, citizenship entitlements, and national sovereignty" (Blackburn 2005, 587).

In this book I propose that such feelings are important to take seriously, not only for the above reasons, but also because they are entry points to understand important characteristics of how emotions and social structures are connected, and how individuals become enmeshed in broader collective ideologies and practices. I consider them to be "structures of feeling" and specifically, what Mark Rifkin (2011) calls "settler structures of feeling." Raymond Williams' concept of "structures of feeling" pinpoints "the ways in which ideologies reflect emotional investments that by and large remain unexamined during our lifetimes, because they have been insidiously woven into the everyday fabric of common sense" (Boler 1999, 181). The concept names the "simultaneously cultural and discursive dimension of our experience," but does not "neglect that these experiences are embodied and felt" (Boler 1999, 29).

Rifkin suggests that longstanding institutionalized frameworks and material relations of settlement create certain "modes of feeling" amongst non-Indigenous people in settler colonies. He argues that:

> Processes and institutionalized frameworks of settlement—the exertion of control by non-Natives over Native peoples and lands—give rise to certain modes of feeling, and, reciprocally, particular affective formations among non-Natives normalize settler presence, privilege, and power. Understanding settlement as a structure of feeling entails asking how emotions, sensations, and psychic life take part in the (ongoing) process of exerting non-Native authority over Indigenous politics, governance, and territoriality. (Rifkin 2011, 342)

Importantly, he asks, "How does that feeling of connection to this place as citizens of the state actively efface ongoing histories of imperial expropriation and contribute to the continuing justification of the settler state's authority to super-intend Native peoples?" (2011, 342). In two ethnographic chapters (3 and 4) I explore how particular characteristics of affect/emotion make these specifically "*settler* structures of feeling" (Rifkin 2011), and not some other kind. Given that the making of Indigenous lands into settler homes is an "experienced material-ity" (Harris 2004) of broader global processes of hierarchical identity-making and material appropriation, tracking them in this book has involved examining how individual and collective emotions—as well as their broader social and legal common-sense frameworks—both reflect as well as reproduce key assumptions and "logics of settler colonialism" (Smith 2012), including the certainty, uncertainty and anxiety that land rights conflict engenders. I discuss notions of certainty, uncertainty and anxiety in more detail in Chapter 2.

DISMANTLING AND REBUILDING

Unsettled Expectations draws on and contributes to critical streams in many intersecting fields. Given that conflict about land rights concerns belief systems, policies and laws at local, regional, national and global levels, in both the past and the present, *Unsettled Expectations* takes an interdisciplinary approach[10] that began with ethnographic research. My background in anthropology and critical feminist theory means that I tend to think of research in terms of how to explore a problem that materializes in face-to-face encounters, and yet links up to broader systems of power. For this reason I began this research with ethnography on the problem of settler-Indigenous relations. I focussed on settler practices and concepts as the critical object of inquiry, building on decades of work in feminist theory, critical anthropology, settler-colonial studies and Indigenous studies and queer theory, showing that it is necessary to examine our own social locations, and to critically analyse normative and authoritative power structures and subjects. In this way, the study of affect is linked to material and historical processes.

Although it is now more acceptable for anthropology to examine colonialism within the context of "settler societies," Simpson (2007, 68) argues that anthropological "analyses of Indigeneity may still occupy the 'salvage' and 'documentary' slot for analysis," and thus participate in the "endurance of categories" from moments of "colonial contact." Except for notable examples, anthropologists carrying out ethnographic work have a tendency to construct the field of enquiry as the local community (or Indigenous community) and create a form of "local community study." They do not, as I have attempted to do here, conceptualize the local sites as case studies of broader settler projects, nation-states and the possibilities of decolonization. This book could also be seen as a contribution to political and legal anthropology, specifically as what Nader (1997, 712) calls an anthropology of "controlling processes," because it focuses on the "transformative nature of central ideas" in a range of sites, it "brings political and economic issues more prominently into present-day anthropology," and it has a methodology "rooted in fieldwork" (Nader 1997, 712). It begins with attention to the "micro-processes" of conflict over land rights to explore how individuals and groups use key concepts as political "common sense" in their everyday lives (Nader 1997, 712). Within this field, it brings ongoing settler colonialism—in the present—into the lens of political ethnography, showing how Western concepts of possession, private property, personhood, certainty and uncertainty are mobilized and contested on the ground in face-to-face human relationships, but also in philosophy, law and government policies.

However, in order to locate this book within its academic context it is necessary to move away from anthropology and look to interdisciplinary analyses. Simpson

(2011, 210) argues that "In the literature, one must range within and also well beyond anthropology for models of cultural and political analysis that take settler colonialism and Indigenous sovereignty as their departure points. These works may be found in Indigenous studies and anthropology, governance studies and political theory."[11] She writes, "In spite of its long history in law and policy studies in 'American Indian Studies,' rarely do we see sovereignty centered within contemporary anthropological analyses of Indigeneity."

This book contributes most clearly, therefore, to an emerging interdisciplinary field of research and writing in Australia, Canada, Aotearoa/New Zealand and the United States that I think of as ex-British "settler studies" (in that they take the settler and settler states as the problem and critical object of inquiry), and that can be considered integral to the broader field of "settler colonial studies."[12] Thus, this book can be located within "settler colonial studies," as informed by critical Indigenous studies, critical race and whiteness studies and feminist theory.[13] It addresses lacunae in settler colonial studies by developing an ethnographic approach to settler colonialism in the present, and by bringing questions of decolonization to the centre of the field. Settler colonial studies as a field attempts to think through contemporary colonial relationships in settler nations, and like much Indigenous theory, works to reveal the "logics of settler colonialism" (Smith 2012). It explores settler colonialism as an historical and empirical phenomenon as well as a conceptual framework embedded in a set of practices that are ongoing. Some of the strengths of settler colonial theory (shared with Indigenous studies) include the important position that, despite constant assertions within settler national mythologies that colonialism is over, settler nations are not *post*-colonial. As Patrick Wolfe (2006) so aptly puts it, "colonization is a structure not an event." Settler colonial theory shows that the oft-repeated settler colonial assertions that colonialism is over and only exists in the past, are "layered over" and work to obscure its "central structural continuity" (Macoun and Strakosch 2013, 428). Indeed, this book (in Chapters 2, 3 and 4) traces how longstanding ideas and concepts that legitimated colonial dispossession are still being mobilized by the people I interviewed, and that the same ideas still inform law and other state-institutions. Colonial frameworks and epistemologies are embedded, as I demonstrate, in "settler structures of feeling" (Rifkin 2011). In this way, I show how settler knowledges, practices, structures, emotions and selves are deeply interconnected and intertwined, in the past and the present. Settler colonial studies has been very effective at providing sophisticated understandings of how settler colonialism reproduces itself in numerous "shape-shifting" (Corntassel 2012, 88) and complex ways and shown it to be "a set of practices as well as an ideology, and an ongoing present as well as a past" (Macoun and Strokasch 2013, 437).

However, settler colonial theory has also been critiqued for a range of issues related to how it may unintentionally reproduce settler frameworks. Macoun and Strakosch, in "The Ethical Demands of Settler-Colonial Theory," provide a nuanced analysis of both the limits and possibilities of settler colonial approaches. When settler colonial theory is "deployed with a neutral descriptive authority, and used by settler scholars to explain not just our own political drives but the entire field of our [settler] relationships with Indigenous people, this can serve to re-enact the central settler fantasy that we constitute and have authority over this space" (Macoun and Strakosch 2013, 437–9). Claims of entitlement and authority over conceptual and territorial space are pivotal to settler colonial projects. Indeed, in this book I trace the repeated assertions of singular authority—a singular "jurisdictional imaginary" (Rifkin 2011, 343)—over the presumed national territory, and I examine how these assertions construct an ongoing "fantasy of the certainty of entitlement." My ethnographic approach to such work undercuts the supposed authority of such fantasies and also demonstrates that, despite the masses of energy it takes to reproduce it, settler colonialism is neither authoritative nor uncontested.

One result of the centring of ethnography in this book is that the analysis is specific and limited. When I read work by other scholars from political theory or other disciplines not grounded in ethnography, in some ways I envy the breadth and free-ranging approach to finding the theories and overarching rules. However, because this book started with, and pivots on, the ethnographic material, the analysis follows what I found at local levels. In this way, although in the text the history of doctrines comes first, the impulse to understand them in the specific way that I do emerges from the ethnographic material. This pivoting on the ethnographic is possibly a weakness because of its specificity. Yet I hope that this specificity is also a strength. This approach may help some readers to link day-to-day experiences to broader historical systems. For this reason, although other theorists centred in law or political theory refer briefly, in condensed form, to many of the legal and political theories I discuss here, I sometimes spend more time explaining them to readers who may not be familiar with them or have the specific theoretical or disciplinary background. Another result of the centring of ethnography in this book is that, in Part Two, led by my fieldwork data, I explore only limited and specific examples of a possible broad range of settler states of feeling. Given that the responses I discuss emerge from rural small-town farming communities that are under siege in the shifting economies of the global, neoliberal world, they represent a particularly land-based and agricultural response. In some senses, these may represent a more "traditional" agrarian settler framings of subjects. Although I do not have the space to explore other more urban, cosmopolitan, left-wing and "progressive" responses to land rights and Indigenous sovereignty, I think it safe to say that concerns would have some similarities, although they would likely be framed and enunciated in different ways.

Contestation and resistance are often not fully taken up in settler colonial theory, an approach that defines itself primarily as a project that focuses on the *critique* and *deconstruction* of dominant ideas and practices. Settler colonial theory has been successful at the *critique* of settler colonialism, but less successful at the more *constructive* project of documenting resistance and imagining alternatives. As Veracini (2011, 211) observes, "the decolonization of settler colonialism needs to be imagined before it is practised, and this has proved especially challenging" within settler colonial studies. These two related but very different projects— critique and construction—are seen by Henderson (2015) as the "two fronts of decolonization." For Henderson, one front is the critical project of "dismantling the master's house," in Audrey Lorde's terms. The other, which is often engaged in by Indigenous scholars, entails what Leanne Simpson (2012, in Henderson 2015) calls "(re)build[ing] our own house." For Simpson, such rebuilding refers to Nishnaabeg re-creation and resurgence. In a broader sense, it implies that while decolonization requires critique, it also needs the constructive project of imagining and living regenerative ways of ways of being. Jo Smith (2013, 106–7) calls this the "realm of politics when politics is understood as 'an art of the possible' (Brydon 2006)."[14] My ethnographic approach in Part Three details the lived relationships of how people are attempting to unsettle settler colonialism and rebuild new kinds of relationships and political imaginaries.

These two thrusts require very different analytical and political stances as part of my own project of understanding the limits and possibilities of decolonizing relations. Part Two, based mainly on analysis of the groups fighting against land rights claims, speaks to and contributes towards "dismantling the master's house" through mapping the logics of settler colonialism, and therefore speaks more to approaches and concerns of settler colonial studies. The concerns of Part Three, in which I examine moves to decolonization and settler-Indigenous alliances, require a more speculative and imaginative approach because, as a recent vibrant body of work on decolonization has shown, the shape of decolonization is necessarily unknown, it is a "place where no one has ever really been" (Reyes Cruz 2012, 153). *Unsettled Expectations* juggles the two fronts of decolonization, contributing both to settler colonial understandings of the complex logics of settler colonialism as well as to imaginings of decolonization often taken up by Indigenous studies. The conceptual lens that links these two thrusts together examines how certainty and uncertainty operate in both these fronts. My unique contribution to settler colonial studies, in addition to my ethnographic approach, is my proposal that certainty and uncertainty are central to the multi-sited logics, practices and "states of feeling" in analysis of the "two fronts of decolonization," the critique and dismantling of the logics of settler colonialism, and the imaginative process of rebuilding. I take up the discussion of certainty and uncertainty in the next chapter.

Notes

1   In this book I use the term "Indigenous" when referring to First Peoples of settler nations including Canada, Australia, Aotearoa/New Zealand and the United States. Whenever possible I use the names of specific Indigenous nations. I may use the terms "Aboriginal," "Indian," or "Native" when citing others or when discussing state policies, law, or legislation that uses those terms.

2   Many of the people I interviewed preferred me to use pseudonyms when I quote from interviews, whereas others preferred I use their names. I have followed their preferences.

3   I recognize that my use of the term "settler" to refer to people both in the past and present is both contested and inadequate. Some suggest that "settler" is too gentle a term, occluding the violence and genocide that settler-colonization entailed, and that a more accurate term would be "settler–invader." There is also passionate debate about whether, and if so how, people of colour are settlers too (Phung 2011; Yu 2011; Sehdev 2001) and the relationship between anti-racism and Indigenous politics and sovereignty in settler nations (Lawrence and Dua 2011; Wright and Sharma 2008–9). These debates are complex and important, given the many (especially racialized) "differences between settlers" as well as the necessity of taking account of "global histories of racialized violence as well as unforced and forced migrations that brought diverse peoples to the Americas" (Byrd 2011). In this book I have not found it possible to develop a more nuanced analysis of the term "settler," or to tease out all the possible categories of "settlerness"; that would be a different project. In this book I have therefore settled on the applicability of using the term "settler" to refer to non-Indigenous citizens of settler-nation states. This is in part because, in my limited project, the people fighting against Indigenous land rights that I interviewed used discourses that mobilized "settler states of feeling," reflecting the "logics of settler colonialism." Others have said to me that the term settler makes them uncomfortable because it is not how people would likely see or name themselves. In my mind, that is precisely why it is important to use the term, because it unsettles the idea of us (settlers) as "good" or "bad" individual citizens who may or may not have "racist" attitudes, and reminds us (hopefully) of the collective land theft that is foundational to our nations and citizenships, and that is ongoing. As Adam Barker (2013) argues, "All of us—every person who lives on and benefits from the theft of Indigenous lands—is a Settler. We all live on someone else's lands, and almost all of us do so illegally … It does not matter if your family has been here since the Mayflower landed, or if you just recently moved to Toronto from abroad: you are part of this. That is how settler colonization functions."

4   The Canadian national anthem begins, "Oh Canada, Our home and native land, True patriot love, In all thy sons command."

5   Based on an analysis of court decisions, Asch concludes: "Canada relies on the 'settlement' thesis to justify its acquisition of sovereignty. This thesis rests on the concept that the territory claimed by the colonists was previously a *terra nullius*" (Asch 2002)

6   Although this book focuses on the "settler problem," it does not mean I ignore what Indigenous people are doing or saying. Yet it is also not an ethnography of the Indigenous communities I worked with, a cultural production that has a problematic history (especially in anthropology) because of the ways in which communities have

been represented (usually by white anthropologists) through a colonial lens, either as deeply "traditional," timeless and harmonious communities, or confused and assimilated, having forgotten their traditions (see Simpson 2014, Chapter 4). Although the communities of Indigenous people I worked with were often filled with tensions and lateral violence regarding membership and other issues, I have chosen not to explore these tensions and lateral violence in this book. Such battles and divisions within communities make constant appearances in the mainstream press and can, and do, feed into settler vilification and refusal of Indigenous sovereignty (statements along the lines of "Well, if they can't even agree between themselves, how can they negotiate with us or have self-government?"). Therefore, when discussing Indigenous peoples, I only reveal what people wanted me to say, and what is necessary for the argument I make in this book. Given that this book is about the politics of relationships between Indigenous and non-Indigenous people, I draw on Indigenous theory and voices in this book in this limited way—for the most part only as they relate to conceptualizing and theorizing these relations. I conceptualize this as Indigenous political theory. My approach holds the risk that I may inadvertently represent the communities in ways that may appear timeless and traditional, even romanticized. The point is that they do draw on tradition in political theory and action in relation to the settler state, but that does not of course fully define or represent the whole community or its lifeways (as if anything ever could). Researching and defining Indigenous communities is purposefully not the topic of this book.

7   For example: Moreton-Robinson 2004, 2007; Nicoll 2004a, 2004b; Frankenberg 1993; Rifkin 2014; Smith 2010; Morgensen 2011, 2012.

8   In focusing on "the settler problem" and resisting the "normalizing logics" that are so self-evident to settlers, the work of Fiona Nicoll (2004a, 2004b) has been invaluable. My questions here are indebted to her powerful analysis in the Australian context.

9   Canada has two forms of "land claims"—"comprehensive claims" and "specific claims." "Comprehensive claims always involve land, but specific claims are not necessarily land-related. Comprehensive claims deal with the unfinished business of treaty-making in Canada. These claims arise in areas of Canada where Aboriginal land rights have not been dealt with by past treaties or through other legal means ... Specific claims deal with past grievances of First Nations related to Canada's obligations under historic treaties or the way it managed First Nations' funds or other assets" (INAC 2010).

10 In order to understand more fully the concepts I found ubiquitous during my ethnographic work on contemporary land rights, I moved on to explore how such apparently axiomatic knowledge about histories, entitlements, nationhood, appropriation and race has been produced over time and space. In this vein, I began to read widely and in many disciplines: anthropologies of law, conflict and property; history; philosophy; law; legal theory; property theory; Indigenous theory; feminist theory; and post-colonial and decolonial theory. I began to trace the concepts, categories and frameworks people used in debates about land rights, in order to examine the work that such concepts do, and have done, to legitimize settler possession and delegitimize that of Indigenous peoples. In other words, I undertook something akin to a Foucauldian genealogy of key colonial ideas and conceptual frameworks that I had first identified in the present.

11 Simpson cites exceptions to this trend, including Moreton-Robinson 2007; Bruyneel
    2007; Corntassel et al. 2008; Coulthard 2007; Biolsi 2007; Cattelino 2008; Landsman
    1988.

12 A small sampling includes: Barker 2009; Baloy 2015; Coulthard 2014; Francis 2011;
    Bhandar 2011, 2015a, 2015b; Goldstein 2008; Furniss 1999; Cowlishaw and Morris
    1997; Cameron 2011, 2015; Bhandar, Fumia and Newman 2008; Black 2015; Black
    and Murphao 2015; Marcus 1997, 1999; Mawani 2005, 2007, 2009, 2012; Cowlishaw
    1999, 2004; Bell 2008; Gilmour, Bhandar, Heer and Ma 2012; Henderson 2003, 2013,
    2015; Henderson and Wakeham 2009, 2013; Coleman 2006; Sugars 2004; Sugars and
    Turcotte 2009; Stasiulus and Yuval-Davis 1995; Wolfe 1999, 2006, 2013; Lawrence
    2004; Razack 2002; Thobani 2007; Povinelli 1993; Bannerji 2000; Mackey 2002, 2005,
    2013, 2014; Jones with Jenkins 2008; Veracini 2007, 2011; Caldwell, Leung and Leroux
    2013; Asch 2014; Epp 2003; Regan 2010; Hugill and Toews 2014.

13 My work also contributes in a less explicit way to the law and society literature, by
    linking philosophical and socio-legal analysis of relations between Indigenous and
    non-Indigenous peoples to subjectivity, emotions and "legal consciousness" (Silbey
    2005).

14 "Politics as an 'art of the possible' frees us from the idea that politics must always already
    know in advance, the model or ideal of social transformation" (Smith 2013, 107). "The
    question then becomes, do we have the strength, imagination and will—as well as the
    capacity for hope ... for this kind of creative labour of imagining otherwise?" (Smith
    2013, 107)

Chapter 1

GENEALOGIES OF CERTAINTY AND UNCERTAINTY

Canada's striv[ing] for certainty reflects a desire that Indigenous peoples assimilate into Canada, that we sever our connection to the Land. Canada asks that we dig up the roots connecting us to the Land... [O] ur Aboriginal Title... is *"uncertain," because it prevents Indigenous peoples from viewing the Land as a commodity to be bought, sold or traded.* (Union of BC Indian Chiefs 2012, emphasis mine)

We recognize that, despite our certainty that decolonization centers Indigenous methods, peoples, and lands, the future is a "tangible unknown," a constant (re)negotiating of power, place, identity and sovereignty. (Sium, Desai and Ritskes 2012, 1)

The people I interviewed for Part Two of this study felt afraid, angry and uncertain as a result of Indigenous "land claims." It was an unexpected crisis they felt would threaten their entire life's work and future. They felt victimized and angry. They did not see themselves as personally responsible for what their ancestors may or may not have done. How is it that they could possibly deserve what is happening to them? They felt betrayed by elites in government who were allowing such threats to their security, property and futures. Land rights for Indigenous peoples appeared to disrupt deep and longstanding feelings they have about their rights and entitlements as citizens within nations, particularly with regards to their own property and their rights to fully control that property in the present and the future.

To understand the discourses and feelings of danger, crisis and uncertainty that people used to resist land rights, it is helpful to explore how scholars have analyzed the politics of the social construction of uncertainty. How people perceive and respond to uncertainty and risk have, in different ways, been seen as "central political question[s] of our time" (Reddy 1996, 224; Marris 1996). Certainty is often conceptualized as an unequivocally desirable and positive state of affairs. Many theorists assert, as if it is a self-evident universality, that all people require certainty, a sense that our lives and futures are secure and not at risk (Marris 1996; Giddens 1990). At the same time, as Marx and Engels (1848, 16) pointed out, capitalism guarantees "everlasting insecurity." Many theorists have explored the uncertainty that characterizes the post-modern, post-Fordist, and/or so-called "post-national" era of "globalization" (Bauman 1997; Beck 1992; Berman 1988; O'Malley 2004). One of the key reasons that the Canadian government seeks to resolve Indigenous land rights is to provide "greater certainty over rights to land and resources therefore contributing to a positive investment climate and creating greater potential for economic development and growth" (AANDC 2010a).

In exploring the ways in which scholars have discussed these issues it is now "almost banal to make the claim that we live in a risk society" (O'Malley 2004, 1). We can see it all around us. Time and effort in our day-to-day lives are spent following health and dietary regimes said to reduce risks of various health problems. We are careful to follow rules and regulations to reduce risks of traffic accidents, and practice "risk prevention" and "risk reduction" for the safety and protection of our children and ourselves. At the same time, "security" against various unknown threats is a major focus of governments and institutions.

Analytical approaches to risk and uncertainty in the social sciences are very diverse. They tend to share the idea, nevertheless, that risk and/or danger is "an increasingly pervasive concept in the ontology of human existence in Western societies; risk is a central aspect of subjectivity; risk is seen as something that can be managed through human intervention; and risk is associated with notions of choice, responsibility and blame" (Lupton 1999). One of the most influential bodies of social theory on risk emerged from what Lupton calls the "risk theorists," most famously, Ulrich Beck, Anthony Giddens and Scott Lash (1994), who have argued that the distribution and sharing of "risk" is at the "very core of an understanding of contemporary advanced societies" (Reddy 1996, 224). Beck proposes that because of modernization, industrial society has become a "risk society," in which the central problem is no more the "production and distribution of 'goods' such as wealth and employment in conditions of scarcity (as it was in early modernity and remains the case in developing countries) but the prevention or minimization of 'bads'; that is, risks" (Lupton 1999, 59).

Such "risk theory" frameworks, although widely accepted in the social sciences, have also been subject to important critiques. Patrick O'Malley, for example, suggests that one problem with many of these analyses is that they present "risk society" as somehow an inevitable "effect of the inescapable 'logic' of modernity, capitalism or whatever" (O'Malley 2004, 7). Risk society is inevitable, these theorists seem to argue, but then they fail to offer an analysis of the diversity of ways in which uncertainty is already being mobilized to govern, and they do not examine precisely how these practices have been linked in past governance.

Anthony Giddens' concept of "ontological security" works in just this way. Giddens (1990, 92 in Silverstone 1995, 5) says that ontological security refers to "the confidence that most human beings have in the continuity of their self-identity and in the constancy of the surrounding social and material environments of action." He further defines it this way:

> A sense of the reliability of persons and things, so central to the notion of trust, is basic to feelings of ontological security; hence the two are psychologically related. Ontological security has to do with "being" or, in the terms of phenomenology, "being-in-the-world." (Giddens 1990, in Silverstone 1995, 5)

According to Silverstone, Giddens argues that trust is a precondition for ontological security, which all people need (1995, 5). Such trust is necessary for "our capacity to sustain an active *anxiety-controlling engagement in the everyday world*" and "implies the ability to manage, counteract or minimise the *various threats and dangers that* appear to challenge us, both as individuals and as collectivities" (Silverstone 1995, 5–6, emphasis mine).

To be sure, Giddens assumes a dangerous world, inevitably full of risks and insecurities, what Siverstone suggests is a "routinised, defended social order... in which the level of risk and uncertainty is an ever-present and palpable threat" (Silverstone 1995, 6–7). Giddens' conception of "ontological security" is therefore normative. It constructs a particular view of a *normal* world of ontological *insecurity* that we all supposedly share, a world that requires constant engagement to *control* the inevitable anxiety of dealing with constant threats and dangers. Such a world triggers images of a society that developed out of specific Enlightenment philosophies and practices and is, consequently, not universal. Presenting a risky and dangerous world as normal and universal also intersects with particular forms of contemporary neoliberal politics.[1]

In terms of examining conflict about land rights, I find the approaches based on "risk theory" less helpful than other approaches that examine how discourses about danger and uncertainty transform and change in specific contexts, and how they intersect with contested power relations and changing expectations. Such approaches are more helpful, both methodologically and theoretically, in terms of analyzing or explaining the ways in which people expressed and mobilized specific fears and uncertainties during my research.

O'Malley argues that it makes political and theoretical sense to develop a "genealogical approach to risk and uncertainty, attending to their natures as the products of contingency and invention" (O'Malley 2004, 7). He demonstrates, with extended detailed examples, how concepts, theories and practices of uncertainty and risk have been mobilized in diverse and variable ways, both historically and in the present. In the context in which people mobilized discourses of risk, certainty and uncertainty in order to make political arguments for and against land rights, I have also found Mary Douglas' approach to the concept of risk illuminating. Douglas argues that "in all places at all times the universe is moralized and politicized. Disasters that befoul the air and soil and poison the water are generally turned to political account: someone already unpopular is going to be blamed for it" (Douglas 1992, 5). For every accident, disaster or death, someone must be found responsible in order to be blamed. Risk discourses can be used to mobilize moral communities to define dangers, to deal with the dangers in particular ways and to assign responsibility and accountability. Thus, such assertions of danger and risk are integral to larger contest over politics and about justice (Douglas 1990, 3, 1994, 44–6, 22–37). In my view, discourses about danger, risk and uncertainty are also discursive devices that construct some political and moral positions as natural and rational, and define opposing positions as irrational, disloyal and dangerous, as we see in the discourses about the dangers of land rights in this book. The imagined dangers of land rights are based less on facts about actual risks and dangers than they are on moral and political assessments of risks and dangers that emerge from historically constructed characteristics of settler colonialism, as I discuss in the next chapter.

Discourses of fear and danger often rely on the (fantasy) construction of a previous state of affairs, an imagined past (even if it is not a reflection of reality) that is then projected as normal, natural, common sense and rational (Mackey 1999a). Change from "the established," the "settled," or expected way of doing things is therefore seen as dangerous and frightening. Put differently, risk discourses have a tendency to be conservative, in that they resist change in part by (re)creating or fantasizing about a "normal" past in which such dangers did not exist. The way people talked about certainty and danger in my ethnographic sites indicates that the so-called "normal" state of affairs is one in which their privileges are unquestioned. They feel they should be able to—and are in fact entitled to—expect and count on those privileges for the future. These conflicts, they might have thought, were supposed to have been settled long ago. In a sense, they feel that they are being placed in a position that they understandably feel is inappropriate. They have always believed that their ownership was certain, secure, settled, and this certainty comes from centuries of ideas and legal practices that have protected settlers, as I discuss in the next chapter.

NEOLIBERALISM AND UNCERTAINTY

In the following chapters, people express anger and loss about social breakdown, a sense of vertigo as their old certainties appear to crumble. Such a sense of anger and loss is not only a result of land rights, because experiences of, and the powerful rhetoric of, risk, danger and uncertainty are also integral to contemporary neoliberal contexts that have become more hegemonic in recent decades: the responses to land rights I discuss here are taking place within specific local and global economic and political contexts, defined by neoliberalism. Thus, some of the anger people express about danger and uncertainty also likely reflects how late modern subjects may experience precarity in this era of flexible accumulation and neoliberal economics, and should thus be understood within the context of a proliferation of "a broader set of anxieties over economic security, citizenship entitlements, and national sovereignty" (Blackburn 2005, 587).

Within this neoliberal context, one of the key reasons that the Canadian government seeks to resolve Indigenous land rights is to provide "greater certainty over rights to land and resources therefore contributing to a positive investment climate and creating greater potential for economic development and growth" (AANDC 2010a). Blackburn (2005) argues that treaty negotiations in late 20th century British Columbia are a form of governmentality that help to regulate populations, mediate "between Aboriginal-rights claims and the demands of global capital," and that they produce "effects of state sovereignty" (Blackburn 2005, 586). Land rights, if not "legally captured" within a land rights agreement, are seen as making property *uncertain* and are therefore threatening to economic development and "capital and state sovereignty." The goal of the land agreements, according to Blackburn, is the attainment of certainty through either 1) *extinguishing* undefined Aboriginal rights, or 2) *fixing, defining* and *codifying* of such rights so they cannot *threaten certainty* (Blackburn 2005). While Blackburn argues that the concern with ensuring certainty emerges in conjunction with neoliberal programs and the legal recognition of Indigenous rights since the 1970s, I engage a longer temporal genealogy of concepts of certainty and uncertainty, showing that certainty is not only a concern for present-day governance and neoliberal states. Indeed, securing settler certainty through law and other means is a much deeper characteristic of the "logic of settler colonialism" (Smith 2012), as I discuss in the next chapter and throughout the book.

Thus, although terms such as "certainty" and "security" can appear to com-municate something unequivocally positive, these terminologies also carry specific meanings which imply the regulation, management and "legal capture" (in Blackburn's words) of some rights, for the freedom and prosperity of others. Blackburn suggests that although certainty is "what is sold to investors" in land claims agreements, it is "not necessarily created for all residents ... whether they are Aboriginal or non-Aboriginal" (Blackburn 2005, 594). More broadly, although certainty is constantly being mobilized as a fantasy and a goal (Blackburn 2005, 594), neoliberal economics at the same time produces day-to-day uncertainty and insecurity in labour, personhood and futures for the entire planet.

Of course, as human beings we *should all* be able to feel secure in our homes and our futures. Yet as feminist theorists of the politics of home (Young 2001, 2002; Weir 2008) have pointed out, having a secure home has often depended upon displacing others from theirs. The secure homes of middle-class women (where childcare and cleaning is taken care of so they may go out and work) are enabled by the underpaid labour of other women, usually women of colour, who sometimes have left their own children and homes behind in "Third World" countries. Peter Marris discusses the "unequal distribution of uncertainty," arguing that "the use of power and resources to displace the costs of uncertainties onto others weaker than oneself" is "fundamental to the management of uncertainty" (Marris 1996). The power to control uncertainty is "unequally distributed," because "the greatest burden of uncertainties tends to fall on the weakest, with the fewest resources to withstand it" (Marris 1996).

Following from the insights above, if we look at the history of relations between Indigenous and non-Indigenous peoples in Canada and the United States, it is possible to argue that the deep uncertainties and insecurities that could perhaps have disrupted colonial and nation-building processes were often displaced onto Indigenous peoples. In general, settlers and their governments did not seriously address or grapple with potential uncertainty about their entitlement to land ownership and the establishment of colonies. Instead, as I explore in the next chapter, assertions of sovereignty based on an imagined and continually theorized superiority made that question both unspeakable and irrelevant, elided in the march of progress. Later, the creation of U.S. reservations and Canadian reserves, as well as the development policies such as the Indian Act in Canada (Lawrence 2004) and the Dawes Act in the United States (Debo 1984 [1940]; Stremlau 2005) reinforced Indigenous peoples' "uncertainties." These programs decimated Indigenous peoples' material autonomy over, and their confident assurance (or certainty) in, their individual and collective relationships to their territories and lifeways. These had been first reduced and then destroyed as settlers took the land, then further devastated through attempts to annihilate their cultures and families through policies and practices of assimilation. The risks and uncertainties of settler societies were thus transferred onto the colonized, resulting in centuries of state-imposed uncertainty, risk and danger to individual and collective selves, as the recent testimonies of residents of the Indian Residential Schools attest.

I use the terms "certainty" and "uncertainty" in this book, therefore, not to indicate axiomatic, self-evident states; instead, I assume that they are socially, culturally and politically constructed in specific historical contexts and are pivotal to broader political strategies. They are also experienced emotionally as "settler states of feeling." I use the terms "*ontological* certainty" and "*ontological un*certainty" in this book in order to refer to the importance of how different ontologies (that is, theories about ways of being-in-the-world) intersect with questions of certainty and uncertainty. I hope to highlight how particular Western settler ontologies construct the relationship between land, property and people, as well as how such ontologies of certainty may be challenged.

Concepts of "ontological *un*certainty" and "ontological certainty" are thus helpful to understand the ways in which people construct and experience the threats and dangers that are attributed to land rights, first, without assuming that such a response is natural or universal, and second, to locate such responses within broader historical genealogies of how such concepts have been used over time, as I do in the next chapter.

PROPERTY AND (UN)CERTAINTIES IN SETTLER COLONIALISM

This book traces how concepts of certainty and uncertainty inform ontologies and intersect with power relations between Indigenous and settler societies over time. Concepts of certainty and uncertainty were central to the Western ontologies that were a necessary condition of the particular forms of British colonialism of North America. They are also, as I explore, pivotal to today's ongoing settler colonialism in related but different ways. In both cases they contribute to creating and maintaining settler fantasies of entitlement and certainty in property. As I discuss in the next chapter, Western notions of private property, as well as hierarchical and racialized categories of personhood, are deeply related to securing certainty in land and ontological certainty for settler society. Such imagined self-order and security is only possible through constructing binaries: the settled order of sedentarist boundaries and fences, versus the chaos and unsettled mobility of a "state of nature" that is believed to exist outside of those boundaries. This is a very Hobbesian vision of the safety and security of reason versus the constant and repressed threat of irrational savagery.

Furthermore, such specific ontologies only *become* certain, or "settled," through powerful legitimating fantasies of mastery over nature and others (in philosophy for example) and specific practices of materially supporting those fantasies (especially about the certainty of property) in law and legislation, as I discuss in Chapter 2. In other words, the ontological certainty of settler entitlement to Indigenous land has been *made to seem* certain, over time and in specific spaces, at the expense of a great deal of energy. In addition to the epistemological work of ideology, significant structural and material efforts (guns, laws and policies) have also gone into creating expectations of ontological certainty in property and privilege for settlers, expectations that have come to be seen as a settled *entitlements* that must be defended. This book suggests that the Western concepts of *terra nullius* and the "state of nature," and the practices that emerged from them, were mobilized to create and defend a "fantasy of entitlement" that provides a sense of the certainty, and the "settled" nature, of existing property relations. This is what I call "settled expectations."

Such visions connect profoundly with how property is conceptualized within Western frameworks. Private property is precisely designed to secure certainty for the owner. Nicholas Blomley says the "enactment of property not only presumes a definitional certainty (*this* is property, *that* isn't), but also invites us to imagine that property and settlement are synonymous":

> The unitary owner at the center of the model is imagined as secure in her entitlements, and the institution of property is rendered a means for preventing discord. The clear markers of ownership and the "established expectations" of property are supposed to work to ensure the "quiet enjoyment" of the land. Property brings certainty. Certainty brings peace and prosperity. (Blomley 2004, xiv–xv)

The ownership model that is central to "legal liberalism" (Blomley 2004, xix) makes it appear as if the question of who controls territory is settled, secure and certain.

Such "definitional clarity of the ownership model is deemed valuable, in part, because it 'quiets' title, promising secure and uncontested relations with others" (Blomley 2004, xix). Many of the origin stories of private property that I discuss in the next chapter tell a similar story: "In the beginning was violence and conflict over resources—the war of all against all, in Hobbesian terms. Private property, so the story goes, was the solution to these conflicts" (Blomley 2004, 23). Yet, as we see in this study, such relations are contested and in fact deeply unsettled.

The legal protection of settler property rights, as Cheryl Harris writes, has "allowed expectations that originated in injustice to be naturalized and legitimated." The material advantages that came from this injustice became "institutionalized privileges, and ideologically, they became part of the settled expectations" of settler peoples, a "product of the unalterable original bargain" (Harris 1992–3, 1777), also known as the "settler contract." Many settler peoples have emotional, cultural and financial stakes in the continuation of that way of life. The nation's (and their own) unquestioned past, present and future ownership of land became an unspoken "settled expectation" that could not and would not be questioned, in daily life or in law. Settling, planting and working the land, and therefore contributing to "progress," is what they did and wish to continue to do. Such work is what was and is valued (by whom?). That this state of affairs would and should continue is an expectation based on specific property ideologies, yet it is surrounded with, and clouded by, centuries of legitimating ideas and practices.

Settled expectations and certainty emerge from having one's ontology of entitlement confirmed through various laws, social surroundings and particular versions of exchange-based (Moreton-Robinson 2000) history and culture. More specifically, however, I think that this sense of certainty emerges from a belief in the fantasy of ownership and control over the past/present/future of one's own body and property. Modernity, as we have seen, works through normalizing the control and certainty of some entitled populations over so-called inferior others: indeed, notions of certainty are pivotal to modernity (Bauman 1991). As we see in the next chapter, the control of space, others and time was essential to the construction of the supposedly universal and superior Western frameworks of state of nature and *terra nullius*. This is where certainty and uncertainty link to Hobbes' notion of the state of nature and the social contract, a contract which is supposed to save people from the specific forms of chaos and uncertainty that characterize it.

SETTLER ANXIETY

I also interpret the uncertainty and crisis I discuss in this book as a form of "settler anxiety" (Tuck and Yang 2012; Simpson 2011; Rifkin 2011; Adese 2012b). This anxiety emerges, scholars argue, because the vibrant presence of Indigenous people is a constant and uneasy reminder that the settler colonial project is incomplete and unsettled. Indeed, the very existence of Indigenous societies, according to Rifkin, "has generated and continues to generate a fundamental tension within the jurisdictional imaginary of the [nation] ... troubling the effort to posit an obvious relation between the rightful authority of the state and the territory over which it seeks to extend that authority." This fundamental tension results in what Rifkin calls an "endemic crisis in legitimizing settler sovereignty" (Rifkin 2011, 343). Vibrant Indigeneities and Indigenous sovereignties are "nightmarish for the settler state, as they call up both the impermanence of state boundaries and the precarious claims to sovereignty enjoyed by liberal democracies such as the United States (Simpson 2011, 211). Indigenous peoples making *a priori* claims to land, sovereignty and ways of being indicates that the settler project is not complete, reveals settler certainties as fantasies of entitlement, and shows how the precarious and illogical claims to settler sovereignty must be constantly reinvented and defended.

Settler anxiety in this case emerges when people feel they must defend and explain what was previously thought to be self-evident, when that which is a "given" is unsettled. Although the people I interviewed undoubtedly felt anxiety about land rights, I do not suggest that such anxiety means they therefore consciously perceive authoritative settler histories as "fantasies of entitlement," or come to realize that claims to settler sovereignty are illogical and unfounded. Rather, such anxiety appears to instead create a defensive hardening of unexamined self-evident assumptions. Rifkin's work is helpful here, as he shows how "official governmental initiatives and framings become normalized as the setting for everyday non-Native being and action" (Rifkin 2013, 324).

In my view, these responses of anxious certainty, no matter how understandable they are as "settler states of feeling," reveal both the persistence and the tenuousness of the settler colonial project and its costs and conditions of possibility. The dilemma is that the arguments made to oppose land rights that I discuss seem to be the only ones available to settlers, perhaps because they are based on such long-standing and unquestioned ontologies and epistemologies. They reveal the powerful limitations of coloniality, showing how colonialism did not only affect Indigenous peoples negatively, but also has harmed the ability of settler peoples to see beyond their own limited vision, a vision that cannot allow the conceptual shifts that may be required for imaging how to decolonize settler-Indigenous relations.

UNCERTAINTY AND DECOLONIZING STRATEGIES

I argue in Parts One and Two of this book that settler colonialism—including philosophy, settler jurisprudence, legislation and settler "structures of feeling"— pivot on axiomatic assumptions about settler entitlement and certainty in land, property and settler futures, as well as on materializing "settled expectations." The question, then, is whether decolonization, for settlers and for settler law, may entail embracing particular forms of (likely uncomfortable) uncertainty, in order to imagine and practice relationships and power in new and creative ways. For this reason, when moving on to the question of how to decolonize settler-Indigenous relations in Part Three, I argue that it is also important to recognize and challenge axiomatic assumptions about uncertainty and certainty. Uncertainty may actually imply something positive, even necessary, for decolonization.

In the literature on risk and certainty reviewed above, uncertainty and risk are generally seen in a negative light, almost always indicating *un*desirable outcomes (Lupton 1999). Yet uncertainty can also been seen as positive and necessary, especially in creative pursuits, where uncertainty often leads to new and unexpected discoveries and motivations to continue. In academic research and writing, in educational pedagogy, in music and visual art, uncertainty can lead to excitement and growth by allowing something new and unexpected to emerge. Some researchers would argue that, if you know in advance what your answers to the questions will be, why do the research at all? Similarly, it is impossible to imagine improvisational jazz without uncertainty. Knowing in advance kills spontaneity and ingenuity; certainty leads to predictability, not innovation. Working through uncertainty is deeply tied to the imagination, inventiveness and responsiveness. Creativity requires one to risk letting go of control and certainty in order to find genuine inspiration in the flow of relations, both with the other musicians and the music itself. Uncertainty allows for creative relationships and attentive dialogue between musicians, known as the call and response. Uncertainty therefore does not necessarily result in the destructive chaos and randomness that is often imagined, since good improvisation is tied to deep and conscientious engagement. Improvisational jazz has to be unscripted, yet it must also be *mindful* in order to be a genuine expression of the musicians listening and responding to each other.

Perhaps embracing anxiety and uncertainty may also offer pathways out of the settled expectations of settler colonialism. Macoun and Strakosch (2013, 432) argue that "[e]xposing the settler colonial project as fundamentally incomplete— and unable to be completed in the face of Indigenous resistance—has the potential to be a profoundly liberating and destabilizing move." The moment of destabilization and uncertainty may open possibilities because it may be "the moment that settler colonialism is revealed as one, very limited, way of understanding and organizing our reality" (Macoun and Strakosch 2013, 438). Even within Western political and philosophical traditions, "it is possible to imagine other ways that two societies might behave and be in one place. If we decide to look outside our own frameworks, and engage with Indigenous people and ideas, we might find even richer political possibilities" (Macoun and Strakosch 2013, 437).

Envisioning the possibilities for decolonization, in Part Three I argue that embracing uncertainty is required in order to unsettle the expectations, axiomatic assumptions and practices that emerge from centuries of embedded colonial and national frameworks that have limited our vision and our ability to relate to others. Uncertainty, in fact, may open channels to listening, relating and creating in new and unexpected ways. Moving beyond the limitations and cages of settled expectations and embracing the potential creativity that "ontological uncertainty" could generate might be one way to help us imagine and practice less defensive and perhaps even decolonizing forms of settler-Indigenous relations.

Sium, Desai and Ritskes (2012, iv) point out that it takes humility and courage to be uncertain, and that to decolonize is to "live in understanding that not everything is known or unknowable." Such humility seems anathema to the epistemologies of certainty that inform settler states of feeling and that underpin settler law. Living without the entitlement to know everything (and therefore be certain) would likely lead to settler discomfort, a discomfort that may need to be embraced instead of resisted in order for settlers to participate in the difficult work of decolonization. Here I am not suggesting that such discomfort and uncertainty replicate the so-called "resilience," "flexibility" and "privatization of risk" celebrated and promoted by neoliberalism (Calhoun 2006). Instead, I am imagining a principled, histori-cally aware stance of self-conscious refusal to mobilize the axiomatic knowledge and action that have emerged from settler entitlement and certainty. This kind of refusal may open a space for genuine attention to alternative frameworks, and seed possibilities for creative and engaged relationships and collective projects.

If decolonization is necessarily a "tangible unknown," a "place where no one has ever really been" (Reyes Cruz 2012, 153), it is therefore also a place that, even in its tangibility and grounded uncertainty, will undoubtedly require engagement with the difficult yet necessary task of unsettling attitudes and practices based on settled expectations. My goal in this book is, in part, to help settlers like myself begin to embrace unsettlement and disorientation as a difficult yet creative first step to engaging processes of imagining and putting into practice the making of a decolonized world. However, it is first necessary to understand the genealogy of colonial and national processes that have secured certainty of entitlement to land for some, and not others, as I begin to do in the next chapter.

TERRA NULLIUS AND THE DOCTRINE
OF DISCOVERY IN EVERYDAY LIFE

Above I discussed how the production of settler certainty was twinned with the institutionalization of Indigenous peoples' "uncertainties." A major sources of settlers' fantasies of entitlement and certainty emerge from philosophies and legal systems based on the doctrines of *terra nullius* and Discovery. While these doctrines, as I show in later chapters, were essential for settler peoples and governments to legitimate their fantasy of certain entitlement to Indigenous territory, they have affected the day-to-day lives of Indigenous peoples in very different ways, specifi-cally through a much clearer awareness of the violence and brutality of how these concepts work, as well as the imperative of changing them. I had the pleasure of meeting Frieda, an Onondaga Clan Mother, and her mother, Ada, through my research. They often talked about the Doctrine of Discovery and provided their views about the importance of understanding it and changing it. Their sophisti-cated analysis of the relationships between ideas and practices provides another rationale for this book.

Frieda and Ada had several times talked about their sense that non-Indigenous people were surprised to meet them and recognize them as *Indigenous peoples*, actually existing in the world. At one public event about Indigenous rights at Syracuse University, Ada nudged me and then gestured around the room. She said, "They keep looking at us. They think Indians should be dead. Gone. But we're not. We're here." Later, when I asked her about that moment, she said "It's the Doctrine of Discovery; it's the basis of it all. They always thought we'd be gone." In this way, Frieda and Ada dealt with the implicit violence of the epistemology of the Doctrine of Discovery in their everyday lives through facing the settler expectation that they would be invisible, that they would simply not exist.

Yet the violence of the Doctrine of Discovery had also, according to Frieda, been forced upon her mother Ada in a more explicit way:

> My mother was harassed here in our yard when she first acquired this place [on unceded Onondaga territory] where we're living, from my grandma. A man came (he was a white man) and he said, "Do you know I could take this place from you at any time?"... He said that. "Because I can. You know, I can if I want to." And she says, "Well I think you need to just leave," and she picked up a rock and threw it past him (because you know she's a very accurate thrower so she could have hit him if she wanted to) but she threw rocks until he left. And he left. *And that's the Doctrine of Discovery*.

> For Frieda, the Doctrine of Discovery is a part of everyday life. She and Ada have a clear and unambiguous sense of the violence that it is responsible for perpetuating. For both, understanding the histories of such ideas and laws and their effects is essential, especially as a means to challenge the underlying assumptions of that belief system that are still active today. Frieda says "people need to look at it and realize that it's still there and it's still being used in law, and then to come to the decision that this isn't a good idea anymore." Colonialism, based on the doctrine, meant that "there were always these people with the right to run over somebody else. And that the others didn't have a right or they were somehow inferior and therefore it's fine if they go away, it's fine if we take what they have, it's fine—they don't matter, right? ... And the law supported it."

> For Frieda, a critical approach to the Doctrine of Discovery is also an important space of alliance and challenge, because it is a history that has not yet been heard. She said, "I think people have to look at things straight ahead, directly, and I think we found some of those keys in our efforts together—the scholastic people and us—and one of those is the Doctrine of Discovery":

It is shocking, and it's been not included in history on purpose because of that. It's purposely left out so that it isn't looked at … so it supposedly does not matter…. And it needs to … be very obvious in the scholarly area as well as the law … They need to look at it straight ahead—and look at it for what it is and what it's done, and not in a minor way…. It has to get to that point where the general public understands, and realizes that the judges are looking at it, the lawyers are looking at it, the legal system is going to purposely look at what has happened with the Doctrine of Discovery and that it was not a good idea.

Thus, the doctrine and its effects need to be examined critically and deeply in the scholarly arena, in law and more broadly, so that the "general public" understands. Frieda has a sense that sharing the story of the Doctrine of Discovery is the first stage of an important form of recognition. Frieda says, "Simply knowing is a real big thing: knowing that the people know. And knowing that … [non-Native] people know; knowing that the world knows, rather than us [Native people] knowing and you [settlers] hiding it."

For Frieda, critical acknowledgement of the silenced histories and experiences of the common-sense and commonly accepted doctrines that have held sway, both past and present, is necessary before thinking about the future. She says, "Let's look at what happened and let's be realistic about it, and *then* let's look at what can be, start looking into the future." From this perspective, there is no possibility of looking *forward* to decolonizing relationships *before* we do some of the challenging but crucial work that I have tried to begin in this book.

In the next chapter, "Fantasies of Possession," I explore the history and foundational concepts of settler colonialism, as well as how such concepts became embodied in law and legislation. These concepts were simultaneously deeply sedimented and transformed in the contemporary local sites of conflict, which I discuss in detail in Part Two: Chapters 3 and 4. In Part Three, "Imagining Otherwise" (Chapters 5 and 6), the final section of the book, we meet Frieda and Ada again, as well as their settler allies who are also striving to unsettle expectations and decolonize relationships and homelands.

Note

1   Perhaps it is therefore not surprising that Anthony Giddens, Ulrich Beck and Scott Lash became influential theorists of the British Prime Minister Tony Blair's infamous "Third Way" approach to politics. Some have suggested that the "Third Way" is "merely a deftly crafted slogan designed to make the capitulation to a conservative agenda intellectually and morally respectable" (Faux 1999).

Chapter 2

FANTASIZING AND LEGITIMATING POSSESSION

In order to understand the significance of the strategies and frameworks used today by activists countering land rights, as I do in Chapters 3 and 4, it is first necessary to sketch a genealogy of past legitimating strategies and conceptual frameworks that have been mobilized for centuries to authorize colonial and national processes of land dispossession in North America. Here I do not provide a "general" or all-inclusive history of colonial and settler-national ideologies, but a very selective genealogy of the relationship between property, certainty and entitlement based on the issues that emerged in the ethnographic research, to be discussed in the following chapters. It builds a background to help understand how many of the people I interviewed might come to have such a sense of certain entitlement and "settled expectations" of certainty, as well as to understand the strategies they use to defend those entitlements. In this chapter I trace how the concept and practice of trying to ensure the certainty of "settled expectations" of entitlement and to deny Indigenous sovereignty has been conceptualized and materialized in philosophy, law and policy/legislation. One goal of this chapter is to demonstrate that racialized colonial philosophies and practices that present-day citizens might want to distance themselves from are not simply an inheritance or legacy of the past, safely stored in an historical archive. These ideas, and the practices that are informed by them, continue to be foundational to, and actively drawn upon in, present-day law and land claims legislation. It is important to keep this ongoing settler-colonial foundation in mind when we move, in Chapters 3 and 4, towards exploring how anti–land claim activists strategize to fight against Indigenous land rights.

I have titled this chapter "Fantasizing and Legitimating Possession" because within it I argue that the colonial rationales and supposedly legal frameworks for asserting and justifying control over the land in North America are, fundamentally, extremely complex and flexible fantasies. Indeed, the rationales for such entitlements to the land are rarely examined within settler nation-states, but instead are simply assumed, especially within the daily lives of many non-Indigenous people. The ascendancy of settler-colonial entitlement and possession, no matter how illogical, emerges from a longstanding and powerful tradition of "conjured fictions" (Borrows 1999, 559) and fantasies of entitlement that required intense and consistent effort and flexibility over time. Through this process, colonial powers conferred upon themselves the authority and entitlement to appropriate and possess Indigenous land. At the same time, complex and contradictory aspects of settler-colonial subjectivity emerged. This is why, as I discuss in the final part of the book, it is so difficult—yet so necessary—to strategically decentre such "sedimented expectation[s] of settler domination" (Bell 2008, 865) in order to develop decolonized relationships. In addition, by being able to understand how these fictions rationalizing settler entitlement came to be seen as certain and self-evident truths—and how they are actually contingent and provisional—we may see that they are actually open to change. Perhaps we may then be able to imagine new and less predictable ways of living and relating in the present and future.

Suggesting that these rationales for possession were, and continue to be, underpinned by fantasies does not mean they do not have powerful material effects; they become more than just fantasies when they are bolstered by actions and law. How did the vast lands of Canada and the U.S. come to be owned and controlled by colonial powers, and not the previously free and independent nations that lived here before 1492? How do vast tracts of land become "owned" by some people and not by others? How does a particular version of ownership and property come to be dominant and widely accepted, and not others? How did previously independent sovereign nations become "domestic dependent nations" in the U.S., with limited sovereignty? Regarding the territories now known as Canada, how can it be that Indigenous peoples have a recognized "inherent right to self-government" (embedded in Section 31 of the Canadian Constitution since 1982), yet must struggle with the contradiction that they only have these rights as long as they can be "*reconciled* with the Crown's assertion of sovereignty over Canadian territory" (Borrows 1999, 557, emphasis mine; see also Macklem 2001; Asch 1997)?

Although the legal frameworks in Canada and the U.S. are extremely complex and decidedly different from one another, one clear similarity in both systems is the legal rationale driving a settler sense of entitlement. As I discuss here, laws were developed to recognize some aspects of Indigenous rights and occupation of their territories, yet such recognized rights were and are only partial, limited and secondary, because the ultimate and higher sovereignty is always the property of the (settler) government. This ultimate, supposedly superior sovereignty, as I discuss below, is variously "invented," "conjured" like a magical "spell," assumed, asserted, and rarely questioned (Borrows 2002). For example, one of the most cited and influential cases in both U.S. and Canadian Indigenous rights law is a United States decision, *Johnson v. McIntosh,* in which Justice Marshall, according to McNeil, "*invented* a body of law which was virtually without precedent" (cited in Bell and Asch 1997, 45, emphasis mine). One of the most criticized elements of Marshall's analysis is his definition and use of the concept of the "Doctrine of Discovery" (based on notions of *terra nullius*), in which colonizers gain sovereignty over land on the basis of the "discovery" of that land, even if the land is already occupied. Despite major critiques of this doctrine and of Marshall's legal reasoning, in addition to changes in subsequent decisions by Marshall, Canadian courts still consistently cite Marshall in *Johnson v. McIntosh* to support the legal presumption of Crown sovereignty. Indeed, that legal decision is seen as "'the *Locus classicus*' of principles governing Aboriginal title in settler nations (Bell and Asch 1997, 46–47; also see Miller, Ruru, Behrendt and Lindberg 2010).

In both Canada and the U.S., then, Crown sovereignty—and thus the legality of settler ownership of land—is most often assumed and asserted (often based on U.S. law), seen as self-evident and rarely questioned in legal decisions or by settler subjects. As I have already suggested, to argue that settler sovereignty is based on "*fantasies* of entitlement" does not mean that such assertions do not have profound material effects in the world. Indeed, such fantasies of entitlement legitimated the unleashing of one of the most extensive colonial processes ever, a legalized grasping for land that has not stopped to this day. This process still powerfully defines the day-to-day lives and imagined futures of all North Americans, although in very different ways depending on their social location. Colonial powers "conjure fictions that vindicate their claims of authority," asserting and assuming colonial and national settler "political and legal ascendancy" (Borrows 1999, 559).

PROPERTY AND "FIRST POSSESSION"

One of the reasons that the idea of land rights for Indigenous people is often responded to in contentious and even violent ways is that it disrupts unquestioned European assumptions about property, assumptions that have been developed through liberal political theory, social practice and law over centuries, and are based on a settled agricultural or commercial society. Such assumptions emerge from specific notions of property, and how within this framework property is meshed with ideas of entitlement, appropriation and personhood.

In current modern Western usage, the term "property" usually indicates the "thing" over which a person claims "more or less exclusive rights of ownership" (Hahn 1998, 4). For anthropologists and legal scholars, however, ideas about property are really about human social relations rather than about the inherent attributes of the object that we call *property*. In other words, property is not a "thing," but instead signifies "a network of social relations that governs the conduct of people with respect to the use and definition of things" (Hoebel 1966 in Hahn 1998, 4; see also Brace 2004; Rose 1994; Nedelsky 1990).[1] Anthropologists have shown that there are, and have been, many possible ways to organize relationships between people with regard to things. I find it useful to consider what property theorist Carol Rose (1994) calls the broader "property regime." For Rose, the term involves an entire historically developed and institutionalized system of beliefs and practices about the correct way to deal with property, as well as the proper relationships between people regarding things. As I discuss below, both *terra nullius* and the Doctrine of Discovery conceptual frameworks underpin colonial appropriation of Indigenous land. They emerge from a culturally specific (British) property and legal regime that differed from Indigenous philosophies and laws, but that became relatively hegemonic through time.

British colonizers "primarily conceived of property 'as individual absolute domination' in which 'all the potential sticks in the bundle of property rights are gathered into a single owner'" (Weaver 1999, 17; see also 2003). Western concepts of property implied sole, individual ownership of actual property, as well as particular "properties" or characteristics of humans and societies (propriety). Some scholars refer to this as an ideology of "absolute dominion," an "absolute ownership norm" (McLaren et al. 2004), in which private property is expressive of "autonomy and liberty," equality and freedom (Brace 2004, 101). The naturalization of such ideologies also implicitly reproduced the assumed superiority of those who shared them.

Although private property is often constructed as a natural and normal property regime in much economic and political literature, Rose illustrates how such naturalness has been formed and maintained over time, arguing that it is important to look at community norms and narrations (stories)—the common-sense beliefs and cultural understandings that hold property regimes together. In doing this, she demonstrates the contradictions and assumptions in the practices and beliefs of private property, thereby allowing for the possibility of alternative property regimes (Rose 1994, see also 2004).

Within Western property regimes, one of the most long-standing and dominant methods of establishing rights to property is the rule of "first possession" (Rose

1994), granting ownership to the party that gains control of the property *before* other potential claimants. Emerging from Roman law, first possession is deeply woven into the fabric of Anglo-American society as the notion of "finders keepers," or "first come, first served" (Lueck 1998). The rule of first possession is foundational to the *terra nullius* doctrine (Berger 1985; Epstein 1979) and represents, as I discuss, a specifically agriculturalist or commercial view of property.

The sixth century *Digest of Justinian* (Watson 1985, 533) is considered to be the key text of Roman law, a text which "all civilian lawyers in England and Europe would have studied in detail" regarding legal precedents for the acquisition of territorial sovereignty and possession (MacMillan 2006, 106). In it, the words *terra nullius* themselves "appear nowhere" (Tomlins 2007). Instead, the basis of *terra nullius* is found in the law of first possession, which states: "What presently belongs to no one becomes by natural reason the property of the first taker" (Watson 1985, book 41). According to this version of first possession, it is difficult to understand how colonizers were able to construe themselves as "first takers," given that the land was already inhabited by Indigenous peoples. How could they possibly see themselves as being "first"?

As we see in the *Justinian Digest* (Watson 1985, 533), colonizers' ability to proclaim their "firstness" was predicated on culturally specific values related to the idea of unimproved nature. Book Forty-One, on the "Acquisition and Ownership of Things" states:

> One can acquire possession of someone else's land without force; it could be that the *land lies vacant through the owner's neglect* of it or because he has died without a successor or because he has long been absent from it. Any of these things which we take, however, are regarded as ours for so long as they are *governed by our control*. But when they escape from our custody and return to their *natural state of freedom*, they cease to be ours and are again *open to the first taker*. (Watson 1985, my emphasis)

In this legal story about entitlement, the term "vacant"—as in *terra nullius* (vacant land)—does not therefore imply "empty." Instead it indicates something that is in a "natural state of freedom" (wild, uncultivated), and is *not governed by human control*. This idea, that land is "open to the first taker" if it is uncontrolled and natural and not governed by human control," is pivotal to *terra nullius* frameworks that excluded Indigenous peoples, because they occupied and used the land and were related to nature in a way that colonizers misrecognized.

First-possession frameworks were therefore culturally specific, in that they conceptualized human beings as outsiders to, and conquerors of, nature. Such concepts of relationship to land in terms of possessive ownership and control are widely believed to have been foreign to First Nations (see Feit, 2004a, 2004b; Nadasdy 2003). Glen Coulthard suggests that land and place for Indigenous peoples "ought to be understood as a field of 'relationships of things to each other'" (Coulthard 2010, 79). Land is "an ontological framework for understanding relationships" (Coulthard 2010, 79) because it

> locates us as an inseparable part of an expansive system of interdepend-ent relations covering the land and animals, past and future generations, as well as other people and communities. This self-conception demands that we conduct ourselves in accordance with certain ethico-political norms, which stresses, among other things, the importance of sharing, egalitarianism, respecting the freedom and autonomy of both individu-als and groups, and recognizing the obligations that one has not only to other people, but to the natural world as a whole. (Coulthard 2010, 82)

Thus, it is important to see that the Western concepts of first possession that undergird the concept of *terra nullius* were based on specific cultural practices and ontologies that from the outset did not valorize different forms of relationship to land. The implication is that the very concept of "first possession" is "Western," in that it is based upon assumptions of a "settled" agrarian society that communicates possession through marking territory, by transforming nature and through the establishment of certainty in the possession of objects through establishing fixed and certain boundaries. In this way, having or claiming "first possession" depended upon mis-recognizing non-agrarian relationships to land.

This is where the relationship between certainty, property and entitlement to possession comes into play. Rose suggests that the "agrarian or commercial people" who recognized the law of first possession were "a people whose activi-ties with respect to the objects around them require an unequivocal *delineation of lasting control so that those objects can be either managed or traded*" (Rose 1994, 19, emphasis mine). If property is not "certain" it cannot be managed, traded or sold. It cannot be used for capitalist ventures.

Such certainty of expectation is what Western property regimes are designed to create. According to Jeremy Bentham, "Property is nothing but the basis of expectation … consist[ing] in an established expectation, in the persuasion of being able to draw such and such advantage from the thing possessed" (cited in Harris 1992–3, 1729). Indeed, "the functional importance of property," according to Merrill and Smith (2001, 363, emphasis mine), "is the *security of expectation* it created with respect to the future control of particular resources." Inherent in the liberal notion of property is the idea that it is secure and certain, not only now, but also into the future. It is therefore tied to *expectations* of certainty.

TRACING *TERRA NULLIUS*

The terms "*terra nullius*" and "Doctrine of Discovery" refer to a set of powerful and ubiquitous conceptual frameworks underpinning the so-called "natural law" foundations of international law.[2] As Fitzmaurice (2006) argues, "the basis of international law is in natural law [i.e., Roman law as discussed above], so when international lawyers coined the term *terra nullius* they did so as a way of summarising the natural law understanding of property." It therefore does make sense to use the terms *terra nullius* or Doctrine of Discovery as long we use them as "short-hand" terms, not to refer to fixed policies and laws, but to indicate complex processes that had numerous inconsistencies and continuities across time and space.[3]

Carol Pateman (2007a) argues that an understanding of the concept of *terra nullius* is essential to comprehending how the British legitimated "planting" colonies in faraway places and transforming them eventually into places called New England, Nova Scotia, and New South Wales, later to become nations such as Canada, the United States, and Australia. In short, through arguments based on various versions of "natural law," colonizers decided that if a land were defined as *terra nullius* it could rightfully be occupied. I have found, when teaching about colonialism in Canada, that when asked about the term "*terra nullius*," many of my students know it means "vacant land," and assume that the colonizers somehow did not see the Indigenous peoples. I have to correct them that settler-colonizers in Canada and other settler states did use *terra nullius*, but not in the original meaning of the term. As Lindberg argues, "European settlers applied the doctrine of *terra nullius* with a unique twist, concluding that such lands were legally vacant despite the presence of bands of people organized according to their own societal custom" (Lindberg 2010, 107). *Terra nullius* did not mean actually "vacant land" (in the sense that it was unoccupied), but that it was *legally* vacant: thus, land not possessed (in specific, culturally recognizable, ways) by either an individual or a sovereign power is open to claims of ownership.

In the early "Age of Discovery," the Spaniards (under the authority of a number of Papal Bulls) conquered lands through "discovery," but only gained sovereignty over them through occupation or possession. Originally, the discovering power had the first right of occupation *if there were no previous inhabitants* ("*terra nullius*"). If the land was inhabited, the so-called "discovering power" had the first right to trade and negotiate issues of allegiance, sovereignty and land sharing with the newly discovered people(s). So, in theory at least, the Doctrine of Discovery was not direct sovereignty over the land, but instead a right, as against other European nations, to negotiate with the people occupying the land, people who were recognized as having certain rights (Stogre 2001; Churchill 2002; Pateman 2007a, 41). Over time, as in the term "vacant" in Roman law, the term *terra nullius* was not used to describe lands that were empty as in uninhabited (Stogre 2001), but instead, lands that were *uncultivated* and therefore *not possessed* or owned as property according to European standards. It did not usually mean actually *seeing* the land as *empty of people*, but instead as *legally unowned* and therefore claimable by Europeans. In other words, the lands were seen as only *occupied*—not *owned*—and therefore *empty of people and societies that mattered*. This "unique twist" meant that Indigenous relationships to land had to be somehow defined as inferior.

Making the land available for settler appropriation, then, required a justifying rationale which depended on an equivalent "fantasy of entitlement" to define Indigenous peoples as inferior and in a state of nature. According to Pateman (2007a, 36), those who defended the colonization of North America often invoked two versions of *terra nullius*: "first, they claimed that the lands were uncultivated wilderness, and thus were open to appropriation by virtue of what I shall call the *right of husbandry*; second, they argued that the inhabitants had no form of sovereign government. In short, North America was a state of nature." This is where "state of nature" and *terra nullius* arguments become co-constitutive of the ongoing racialized rationales that are still drawn on today.

Thomas Hobbes' (1588–1679) political theories of governance depend upon the conceptualization of the state of nature as a pre-political, chaotic and violent environment, a "natural" state that Indigenous peoples were seen to embody. In *Leviathan*, Hobbes presents his theory of the foundation of legitimate governments. Essential to his theory is the construction of its opposite: the "state of nature," in which

> there is no place for industry, because the fruit thereof is uncertain, and consequently no culture of the earth, no navigation, nor use of the commodities that may be imported by sea, no commodious building, no instruments of moving and removing such things as require much force, no knowledge of the face of the earth; no account of time, no arts, no letters, no society, and which is worst of all, continual fear, and danger of violent death, and the life of man, solitary, poor, nasty, brutish, and short. (Hobbes 1651, 46)

Hobbes' social contract theory suggests that to escape the uncertain state of nature, people form a social contract in order to establish a civil society beneath a sovereign authority. In doing so, they consent to give up some rights to the "absolute political authority" in order to maintain social order and escape from the state of nature which is "neither propriety nor community, but uncertainty" (Hobbes 1996, 152, cited in Asch 2014, 128). If America was "a state of nature," it was *not governed by human control*, and was thus *terra nullius* and "open to the first taker," according to Roman law. That taker, if seen to be more civilized, was entitled to appropriate that land into private property. James Sákéj Youngblood Henderson (2000b, 12) stresses the pivotal role of "state of nature" theory to colonialism when he argues that "modern European political thought has its roots in 'state of nature' theory. Hobbes' vision of the state of nature remains the prime assumption of modernity, a cognitive vantage point from which European colonialists ... justify modern Eurocentric scholarship and systemic colonization." Further, as we will see in forthcoming chapters, it is still used today by activists countering land rights in order to delegitimize Indigenous personhood and land rights.

LOCKE'S IMPROVING LABOUR, PROPERTY AND PERSONHOOD[4]

European philosophical approaches to property conceptualize and evaluate different categories of personhood in relationship to it. For Hegel, private property is something everyone must have in order to develop freedom and individuality (Waldron 1990, 351). It is a necessary condition of personhood and active citizenship. I use the term "personhood" here to emphasize the process of how—and through what specific ideas and frameworks—socially located peoples and societies are accorded (or not) categories of social recognition, inclusion, citizenship and rights. I therefore focus less on individual personhood and more on how people, ideologies and processes of conflict construct cultural, political and legal categories of human subjects (see Nedelsky 1990, 1989, 1994; Davies 1999; Brace 2004; Mackenzie and Stoljar 2000).

Culturally and historically specific concepts of property, developed in the colonial context, informed influential philosophical notions of the value of persons and rights to citizenship. They elaborate an ideal of normative subjects, suggesting what kind of person is deserving of ownership of land and of citizenship. The ideals of improvement, individualism, civilization and "productive elaboration" became essential to what Asad (2003, 167) calls the "civilizational identity" that emerged from Europe, and that has, in turn, been generalized and "globalized" in many ways. Property is central to the narrative and identity of Europe, "not only in the sense familiar to political economy and jurisprudence, but in the sense of the particular character, nature, or essence of a person or thing" (Asad 2003, 168). Certainty and the transformation of nature into property were integral to this "civilizational identity" in settler colonies. Brenna Bhandar argues that "raciality and property ownership were co-constituted through a tautology repeated throughout European colonies ... Properties circulated amongst and were unevenly attached to subjectivities of both coloniser and colonised" (Bhandar 2011, 229).

Rose (1994) argues that versions of identity based on property ideologies are deeply embedded in people's subjectivities, since one's perceptions of property and property rights are fundamental to broader world views. While many of these ideas are today treated as self-evident and universal frameworks, appearing constantly in opposition to land rights, in the past they were carefully developed, articulated and argued over by liberal political philosophers such as John Locke in the 18th century. Locke argued that God rewards the transformative productive labour of industrious people with property:

> God gave the world to men in common; but since he gave it to them for their benefit, and the greatest conveniences of life they were capable to draw from it, it cannot be supposed he meant it should always remain common and uncultivated. He gave it to the use of the industrious and the rational (and labour was to be his title to it). (Locke 1690, 34)

The role of labour in transforming nature into property was a task commanded by God, and such godly labour then resulted in entitlement to property.

> God, when he gave the world in common to all mankind, commanded man … to subdue the earth, i.e., improve it for the benefit of life, and therein lay out something upon it that was his own, his labour. He that in obedience to this command of God, subdued, tilled and sowed any part of it, thereby annexed to it something that was his property, which another had no title to, nor could without injury take from him. (Locke 1690, 33)

God, in Locke's voice, mandates that improving, productive labour is the key to entitlement to property. So mandated, colonizers felt the entitlement, even the duty, to appropriate, enclose, develop and "subdue" the "vacant lands" of America that were regarded as lying to waste by the inhabitants, who were seen as "actively neglecting" the land (Brace 2004, 34). Such versions of personhood differ from Indigenous notions of personhood (see Povinelli 1993).

The cultural specificity of these approaches to property is apparent in the differences between how British colonizers conceptualized and legitimized their colonial process through images of "planting," instead of the Spanish colonizers images of "conquest." British colonizers did not tend to use a language of conquest, and according to a number of scholars (including Tully 1994; Pagden 1995), direct conquest was "never the doctrine of the Crown" (Tully 1994, 172). Pagden (1995, 88, cited in Pateman 2007a, 44) argues that the British "increasingly came to regard conquest as unsustainable in fact, and morally undesirable in theory." Instead, they mobilized arguments around planting and husbandry, using the "agriculturalist argument" (Pagden 1995, 78), or the "right of husbandry" argument (Pateman 2007a). These "settled" or "planted" justifications were a way to ideologically distance the British from the Spaniards, whose colonies they saw as being founded on violence and destruction, instead of on planting and "improvement" (Pagden 1995, 80).[5]

Seed's (2006) fascinating research explores differences in the "ceremonies of possession" enacted by different colonizers of the "New World" between 1492 and 1640. For example, the English first engaged in "turf and twig" ceremonies that stemmed from sixteenth century gardening rhetoric, land ownership practices and agricultural fertility rituals. Soon, the most important, consistent and obligatory way of claiming and justifying discovery and possession was by building a dwelling, planting a hedge around fields, or an activity demonstrating use of (or intent to use, i.e., clearing) the land. This British practice began to be seen as "planting" colonies.

> Sixteenth- and early-seventeenth-century Englishmen usually constructed their right to occupy the New World on far more culturally and historically familiar grounds: building houses and fences, and planting gardens. (Seed 2006, 18)

This particular version of marking one's possession emerged from a specifically English history of "peculiar fixity" that was different from elsewhere in Europe (Seed 2006, 18). Mundane activities of boundary marking created legal rights of possession and ownership over seemingly unused land. This included planting hedges and constructing fences, as well as demonstrating use and improvement of the land, markers which also signified *private* ownership of land. Thus, from the start of the colonization of the New World, enclosure indicated individual, private ownership and private property (Seed 2006, 19–20). Such acts of survey, enclosure and planting were, at the time, often called "improvements." Although today improvement often means simply making something better, in the English context of the time the word signified "fencing in large tracts of previously unenclosed land" as a way to claim it in a "culturally powerful way." Later, "improvement" included husbandry and gardening, and gardening inside a boundary "began to signify possession" (Seed 2006, 24–25). The garden, as a sign of possession, "represented the entire colonial ambition to possess the land by establishing a part of the project in a central and visible way. No other country used the garden in the same way" (Seed 2006, 29).

Improvement and possession through enclosing and planting gardens was also associated with specific techniques of English agriculture that Native peoples did not employ: "subduing" and "replenishing" the soil. Subduing usually meant the use of implements, often the Anglo-Saxon plough. Replenishing meant enriching or fertilizing the soil, usually with animal manure, a familiar English fertilizer (Seed 2006, 31–2). The verb *to manure,* in sixteenth-century English, meant "to cultivate" and more significantly, "to own" (Seed 2006, 32).

The use of the terms "subdue" and "replenish" were very significant in this context, having their origin in the book of Genesis. They also reverberate with the Roman law of first possession that I discussed earlier, in which land that was not "under the control of humans" was perceived as unowned and, thus, free for the taking. One of the most popular biblical quotations used in the English occupation of the New World was Genesis 1:28: "Multiply and *replenish* the earth, and *subdue* it" (Seed 2006, 32). Indeed, this scriptural, god-given rationale did important legitimating work, as evidenced in how Locke uses it. This interpretation of Genesis "justified English title to the Americas" (Seed 2006, 35). Invoked in Massachusetts laws and countless writings by early English settlers and colonial advocates, the terms found in Genesis, and the resulting implication that to subdue land was to possess it, was integral to their understanding of the legitimacy of English domin-ion over the New World.[6] Further, it "continues to be invoked as the foundation of English property law" (Seed 2006, 35). Consequently, a very specific local European cultural interpretation of the relationship between land, labour, God and entitlement to property was transformed over time to become a major—and sup-posedly universal—legitimating rationale for the appropriation of and dominion over Indigenous land. "As culturally specific as the understandings" of planting and possession were, they were to used to "deny Indigenous peoples of the world possession of their lands (Seed 2006, 38–9). Planting and husbandry as "produc-tive labour" are central to Locke's theories, which Mills (1997, 67) argues are in turn "the central pillar of the expropriation contract," within which "Aboriginal economies did not improve the land and thus could be regarded as nonexistent."

Colonizers saw such outsiders to the improvement process as less than human beings. Native Americans, having "failed to subdue the earth" and having given themselves "up to nature, and to passivity," had no right to consent or refuse. Indigenous peoples became, conceptually and legally, wandering nomads (Arneil 1996; Basset 1986), "not labourers or improvers but occupiers of vacant lands" (Brace 2004, 34). They needed to be civilized, and in Takaki's words, "converted into Lockean people" (cited in Brace 2004, 35)[7] who would be rational, individual-ist and self-reliant, people who would "subdue the earth" and improve it through labour. Such distinctions defined what kinds of societies and civilizations were accorded respect and sovereignty. Locke's *Second Treatise* is known as a seminal work in the liberal tradition, and is one of the key sources for "conventional Western conceptions of human rights" (Donnelly 1990, 33). Locke bases his theorizations, as do many liberals, on what Donnelly calls a "radical, property based individual-ism," or what C.B. Macpherson famously calls "possessive individualism." For MacPherson, the "possessive individual" lies at the heart of the liberal theory of the seventeenth century. Within liberal theory the individual is conceived "as essentially the proprietor of his own person or capacities, owing nothing to society for them." MacPherson argues that for liberals such as Hobbes and Locke, "The human essence is freedom from dependence on the wills of others, and freedom is a function of possession" (cited in Dean 2013, 69–88).

In this way, culturally specific ideas about property, labour, personhood and morality were important for the creation of differential categories of social being, cultural belonging and political authority. Ideas about property and rights, tied as they were to notions of "improving labour," were used by these colonizers to entitle themselves to appropriate the land and to continue to define Indigenous peoples as savages. In other words, Indigenous peoples were defined as savages because they did not know how to own land in a possessively individualistic way that European colonizers defined as proper. As such, their inability (or unwillingness) to control land was interpreted to mean that they needed to be under the control of colonizing, sovereign, settler subjects. Ultimately, then, ideas about property and personhood were (and continue to be) intimately connected, as legitimating strategies for ongoing colonization.

For Locke, rational societies must establish private property, they must give incentives to industriousness, they must develop reason, and, finally, political power must be institutionalized in particular ways (Parekh 1995, 84). They have clearly defined characteristics based on European structures and ideals. Locke argued that "Indian" nations, even if they called themselves nations, were not true political societies because they lacked sovereignty and a singular unified central authority. Because they did not have private property and had not built states, Indigenous societies did not conform to the law of nature that applied in this historical phase, as defined by Locke. There was therefore no need to respect their territorial integrity. Such an approach depends on a failure to recognize the governments that did exist and a deep misunderstanding of Indigenous societies. Such theories about the lack of law and government in Indigenous societies had, of course, "certain self-serving implications for Europeans" (Henderson 2000b, 20–21) because they could then legitimate claiming sovereignty over the land. For Locke (or for Britain) it was therefore not contrary to "civilized" ideals to take Indigenous land in the name of progress and through the laws of natural and universal history. An unquestioned sense of superiority and entitlement is embedded in such frameworks. However, it wasn't only philosophers such as Locke who had a sense of authority to define others as inferior and therefore not entitled to land. International law at the time, which was European law, "regarded North America as vacant because it viewed Aboriginal nations to be inferior to European nations" (Macklem 2001 in Asch 2002 footnote 29; Pearcey 2013). Locke's ideas mirror the assumptions of the Doctrine of Discovery. Indigenous people were constructed as peoples whose land could be taken as a logical, rational and moral progression of colonial superiority and entitlement. Indeed, this new philosophy of universal history based on the state of nature justified a range of violent, genocidal practices as an inevitable result of ideologies of progress. Further, such practices, even if seen as somehow unjust, were also seen as part of the inevitable dying off or extinction of an inferior people who did not labour on the land.

As discussed, the key issue is that the colonizing nations function on the legal presumption that they are entitled to underlying sovereignty over the land, and that the rights of Native people are secondary to these sovereign nations. Further, and as I have shown, within such conceptions Indigenous peoples were dehumanized, defined as inherently lower on a scale of civilization, failing to relate properly to land, progress, cultivation and boundaries (and thus property), living in a state of disorder and chaos, not understanding or practicing correct individual personhood and unable to govern themselves with reason.

A great deal of effort went into naturalizing the idea that culturally specific ways of relating to land and people was universal and proper, and to defining alternate worldviews and practices as moral "failings." This supposedly universalized framework provided a persuasive and authoritative fantasy of entitlement and, more importantly, a sense of certainty about the correctness and inevitability of European settler domination and land ownership. These frameworks are based on "fantasies of mastery" and "epistemologies of domination" (Bell 2008, 862). As we have seen, such fantasies of possession and entitlement are "more than just fantasies," however: they emerge from an Enlightenment legacy based on common-sense epistemologies of mastery that reproduce a way of knowing that naturalizes "relations of unequal power" (Bell 2008, 862) and reproduce specific understandings of reality/the world (including human relations to each other and to land) as both certain and universal. In this way, they exclude alternate worldviews by deeming them "primitive" and "traditional," while contradictorily claiming to produce universally valid "truth" by denying their own basis in specifically located traditions.

Such settled expectations and epistemologies of mastery are characterized by the entitled desire to own, bound, improve, appropriate, define, subdue and control both land and so-called inferior beings in specific ways. These approaches, deeply linked to western notions of property and personhood, also secure a fantasy of certainty that allows settlers to expect that, because of their superiority, they would naturally continue to own the land and that Indigenous peoples would inevitably disappear.

Such certainty of expectation is what Western property regimes ensure and perpetuate. Such regimes are built to protect established expectations and secure certainty in the present and future. Yet such expectations must be enforced somehow. Macpherson, (1978, 3) argues that what "distinguishes property from mere momentary possession is that property is a claim that *will be enforced by society or the state, by custom or convention of law.*" I now move on to explore how many of the expectations of certainty over property and privilege I have discussed here have been secured in law over time.

LAW AND CERTAINTY

The fantasies of certain entitlement that I have discussed require political, economic and legal muscle in order to make them into more than just fantasy. In particular, they need law to turn expectations and fantasies into material certainties. The patterns of settled expectations of certainty in property and privilege discussed above underpin jurisprudence about Native title and land rights, including landmark cases since Calder, cases that are often seen to have fundamentally "expanded the recognition and protection" of Aboriginal rights (Blackburn 2005, 589) in Canada. At the same time, these cases continue to reproduce what Gordon Christie calls a "jurisprudential colonial narrative" (Christie 2005, 1), a narrative that provides the conceptual underpinning animating the settler states of feeling that I discuss in Chapters 3 and 4.

The (1763) Royal Proclamation has often been called the "Indian Bill of Rights," because it appears to acknowledge the pre-existing rights of Indigenous nations, implying Crown recognition of Indigenous nationhood. Yet, at the same time that it recognizes some rights, it authoritatively undercuts the most "fundamental" of these rights when it "proclaims Crown sovereignty and ownership over vast reaches of Aboriginal territory (including lands into which at that time no European had ventured!)" (Christie 2005, 4). The Proclamation seems respectful because it recognizes Indian Nations as being in "possession of" land. Yet immediately, speaking in the voice of the Crown, the Proclamation declares that those lands are "Parts of Our [Crown] Dominions and Territories." Therefore, at the precise moment of apparent recognition of Indigenous nations on one hand, it simultaneously transforms unceded Indigenous lands into Dominion territory, on the other. These territories were seen to be only temporarily occupied by Indigenous peoples (and it was assumed that they would eventually be ceded only to the Crown). This move, Christie (2005, 5) argues, "unilaterally undercuts Aboriginal sovereignty" by "enveloping Aboriginal nationhood within Crown sovereignty." The sense of Crown entitlement lies in part in what the Proclamation assumes—yet does not explicitly explain or justify: its powerful silences communicate the unspoken assumption that the Crown is naturally entitled to its superior sovereignty. John Borrows points out that the Proclamation "illustrates the British government's attempt to exercise sovereignty over First Nations while simultaneously trying to convince First Nations that they would remain separate from European settlers and have their jurisdiction preserved" (Borrows 1997, 171). In this way, the Royal Proclamation created, structured and protected Crown fantasies of certain entitlement to future title through the establishment of a jurisdictional imaginary that may have recognized, but at the same time encompassed, the sovereignty of Indigenous nations. At the same time, the full, rich, collective place-based sovereignty of Indigenous peoples becomes irrelevant within settler law, simply through the colonizers' unquestioned entitlement to define entire nations on their own terms and as implicitly inferior. Indigenous nations exist, they are "recognized," but at the same time they are carefully and "legally" (according to colonial and national law) put in their subordinate place. The Royal Proclamation, as Pasternak (2014, 156) argues, "cements an imperial property right: preemption, which is essentially the right of discovery."

Indigenous peoples are first contained within colonial jurisdiction, and later further legally defined in the U.S. as "domestic dependent nations" in 1831 (case of *Cherokee Nation v State of Georgia*) (Laforme 1991). In Canada's 1888 *St. Catherine's Milling and Lumber Company v The Queen* [1888] UKPC 70, [1888] 14 AC 46 (12 December 1888) the Crown encompasses Indigenous lands and title, bestowing Indigenous nations with the mere right to use and enjoy the fruits of the land, yet always depending on the Crown's "good will" (Christie 2005, 9). The court argued that Aboriginal title was only a restriction on underlying provincial Crown title, and would be extinguished when surrendered by treaty. The Court ruled that the treaties transferred Crown lands to exclusive provincial control while eliminating Indian interest in those lands. This is because "post-treaty-making, the land was not federal land, over which the federal Crown could issue licenses. Upon surrender by the treaty nations, this land became provincial land" (Christie 2005, 5). One "vitally important subtext" of the dispute about jurisdiction in the St. Catherine's Milling case, Christie argues, was that the Court interpreted the wording of the Royal Proclamation "not as signalling *recognition* of pre-existing claims," but instead as a "*granting* of rights to pre-treaty Indians" to use and occupy lands reserved for them by the Crown. The difference between recognizing pre-existing rights and "granting" temporary rights transfers superior power to the Crown. Indeed, reserving lands was, significantly, understood to be "nothing more than a gracious extension of the good will of the Crown" (Christie 2005, 5). This kind of reasoning is still common sense today, especially when people speak of the government solving land "claims" by "giving" First Nations huge settlements, or suggesting that Indigenous peoples "claim" settler land rather than "*reclaim*" their pre-existing land rights.

The assumption of an ultimate, supposedly superior, sovereignty continues to inform legal decisions to this day, even though it is a common perception that Canadian law is at the forefront of the recognition of Indigenous rights, especially since *Calder* in 1973. If we examine legal cases after *Calder* in terms of if and how they defend certainty for settler property, they ultimately continue to play out the same fantasy of Crown entitlement, making fantasy into law, and providing certainty to settler society through the careful *limiting* of Indigenous title and sovereignty. *Calder* was a landmark decision because it changed the definition of Indigenous land rights from what it had been previously—a personal and usufructory right—to a notion of Aboriginal title, a legal right. Yet the specifics of Aboriginal title were not defined. In 1982 the *Canadian Constitution Act* introduced Section 35, which stated that the "existing Aboriginal and treaty rights of the Aboriginal peoples of Canada are hereby recognized and affirmed," even though the meaning of Aboriginal title was still unclear. In 1995, the Government of Canada recognized the inherent right of self-government as an existing Aboriginal right under section 35 of the Constitution Act, 1982. However, since then, pivotal court decisions have consistently interpreted these *inherent* rights so that they can only exist as long as they can be *"reconciled with"* Crown sovereignty (Borrows 2002, 8). Once again, Indigenous people were required to adapt, adjust and reconcile themselves to the primacy of state sovereignty, which is unquestioned and certain in law.

In the Supreme Court decision in *R. v Sparrow* [1990] 1 S.C.R. 1075, the Court decided that Aboriginal rights that were in existence in 1982 would be protected under Section 35, and could not be infringed without justification, on account of the "fiduciary obligation" of the Crown to Aboriginal peoples in Canada. It thus requires that the Crown exercise restraint when applying its powers in interference with Aboriginal rights. Thus, on the one hand, Sparrow recognized Indigenous rights. On the other hand, at the precise moment of recognition, we also see the limiting of, and encroachment upon, these rights. The implication of *Sparrow* is that Aboriginal rights may be encroached upon given sufficient reason, which means that these rights are therefore not absolute. Thus, while Aboriginal rights were *recognized* within the law, they were also *limited* in specific ways. Although the Crown would now be required to justify its infringement of Aboriginal rights on the basis of the "Honour of the Crown," the measuring and assessing of that infringement is still *within the power of the crown*. In *R. v Sparrow,* Justice Lamer stated that, even if the British policy was to respect that Native people occupy their traditional lands, "there was *from the outset never any doubt that sovereignty and legislative power, and indeed the underlying title to such lands vested in the Crown."*

Similarly, in the Supreme Court of Canada case, *Delgamuukw v British Columbia* [1997] 3 S.C.R. 1010, a decision often proclaimed as a breakthrough for Indigenous rights, Chief Justice Lamer reminds readers that Indigenous rights "are aimed at the *reconciliation of the prior occupation of North America ... with the assertion of Crown sovereignty* over Canadian territory. Such "reconciliation," as we have seen, has meant that Indigenous people's lifeways and relationships to territories must still always reconcile themselves to occupying an inferior position in relation to Crown sovereignty, entitlement and assumed superiority.

Underlying these judicial rulings, as Christie suggests, it is evident that there is "never a flicker of doubt" in the Court's mind that it is the Crown that has sovereignty, and the Crown decides "what land 'means,' to what uses lands may be put, and how people…will live in relation to lands and resources" (Christie 2005, 15). The Crown's superior sovereignty is enacted on lands, peoples and the relationships between them. Borrows suggests that while the case "somewhat positively changed the law to protect Aboriginal title, it has also simultaneously sustained a legal framework that undermines Aboriginal land rights. In particular, the decision's unreflective acceptance of Crown sovereignty places Aboriginal title in a subordinate position relative to other legal rights" (1999, 537). Borrows says (1999, 585–6):

> In *Sparrow*, the Court held that prior to the enactment of the *Constitution Act, 1982*, the federal government could extinguish Aboriginal rights without the consent of a group claiming the right. The final section of *Delgamuukw* confirmed this power … The Court arrived at its conclusion without ever questioning whether extinguishment was "a morally and politically defensible conception of Aboriginal rights." It simply assumed that "in a federal system such as Canada's, the need to determine whether Aboriginal rights have been extinguished raises the question of which level of government has jurisdiction to do so."

In other words, by using precedent to define acceptable questions in the Court, the discussion focused only on debates within Canadian jurisprudence about what level of government (federal or provincial) has the right to extinguish Aboriginal rights. It did not allow for a discussion of the legitimacy of the very right itself.

On June 26, 2014, the Supreme Court of Canada (SCC) released the long-awaited Tsilhqot'in decision. This decision provoked widespread jubilation from First Nations because the landmark decision "recognized that the Xeni Gwet'in Tsilhqot'in People have Aboriginal Title to a large part of their traditional territory" (Diabo 2015). An in-depth discussion of the case is not possible here, yet aspects of the decision are potentially of real benefit for the legal "recognition" of land rights. These include: 1) the decision did not subscribe to the "postage stamp" theory of Aboriginal Title, 2) it recognized that consent of the Aboriginal Title holders is required for activities in the territory, and 3) it recognized that the "beneficial interest" in the Aboriginal Title territory belongs to the Aboriginal Title holding group and not the Crown.

In terms of the argument of this chapter, one of the pivotal issues in the decision is that it explicitly states: "The doctrine of *terra nullius* never applied in Canada" (Tsilqot'in decision, para 69). However, on carefully reading through the decision, it is clear that the Crown's *superior* sovereignty is still consistently assumed and defended, and it assumes Aboriginal rights must still be reconciled with that superior sovereignty. How can that sovereignty be constructed as superior without the doctrines of *terra nullius* and discovery? As I have been arguing, the entitlement of self-ascribed "superior" European power is a fantasy, underpinned by racialized assumptions about the inferiority of Indigenous occupation and use of the land. Without those assumptions, there is no possible way to imagine that that Crown has a radical underlying sovereignty that magically crystallized when they asserted it. Thus the decision does not repudiate the Doctrine of Discovery or question the Crown's legal entitlement (Diabo 2015). *Âpihtawikosisân,* discussing the decision, writes:

> *Terra nullius,* on which the Doctrine of Discovery heavily relies, was found to have never applied in Canada. So the Court has once again told us how Canada did NOT gain sovereignty over the lands, but remained consistently vague on how Canada DID gain this sovereignty. Other than saying, as always, that when sovereignty was asserted by the Crown, it crystalized. (*Âpihtawikosisân* 2014)

The effects of the decision are not yet known. However, even if the decision is potentially an improvement on current legal possibilities, the question is whether—and if so, how—Indigenous peoples can or cannot access it. Diabo and Pasternak (2015) suggest that litigation on the basis of the decision will be impossible for most groups because of the cost, but more importantly, the government has made it clear that it will ignore the decision, regardless of what it might be, and prefers to continue to negotiate through their Comprehensive Land Claims Policy.

Although the legal decisions I have discussed are flexible and constantly changing, they are also located on a continuum with Locke and Hobbes' foundational visions because they embody colonial visions of land, power, property, personhood, people and their interrelationships. They are informed by deep-seated assumptions about the superiority of colonial epistemologies and persons, and the resulting sense of entitlement of colonial powers to function on the legal fiction that they are entitled to underlying sovereignty and ownership of the land. This sense of entitlement depends upon the construction of Indigenous personhood and governments as naturally inferior, and enveloping them within the jurisdiction of the nation-state. The "imperative of dehumanization" (Lindberg 2010, 117) of Indigenous personhood and governance embedded in the doctrines of Discovery and *terra nullius* were mobilized soon after Confederation in Canada, with the 1867 Indian Act, which first of all defined and, as Lawrence (2004) contends, actually "created," "Indians." In this Act, personhood is specifically refused to Indigenous peoples in Section 12, which states: "The term 'person' means an individual other than an Indian, unless the context clearly requires another construction" (cited in Lindberg 2010, 117). At the same time, Indigenous peoples and governments were constructed as a kind of naturalized property of the nation-state—"owned and moveable objects and controllable absolutely" (Lindberg 2010, 113). The settler state ensures its own entitlement to a superior position of power through defining Indigenous peoples as inferior and controlling their relationships to their land and to the state.

Although it is often suggested that the "legal terrain has slowly expanded the recognition and protection of the rights of Aboriginal people since 1973," especially with regard to *Calder v. Attorney General of British Columbia* (Blackburn 2005, 589), such "recognition" is contradictory when Indigenous rights must always be "reconciled" with the Crown's underlying and superior sovereignty. This is settler law, even if such claims have not been proven, or if Indigenous people are not themselves "reconciled" to that interpretation. In this way, jurisprudence has legally entrenched and attempted to materialize the fantasy of certainty and stability for settlers, always encompassing Indigenous nations into the "jurisdictional imaginary" of the settler nation. Law was and is still pivotal in establishing and maintaining the "fantasy of entitlement" and the "settled expectations" of settler society.

LAND RIGHTS, EXTINGUISHMENT AND THE SEARCH FOR CERTAINTY

Part of the process of the "recognition" of Indigenous peoples rights celebrated by many and recently critiqued by Coulthard (2014) and others, is the land claims policy and process. Although, as mentioned, when I began this work there was some hope that land claims might be an entryway to some form of decolonization, this has not, however, been the case. In part, this has to do with the continued and explicit search for Western forms of "certainty" associated with the official land claims process.

In a recent (2015) report to the Government of Canada on "Aboriginal and Treaty Rights," specifically assessing the comprehensive land claims process and Canada's 2014 Interim Policy (AANDC 2014), Douglas R. Eyford provides a summary of the history of treaty-making and land-claims in Canada. It is striking how often the term "certainty" makes its appearance—including in a section specifically on the "certainty techniques" used in the land claims process—indicating how important the attempt to secure certainty has been, and continues to be, for the settler state. When Eyford (2015) describes land claims policies, he does not hesitate to state baldly that "Comprehensive land claims agreements ... are designed to provide certainty and predictability over land and resources." Here, from the outset of the report, it appears to be self-evident that certainty is an unequivocally positive thing. Yet, it is important to ask: certainty and stability for whom? It is clear throughout the report that the goal of land claims policy is certainty and stability for the *state*, specifically in order to promote a stable environment for capitalist investment. Yet when Eyford (2015, 3) says that "Modern treaties, where completed, have improved socio-economic outcomes for Aboriginal beneficiaries," he implies that the certainty of land agreements is also a good thing for Indigenous people. Certainty in land claims policy, as I discuss below, depends upon the extinguishment of undefined Aboriginal rights. This process of state pursuit of certainty, over the objections of Indigenous peoples, has a revealing and shape-shifting quality made up of fantastic imaginings and absurd turns of phrase.

Canada, indeed, has a long history of searching for certainty—a certainty which has required Indigenous people to extinguish their Aboriginal rights and title in exchange for the settlement of land claims. Writing in 1997, Asch suggests that the government follows a policy that "historically sought the extinguishment of Aboriginal title in treaties ... [and] still requires extinguishment as a condition for settling outstanding claims" (Asch 1997, 208). In other words, in order to sign a land agreement, the government requires that Indigenous people sign away (surrender) future and potential Aboriginal rights or title, other than those specified in the agreement. The goal of "extinguishment" in land settlements has often been to remove *undefined* and thus *uncertain* Aboriginal rights and turn them into *fixed, definable* and *certain* or *predictable* rights. Land rights, if not "legally captured" within a land rights agreement, are seen as making property *uncertain* and are therefore threatening to economic development and "capital and state sovereignty." The goal of the land agreements, according to Blackburn, is the attainment of certainty through: 1) *extinguishing* undefined Aboriginal rights, or 2) *fixing, defining*, and *codifying* such rights so that they cannot *threaten certainty* (Blackburn 2005).

As Asch (1997, 212) points out, this specific conceptualization of Aboriginal rights, and the assumption that their "ultimate definition must be a product of judicial interpretation and constitutional amendment," reaches back to the long-standing assumptions of Crown superiority that I have been discussing: first, that the "Canadian state holds underlying title to all of Canada," and second, that Crown sovereignty is "fixed and supreme" and that Aboriginal rights are and should be "subsumed under its jurisdiction" (Asch 1997, 212).

Blanket extinguishment of Aboriginal title was a requirement for the land cession treaties that had spread across what is now southern Ontario and then westward along Lake Huron and Lake Superior, in addition to the eleven treaties the Canadian government negotiated from 1870 to 1921 (Morse 2002). The requirement for blanket extinguishment began to change after 1973 with the minimal recognition of Aboriginal rights after the Calder decision. At that time the Government of Canada began a process of settling what they call "comprehensive claims." Michael Asch suggests that the goal of comprehensive claims settlements within federal policy is to "replace uncertainty with certainty and to resolve debates and legal ambiguities—the central one being the undefined nature of Aboriginal rights" (Asch 1997, 231). The goal is to provide "confirmation from Aboriginal groups that the rights written down in claims settlements are the full extent of their special rights related to the subjects of the agreement" (Federal Policy 1993, 9 cited in Asch 1997, 213). Such a clause is intended to counteract the possibility that if the courts were to, at a later date, interpret Aboriginal rights more broadly (and generously) than in the claim agreement, Indigenous groups could not expand their claim. The goal is to prevent Indigenous signatories from asserting "both the rights they obtain through a settlement and their [uncertain and undefined] Aboriginal rights and title" (Asch 1997, 213). The government itself describes it this way:

> When the comprehensive land claims policy was introduced in 1973, its primary purpose was to address the *ambiguity* associated with Aboriginal rights and title so that governments, Aboriginal people and third parties would know, with a high degree of *certainty*, how land and resource rights were held and by whom. This was achieved by extinguishing or exchanging all of the undefined Aboriginal rights of the particular Aboriginal group and replacing them with rights clearly set out in a treaty. This is often referred to as the "release, and surrender" certainty technique. (Government of Canada 2005, my emphasis)

Here it is possible to discern an explicit government statement of the desire to replace ambiguity with certainty and fixity through extinguishing Aboriginal title.

Indigenous peoples of course were, and continue to be, consistently dissatisfied with extinguishment. The result of their concerns, Eyford writes, was the development of new "certainty models" or "certainty techniques." He writes (Eyford 2015, 73–4) in a section entitled "Canada's Current Approach to Certainty": "Canada acknowledged that legal certainty was possible without requiring a surrender of rights and sought to develop alternatives that were as *legally effective* as cede, release, and surrender" (emphasis mine). These "certainty techniques" include the "Modification of Rights Technique" and the "Non-Assertion of Rights Technique." What does it mean when a policy is proposed as an *alternative* to surrender and extinguishment and at the same time is guaranteed to be as "legally effective" as surrender and extinguishment? Does it mean that the *legal* result is the same as extinguishment? Are these "certainty techniques" really an alternative to surrender and extinguishment, or do they produce the same result, albeit dressed in different language?

THE MODIFICATION OF RIGHTS CERTAINTY TECHNIQUE:
THE NISGA'A AGREEMENT

What does an agreement for *modified rights* actually look like? The 251-page Nisga'a Agreement offers an example of how rights are limited and controlled and yet supposedly not "surrendered." On page 20 the agreement states that it "constitutes *the full and final settlement*" of Aboriginal rights of the Nisga'a Nation (Government of Canada 1999, 20, emphasis mine). Then the agreement goes on to discuss the modification of Nisga'a Section 35 rights:

> Notwithstanding the common law, as a result of this Agreement and the settlement legislation, the Aboriginal rights, including the Aboriginal title, of the Nisga'a Nation, *as they existed anywhere in Canada before the effective date, including their attributes and geographic extent, are modified, and continue as modified,* as set out in this Agreement.

The document clarifies that the goal of the Agreement is "certainty," and that this goal is achieved by "modifying" the "Aboriginal title of the Nisga'a Nation anywhere that it existed in Canada before the effective date" of the agreement, to "estates in fee simple" in "those areas identified in [and limited to] this Agreement as Nisga'a Lands or Nisga'a Fee Simple Lands (Government of Canada 1999, 20–21). In other words, any undefined Aboriginal rights have been converted or "modified" into fee simple property. Undefined title has been effectively extinguished during this modification. In addition, the "back-up release" mechanism ensures there is no future uncertainty, as it indemnifies anyone in the present or future against further claims (Government of Canada 1999, 21). In other words, if, despite the agreement, any undefined rights remain or appear, they are effectively extinguished because the Crown is protected in perpetuity.

Such a "modification" of rights seems akin to a convoluted performance to ensure certainty and security through a more subtle form of continued extinguishment and limiting of unspecified rights. Indeed, this seems to be the goal of the government, which is evident in the way it communicates the results of land claims negotiations to citizens.

For example, the Federal Treaty Negotiation Office published a press release about the Nisga'a agreement addressed to Canadian Taxpayers (Government of Canada 2008), assuring settler citizens that national progress and economic development are not threatened by uncertainty. Entitled "Certainty," it begins by defining "the Issue" in this way:

> Canadian taxpayers are investing a lot in the Nisga'a Final Agreement.
> The Nisga'a are getting land, resources, a new form of government and

substantial cash transfers. What do other Canadians get in return?

THE ANSWER: The Final Agreement provides all Canadians *with certainty as it relates to lands and resources* originally claimed by the Nisga'a and to the relationship between federal, provincial and future Nisga'a laws....

A healthy economy is something we all want and is fundamental to every community's success. But economic prosperity is only possible where investors feel secure that their investments will not be jeopardized by disputes over land and resource rights.

There's *no vagueness* about the Nisga'a Final Agreement. The Final Agreement is a *full and final settlement* of Nisga'a Aboriginal rights.

Q: Does the wording in the Nisga'a Final Agreement provide the same level of certainty as the clauses commonly found in the treaties of the past?

A: This wording ensures that all the rights of the Nisga'a are set out clearly in the Treaty for everyone to understand. This is *consistent with the objective achieved historically through treaties.* (Government of Canada 2008)

This statement is informative. If the historical objective of treaties was extinguishment of Aboriginal title, and the Nisga'a treaty is guaranteed to provide the "same level of certainty" and is "consistent with the objective achieved historically" with treaties, we must ask how, then, are such "modified" rights different from extinguishment?

THE NON-ASSERTION OF RIGHTS CERTAINTY TECHNIQUE: "AS IF THESE RIGHTS DID NOT EXIST"

In my mind, the strangest, most bizarre and potentially the most infantilizing and humiliating (for Indigenous peoples) of the "certainty techniques" used by the government is the "Non-Assertion Technique" used in the Tlicho agreement. The government says that "With this technique the Tlicho nation does not surrender Aboriginal rights, rather *they agree not to exercise or assert* any land or natural resource rights other than the land and resource rights set out in the agreement" (Government of Canada 2005, emphasis mine). In effect, while the treaty group is not forced to *surrender* rights, they are required to voluntarily commit to defining and limiting their rights. The Tlicho Land Claims and Self-Government Agreement Section 2.6 is entitled "Certainty," and states that the Tlicho "will not exercise or assert any Aboriginal or treaty rights" other than any right set out in the Agreement." This, the agreement states, will "enable all other persons and governments to exercise and enjoy all their rights, authorities, jurisdictions and privileges;" and "release all other persons and government of any obligation ... *as if those rights did not continue to exist.*"

How can the government propose that inherent Aboriginal rights supposedly "exist" and are recognized by the Crown, and at the same time have the agreement say that legally it is "as if those rights did not continue to exist"? How can rights continue to "exist" if it is legally agreed that those rights are chimeras? The Eyford report that I discussed earlier says that the non-assertion certainty technique was developed to appear as an *alternative* to extinguishment, but at the same time to be "as *legally effective* as cede, release, and surrender" (Eyford 2015, 73–4 emphasis mine): in other words, extinguishment. It is hard to imagine that the government would expect Indigenous people not to see that these certainty techniques still remain rooted in the principle of extinguishment, when they have been fighting against such surrender of title for centuries. The humiliating difference is that Indigenous peoples are now forced to voluntarily agree that they will not assert their "uncertain" rights in order to establish a land claim.

Understandably, although some land claims have been signed, the resistance to extinguishment policy and the notion of certainty is also strong (See Manuel and Derrickson 2015; UBCIC 2014a, 2014b). The Union of British Columbia Indian Chiefs (UBCIC 2012), for example, questions the very terms of the debate. A legal report written for UBCIC and sent as a submission to Eyford states,

> Canada seeks to negotiate modern treaties with Indigenous peoples in order to achieve "certainty" over lands and resources so that economic development can take place. There is no reference to Indigenous peoples' objectives in entering into negotiations with the Crown with respect to lands and resources. (McIvor 2014, 4)

Indeed, Indigenous peoples have almost always entered into relations with the Crown with the objective that the Crown should, as they themselves do, begin with the presumption of the existence of historic and ongoing title to their territories (see Lindberg 2010). Instead, the intention was to negotiate sharing. Indigenous peoples "generally did not have a concept of land ownership that would have included authority to transfer absolute title to the Crown. They received their land from the Creator, subject to certain conditions, including an obligation to share it with plants and animals," because the "land belongs not just to living Aboriginal people but to past and future generations as well" (Lindberg 2010, 112). Leroy Little Bear writes:

> In summary the standard or norm of the Aboriginal people's law is that land is not transferable and therefore is inalienable. Land and benefits therefrom may be shared with others, and when Indian nations entered into treaties with European nations, the subject of treaty, from the Indian's viewpoint, was not the alienation of land but the sharing of the land. (Little Bear, cited by Lindberg 2010, 112)

It is therefore not possible to imagine Indigenous people entering negotiations without a previous assumption of the objective of maintaining ongoing relationships to their lands. Lindberg (2010, 112) writes: "Although Canadian Law allows for the surrender of Aboriginal title to the Crown, this does not mean that it is surrenderable under Aboriginal law." Discussing the signing of treaties in the mid to late 19th Century, Lindberg is clear that "The notion of transferring, selling, releasing or surrendering land—much less a sale or transfer of that land (and relationship with the Creator) 'to white people forever'—is a foreign concept and is not comprehensible or translatable within Indigenous laws and legal orders" (Lindberg 2010, 110–111). Drawing on a similar logic, the UBCIC assessment of the Interim Policy report to Eyford recommends "all negotiations between Indigenous peoples and the Crown should be based on the presumption of Aboriginal title." And "rather than requiring that Indigenous peoples establish proof of Aboriginal title, there should instead be a reverse onus on the Crown to prove that lands are *not* subject to Aboriginal title" (McIvor 2014, 5–6). Such an approach may sound unimaginable for the Crown today, but it in fact makes sense within sophisticated Indigenous legal regimes that are comprised of complex conceptualizations of "responsibility, legal obligations, reciprocity, and interrelationships" (Lindberg 2010, 90). If, as I have shown here, the settler state's claim to land is a fantasy of entitlement, it would make more sense that the settler state be required to prove the basis of its right to the land, and be required to prove it based on Indigenous legal traditions. As Glen Coulthard suggests, land claims processes reflect and reproduce *settler-colonial* relationships, in which power is structured within a "relatively secure or sedimented set of hierarchical social relations that continue to facilitate the *dispossession* of Indigenous peoples of their lands and self-determining authority" (Coulthard 2014, 6–7, emphasis in original). It enacts what Pasternak (2014, 160) calls "jurisdictional termination" or jurisdictional extinguishment.

Given the history of extinguishment that I have outlined here, it is difficult to imagine Indigenous peoples entering into such "land claim" negotiations willingly, especially if "certainty" still means extinguishment. The problem, however, as Manuel and Derrickson point out, is that "there is no official alternative to the Comprehensive Claims process," a process that "allows Canada to have its cake and eat it too: demanding that First Nations be willing to extinguish their Aboriginal title and rights before they enter negotiations" (Manuel and Derrickson 2015, 202).

Still, many First Nations are refusing to enter into such negotiations, asking questions about what certainty means, and whom it is for. The UBCIC released a statement entitled "Certainty: Canada's Struggle to Extinguish Aboriginal Title," that examines the notion of certainty proposed by the federal government:

Canada's striv[ing] for certainty reflects a desire that Indigenous peoples assimilate into Canada, that we sever our connection to the Land. Canada asks that we dig up the roots connecting us to the Land and replant them through treaties.

Canada cannot understand our Sacred connection to the Land, our Aboriginal Title. It is "uncertain," *because it prevents Indigenous peoples from viewing the Land as a commodity to be bought, sold or traded.*

From Canada's perspective, our Aboriginal Title has to be changed, altered, and defined in a treaty so that it fits with Canadian laws and ideas about Land.

For Indigenous peoples, our Aboriginal Title and connection to the Land is certain, it is in the bones of our grandmothers buried in the earth, and in the blood which beats in our hearts:

Our Sacred connection to the Land is certain. (UBCIC 2012)

Clearly, certainty and uncertainty can be conceptualized in many complex and contradictory ways, revealing distinct ontologies and epistemologies. Here, the particular settler ontology of certainty in land I have traced in this chapter is revealed as culturally specific and not universal. Settler certainty is seen as a strategy to assimilate Indigenous peoples into a particular capitalist mode that by turning land into a commodity would sever Indigenous peoples' "sacred" and certain "connection to the Land."

In this chapter I have followed the thread of how settler expectations of certain entitlement to territory were embedded in colonial philosophies and have materialized in jurisprudence and in land claims policy. Western property regimes, as Blomley points out, entail the bordering and fixing of property. It is supposed "that for every parcel of land, a singular and determinate owner can be identified, clearly distinguished from others by boundaries that distinguish his or her property interest from other owners, nonowners, and the state" (Blomley 2008, 1826). Within this "peculiar fixity" (Seed 2006, 18), boundaries must remain fixed and certain so that the property-holder's entitlement remains clear, and to make the land a commodity that has a particular exchange or market value. In the settler colonial contexts I discuss, such certainty in property, enacted through philosophy, law and land claims policies, has been, and continues to be, pivotal in establishing and maintaining the "fantasy of entitlement" and the "settled expectations" of settler society. In the next part of the book (Part Two), I move on to explore how such ideas were mobilized in resistance to land rights.

Notes

1 Recent anthropological work on property critiques the implicit separation of people and things in this definition, especially in an era of intellectual property, bio-prospecting and new areas of "propertization," such as software and body parts. Excellent collections that address this issue are Verdery and Humphrey 2004, and Benda-Beckmann et al. 2009.

2 See Pearcey (2013) regarding how these ideas still underpin international law today.

3 Carole Pateman (2007a, 39) contends that in North America, *terra nullius* was implicit in practice rather than framed in law. She argues that whereas *terra nullius* became the law of the land in Australia, there was a more "tempered logic" in North America, where Indigenous nations were given some recognition. Despite the differences, she suggests (Pateman 2007a, 37) that the legitimacy of both settler states was "ultimately based on the claim that ... they were created in *terra nullius*."

4 Although in this section I take a critical approach to the theoretical frameworks developed by Hobbes and Locke, they are of course not the only liberal theorists whose ideas could be seen to undergird settler colonialism and the conflicts about land rights I discuss in the next two chapters. One example would be John Stuart Mill's notion of the "civilizing" mission (Mill 1977 [1836]), which I do not have space to detail here.

5 The differences extended beyond those of the British and Spanish. In order to claim possession, each European power engaged in different practices of discovery and possession that emerged from local histories and belief systems, which they each assumed were understood by all others (Seed 2006, 3). The French, for example, engaged in theatrical rituals modelled on royal coronation and city entrance ceremonies that thousands had witnessed in France, whereas the Spanish made solemn speeches created from traditional Iberic Islamic traditions of declaring war, a practice mirrored in the recitation of the "requierimiento" to Indigenous peoples. The Portuguese and Dutch asserted versions of nautical and mathematical knowledge (Seed 2006).

6 For an analysis of Christianity and the Doctrine of Discovery see Newcomb (2008).

7 Such impulses to "civilize" continue to exist, as seen in the Indian Act in Canada and other legislation, which sought to turn Indigenous peoples into agricultural peoples and settle them as an integral part of improving and civilizing them (Lawrence 2004; Miller 1991, 2000; Borrows 2008).

Part Two

ONTOLOGICAL UNCERTAINTIES AND RESURGENT COLONIALISM

The legacy of terra nullius sticks to our shoes with the dirt as we walk over Indigenous sovereignties everyday. (Nicoll 2004a, par 1)

INTRODUCTION

Unsettled Feelings and Communities

How do uncertainty and anger around land rights become embodied in particular actions, vocabularies and symbols? What do these particular responses to land rights tell us about what is at stake in these conflicts? What might they indicate about the challenges and complications of working to decolonize relationships between Indigenous and non-Indigenous peoples? The goal of this, the second section of the book, is to explore how people mobilize in order to counter Indigenous land rights, and to analyse how they argue against them within the context of my argument so far. In this introduction, I introduce the local conflicts I studied, including the standing and influence of the anti–land rights groups in their communities. The next two ethnographic chapters explore how the anti–land rights activists in local communities defend their settled expectations in the context of conflict about land rights.

LAND CLAIM CRISES

Both the Caldwell First Nation in Southern Ontario, Canada, and the Cayuga Indian Nation in upper New York State, U.S., have been landless for over 200 years. Both groups made land claims in the Great Lakes region of North America and both at one point succeeded in federal legal decisions. If implemented, neither claim would have included defined pieces of land as settlement. Instead, the nations would receive compensation money with which they could then purchase land on the so-called "open market." As a result of their land claims, both nations have experienced explosive and angry responses from non-Indigenous residents in the areas under claim (Mackey 2005).

In the agreement, the Caldwell First Nation, a band of about 255 people, were to receive $23.4 million for the purpose of buying 4,500 acres of land over 25 years, land which would (if approved by the government) then become the Caldwell Indian Reserve. The Caldwell First Nation people are also known as the Chippewas of Point Pelee and Pelee Island. The basis for the claim, in a nut-shell, is that when the chiefs of the Chippewa, Ottawa, Huron and Pottawatomi Nations sold over two million acres of Southwestern Ontario to the Crown at Detroit in 1790, the Caldwell Chief (Quenesis Caldwell) was not present. Through this agreement, the Caldwell First Nation would finally become party to the 1790 treaty.

The most unusual part of the agreement is that the Caldwell Band would be reimbursed with money, not land, and would be required to *purchase* all of the land for their reserve. They would be able to purchase land in any part of the area covered by the treaty of 1790 (South of the Thames River), and they focused on an area south of Blenheim. The agreement in principle would have become a final agreement once it was ratified through a vote of the Caldwell members. Blenheim is a town of 4,500 people in a very prosperous and fertile farming area south of Chatham, Ontario. At first glance it seems like the "heart of the golden acres," which is how it is described in local tourist brochure: the town has green fertile fields, beautiful century farmhomes with tidy yards and carefully mown grass, prosperous barns and silos, and a sense of stability and respectability.

When the agreement in principle (hereafter AIP) was announced, some residents formed the Chatham-Kent Community Network (hereafter CKCN) to oppose it. The CKCN describe themselves as a group of "citizens and stakeholders," "seeking to change the current flawed land claim settlement process to be more open and consultative." Early in 1999, the CKCN printed signs saying "NOT FOR SALE" and local residents put them up on their properties. These signs appeared all over fenceposts and under mailboxes on some of the most respectable and beautiful farms in the area. Members of CKCN sent submissions to Jane Stewart, then Minister of Indian Affairs, wrote letters to politicians at all levels, and hired lawyers to start a legal action against the federal government about the claim. They also set up a development trust company that has signed a "first right of refusal" agreement with many farmers to prevent their land from being sold to the Caldwell First Nation. The municipal mayor and the federal member of Parliament were vocal opponents of the claim, and the municipality set up a Task Force to investigate the agreement and filed a suit against the government.

For their part, Caldwell members experienced psychological and physical vio-lence in the form of: a) graffiti and other vandalism to their buildings, b) threats and recurring phone disturbances, and c) during some periods, nightly surveillance and harassment of band members and band buildings. When I first visited the

Caldwell Chief, Larry, and his wife Theresa, they showed me the one-way glass they had installed at their home so that they could see the cars that regularly stopped on the road and simply sat and watched the house for hours. The people in the cars also sometimes threw firecrackers or yelled drunkenly. One night, someone fired paintballs at their house. From the outset, many of the Caldwell interpreted the resistance to their claim as a form of "racism," especially the "NOT FOR SALE" signs. They organized a March Against Racism, and thereafter, a number of signs were posted on the fence of their Band Office, saying "defend Indian Rights against racism," "Racist 'not for sale' campaign" and "Stop Racism."

At around the same time, in Union Springs and Seneca Falls, in upper New York State, opposition to the Cayuga Nation Land claim was reaching a peak. The Cayuga Nation had reclaimed 64,000 acres of traditional territory on the northern edge of Lake Cayuga. The claim was based on challenging a New York State treaty which was then illegal because of the 1790 Indian Non-Intercourse Act prohibiting all Indian land transactions that did not have the federal government's approval. U.S. District Judge Neal McCurn ruled in 1994 that New York State had illegally acquired 64,015 acres of tribal land in Seneca and Cayuga counties by entering into invalid treaties with the Cayuga Nation without receiving congressional ratification as required by a 1790 law. In 2000 a jury awarded the two tribes $36.9 million in damages for the current worth of the land and the loss of 200 years of rental value. Judge McCurn added $211 million in interest in 2001. The claim was later rejected, and then appealed, and finally in 2013 the appeal was rejected on the basis of the Sherrill decision (mentioned in the introduction to the book). In the late 1990s and early 2000s, resistance to their land rights case was explosive, and was organized by a group called Upstate Citizens for Equality. All over the area, handmade signs (Mackey 2005) saying "NO SOVEREIGN NATION—NO RESERVATION," "ONE NATION," and "EQUALITY IS NECESSARY FOR JUSTICE" sprouted against the claim. They organized demonstrations, petitioned local, state and federal governments, hired lawyers, began court cases, attended local meetings and court hearings, held moneymaking events such as bottle-drives and persisted doggedly to have the claim rejected (see Mackey 2005).

CKCN AND UCE IN THEIR COMMUNITIES

People have asked whether the CKCN and the UCE were "representative" of their communities and of "settler" citizens in general. It is impossible to say if a numerical majority of people might have shared their opinions. In any case, the statistical relevance of such views is not a point I am trying to make here. The study of a small right-wing special interest group is a very different project, with quite different significance, than what I am doing in this book. Instead, I argue that the sentiments expressed by these groups are part of a much broader settler ontology and epistemology. Their viewpoints are worth studying because they are entry points for understanding foundational undercurrents in broader settler societies. They represent the kinds of deep-seated and axiomatic emotions and ideas that many people hold, and are therefore necessary to recognize and name as integral to the complex challenges of working through decolonization.

In this book, while I do try to explore the relationships between colonial ideas about property and personhood and the ways in which people experience land rights today, I of course do not suggest that the present-day opponents of land rights that I interviewed had literally studied Locke's and Hobbes' ideas, and were then using them to fuel their arguments. My intent is to suggest a different, much less literal, source and mobilization of such ideas. Specifically, my argument is that such ideas have purchase because they have, over time, become subtly yet deeply infused in common-sense settler thinking for many reasons, including the jurisprudence about Indigenous issues discussed in previous chapters.

It is, however, necessary to briefly discuss how UCE and CKCN stand in their communities, particularly the question of whether or not such groups had a broader kind of authority and influence within their contexts, which I suggest they did. When I was doing my fieldwork in both places, simply driving through the areas indicated the powerful influence of such ideas because of how ubiquitous the signs were that were posted on the mailboxes of prosperous and poor farms, large and small barns, cottages and modern homes. In both places the organizations include homeowners and landowners: farmers, business people, workers in local factories and businesses, homemakers, teachers and public servants. The groups are organized and led, however, by particularly influential local commercial farmers and business people, and they also have the support of local politicians. The CKCN, for example, found money to rent an office in town, equipped with photocopy machine, desks and staff. They also put out many press releases and flyers, retained legal counsel and were involved in supporting the legal claims against the federal government. They eventually organized a property development corporation. The financial resources needed for such a venture must be immense, as land in the area sold in the 1990s for from $6,000 to $8,000 per acre. One member of CKCN told me that they had raised over $170,000 to support one of their legal challenges to the claim. From all of the above, it is safe to surmise that they had influence and support from other community members.

In both places, when I interviewed people who saw themselves as neutral (siding neither with UCE, CKCN nor with the Indigenous peoples) they talked about how deep and widespread the influence of the organizations was at the time, and how it affected their lives and the lives of everyone in the town. For example, when I interviewed Kate and her daughter Sarah about the CKCN in Blenheim, Ontario, they began by saying that they did not usually speak to anyone in town about their thoughts and feelings about the conflict, because of fear of confrontation and of being "pegged a Caldwell supporter." This indicates that there was likely a level of community hegemony on the issue. They were relieved to talk with me, they said, because they felt could talk freely about their views on this issue for the first time that they could remember, because they saw me as a non-judgmental researcher. They thought of the subtly enforced silence in the community as a kind of social control resulting from the influence of the more powerful members of the community (who support CKCN).

They also thought that those influential people managed to organize protests against the land claim before it was even officially announced. Sarah said that there was "a lot of muscle involved in the beginning." By this she meant that a group of influential people in the town had known what was coming—maybe through their government connections—and they had organized meetings and "rallied the gang," as she said, before the first public meeting. Kate and Sarah implied that the CKCN were very influential in the town. Kate said that the farmers against the Caldwell are not "Mom and Pop" farmers: "you can buy stocks in one of the big farms. That's big business; that's not [Mom and Pop] agriculture anymore."

Kate, Sarah and others I spoke with talked about how the politics of day-to-day life changed in the town because of the conflict. They said they did not attend certain local parties or events, or even go to the golf club in town, because they knew the conversation would inevitably come round to the Caldwell issue. They knew that if they did not explicitly take the side of CKCN they would be treated badly and turned into local pariahs. Kate said that earlier in the conflict she was planning to have some of the local farmers at her house for an event. While preparing, she put out a candle she had bought that looked like the face of an older Indigenous woman, whose face and wrinkles moved when the candle is lit. A family member told her that if she left that candle out, the guests would think she was "pro-Caldwell." She quickly put the candle away. Although this example of the candle may seem tiny and insignificant, it indicates a powerful fear that even the banal aesthetic choice of an image associated with indigeneity could be construed as a political choice that confirms or denies community loyalty.

The social control of the CKCN based on the land claim goes even further because people who unwittingly sold land to the Caldwell First Nation were treated as disloyal traitors. One family, I was told, was refused service at the meat market in town and had to go elsewhere to buy his meat. As I spoke to more people over the following years, there were constant references to the woman who had "sold to the Indians." She was consistently sidelined and excluded, not only because she had sold the land, but also because a Caldwell member had published something that called her a "nice lady." Rumours and gossip circulated about other people who had "sold to the Indians." In this context it is significant that the main signs sponsored by CKCN and placed all over the area said "not for sale." Another sign, posted in a field near Rondeau Bay, said "Don't sell your soul for a buck."

The recurring exclusion of those called "sellouts" revealed how "community" was built through judging inclusion or exclusion based on one's attitude to the land claim. One CKCN member I interviewed talked about a man who had "sold out" to the Caldwell:

> He has *broken many people's hearts,* because some of the people who thought he was their friend, you know, the day before the news broke that he sold the land he was telling that he wasn't selling, you know, stuff like that. *He lied to them, his friends. He lied to them.* His friends trusted him, and he lied to them.

This description indicates how polarized relationships became, and how personally people took other community members' decisions to sell or not sell. Any kinds of alignment with the Caldwell was seen as deep disloyalty to personal and community relationships, indicating both the strength and the emotional depth of the anti-Caldwell sentiment. Such examples of the social (mis)treatment of people who were perceived to ally themselves with the Caldwell band illustrate how publicly supporting the viewpoints of CKCN (against the land claim) became a necessary condition of being seen as part of the "community." Such a situation may or may not indicate numeric support of CKCN. It does, however, indicate that they had strong and authoritative influence on what was considered proper behaviour in the "community."

In addition, Kate and Sarah told me that there had been a major split in the church in town over the issue. The church had been trying to hire a minister for over two years and had finally found a candidate. At the last moment, after they had offered him the job, someone discovered that his grandmother had been married to a Caldwell. Word got out, and an emergency meeting of the congregation was held. People argued for hours and a large group wanted to break his contract. When the congregation as a whole decided to hire him anyway, many longstanding members of the church walked out and did not return. In terms of the community standing of the CKCN and how powerful their influence in town might be, the above indicates that their influence is not just that of a few marginal extremists, but integral to the texture of the town.

In a similar way, the UCE had a powerful and ubiquitous presence around Cayuga Lake, especially from 1999 to 2005. As I discuss in the beginning of this chapter, UCE held a car rally in 1999 with over 1000 cars participating. Soon after, a meeting at the chiropractic college attracted up to 4000 people, most of them willing to fight the land claim. At this time handmade signs were seen everywhere in the counties surrounding Cayuga Lake.

Jack Rossen and Brooke Hansen, both originally from outside the area but now professors at a local college and founding members of SHARE, a group dedicated to supporting the Cayuga (discussed in detail in the final chapter) said that during that time the UCE presence in the community was overpowering. Jack said that one could see a "proliferation" of signs. This was "before they standardized the UCE signs and everybody was just writing their own slogans and some of them were very creative ones." Brooke described the environment as "a charged atmosphere, and charged atmospheres are catalysts, where sparks ignite into flames." For Brooke, the "catalyst" for getting SHARE organized was precisely the ubiquitousness of the signs, and how people seemed to be taking up the ideas expressed in them. Julie Uticone, also a founding member of SHARE and a hairdresser who grew up in the area, experienced this period in a more personally devastating way. When she came out as a supporter of the Cayuga, she was assumed to be a critic of UCE and of the important local people who were members. She was then pegged as a traitor to her own community. Her business suffered, and her family became deeply divided.

Thus, although it is not possible to indicate the numerical or statistical significance in terms of their representativeness of the population, UCE and CKCN did have a powerful influence in their local areas. They seemed to offer a very persuasive way of conceptualizing and protecting the settled expectations of non-Indigenous peoples, an approach that had broad and ongoing support amongst many and that seems to be fed on anger and fear about uncertainty.

As I continue to discuss responses to land claims in the next chapter, I examine them as expressions of settler "structures of feeling." They are *settler* "structures of feeling" when they reflect and/or reproduce foundational conceptual frameworks that are essential to settler colonial and national projects. This is specifically the case when, first, they naturalize the assumption that settlers are entitled to the appropriation and ownership of Indigenous territories; they often defend this entitlement using the racialized frameworks discussed in the previous chapter, including the assumption that Indigenous lifeways and relationships to land and each other are necessarily inferior, in specific ways. Second, in a related way, they normalize the assumption that non-Native governments and people naturally should have authority over "Indigenous politics, governance, and territoriality" (Rifkin 2011, 342). This is often realized through a strong sense of home and community that is based on culturally specific settler frameworks that are seen as natural, and that Indigenous peoples should assimilate into. Finally, they are specifically *settler* "structures of feeling" when they draw on and reproduce what I see as *the* pivotal settler colonial and national assumption: that the Crown *always-already had and continues to have superior underlying title to Indigenous lands*. In other words, when they assert and defend the certainty that Indigenous territory is always-already domestic space within a superior jurisdiction, and thereby enact the subordination of Native polities to the "jurisdictional imaginary" (Rifkin 2009) of the settler state.

Chapter 3

DEFENDING EXPECTATIONS

This chapter explores how uncertainty and anger around land rights issues becomes embodied in particular actions, vocabularies and symbols. As discussed, it makes people feel uncertain in regards to their settled expectations about their lives and futures, and they feel angry about having to feel that uncertainty. When they defend their expectations and try to re-assert what they had previously felt to be certain, I show here that they end up re-asserting many of the key settler colonial assumptions and strategies we have seen in Chapter 2. Here I explore the specific ways in which they do so. I argue that their defensive strategies illustrate contemporary "settler states of feeling," and indicate, in a larger sense, that settler colonialism is ongoing and deeply embedded in settler subjectivities.

A video produced by the Ontario public television station (TVO) about the land rights conflict in Chatham-Kent opens with a shot of a Victorian-era farmhouse in Chatham-Kent with a "NOT FOR SALE" sign posted on the mailbox. It then cuts to a medium shot of a white woman and her daughter in a big homey farm kitchen. The woman (Mrs. Dearman) says that when she first heard about "Native people coming to the area" she was happy that they were "leaving the reserve and joining the community." But then, "when I heard they wanted a reserve…. I started to get frightened." To just "drop a reserve in our community," she continues, simply won't work.

Most striking in the above quote is that she constructs "community" and "reserve" as opposites. Native people *leave* "the reserve" and come *to* "*the* community." The definite article *the* in "*the* community" implies a more general, national community and thus the reserve is considered to be outside of the Canadian com-munity. When she says "drop a reserve in our community" it shows that, for her, a reserve is by definition *not* a "community." It is, instead, something that threatens to rupture her community.

Indeed, from the outset of the conflict, CKCN members such as Mrs. Dearman's husband persistently and repeatedly focused on the so-called "danger" that a reserve poses for their community. The CKCN's opposition to the Caldwell First Nation claim in Chatham-Kent was consistently based on discussion of the CKCN's attachment to specific pieces of land, and specific local issues that, as I discuss later, they also sometimes expanded to include the entire territory of Canada. UCE members' opposition to land claims in New York, on the other hand, drew on patriotic practices and discourses that focused almost exclusively on the risks and dangers to the American nation (see Mackey 2005). The different focus of opposi-tion in the two contexts can be seen in the signs that both groups produced. The UCE sign highlighted nationalist imagery of the American flag and proposed "NO SOVEREIGN NATION," while the CKCN signs simply stated "NOT FOR SALE."

Even the name, the Chatham-Kent *Community* Network, defines the organi-zation in terms of ties of local identity and community, whereas the UCE defines itself as Upstate *Citizens for Equality*: the organization is still local (Upstate), but is clearly also framed in terms of national (and universal) ideals such as citizenship and equality. Although CKCN members, similar to UCE members, see themselves as national citizens and make national claims, CKCN begins by asserting their *local* identity and heritage as the site of community authenticity that must be protected from the dangers of land claims.

COMMUNITY HERITAGE IN DANGER

Soon after the announcement of the Caldwell Agreement in Principle, the CKCN prepared a report to the Department of Indian Affairs which began by arguing that the land claim threatened their local culture and "heritage," a culture based on farm-ing and intensive agricultural production. The CKCN report also highlighted the hard work of the English and Dutch settlers of five or six generations ago. It told of the "struggles of these families" and the amazing "feats" they had to perform, such as "attacking six foot trees" to "get to the soil on the forest floor." They linked the past to present, suggesting that the hard work and determination to survive and overcome challenges still "prevails in today's generation." In this way they began to define the local community through characteristics related to labour and land—specifically the labour of intensive farming. Many people described the Caldwell members as outsiders because they did not share this culture based on hard agricultural labour and "interdependence." One of the key aspects of the philosophies and laws

I discussed in previous chapters is the way in which specific kinds of productive labour were valued and seen to be the basis of civilized behaviour and civilized society. We have seen how land becomes private property through the work of farming, gardening and fencing. Such ideas have often been reproduced and made into individual, family and community mythologies through specific and repeated narratives of how people laboured hard and overcame obstacles to settle the land and build a future they could count on. These particular kinds of stories are one version of a larger field of possible heroic settler narratives that are essential to the nationalist mythologies of nation-states.

The notion of a "community culture" based on agriculture recalls the agrarian seeds of Western property law and the colonial notion of "planting colonies" that I discussed in the previous chapter (Seed 2006). This was a culturally specific British way of claiming ownership of land and territory in which "subduing" nature, planting, fencing and making "improvements," was seen to secure private property rights. Significantly, the perceived lack of such "improving labour" by Indigenous peoples was one key criteria used to deny them possession of their lands. In my fieldwork, as I discuss later in the chapter, many people I interviewed also denied that Indigenous people were hard-working agrarian and agricultural people, as part of a strategy to delegitimize their land rights.

In the CKCN report to the Department of Indian Affairs, they list some of the "traits of everyday life" and "cultural heritage" that they argue are under threat of "extinction" from the land claim (CKCN 1999b). Especially interesting is the list of specific activities that they suggest are at risk:

- The local coffee shop and restaurants, where news in the community is communicated
- The school bus picking up and dropping off children
- Fishing at the back of your farm with grandchildren
- Neighbours plowing out drives
- Community dinners that feature wild game and a feast of fresh perch
- The infamous wave as people you know, and people you don't know, drive by
- The noise of the Canada geese as the flocks migrate south (CKCN 1999b)

The submission suggests that one only needs to spend time in the area to "realize the loving, sharing and generous community they are in," and that community is threatened by the possible presence of a reserve (CKCN 1999b, 12).

Why can Indigenous people not be included in this "loving, sharing and generous community"? Would waving at Indigenous peoples really be dangerous? How could and would their presence actually threaten or "extinguish" coffee shop gossip, school buses, fishing, wild game and perch dinners, or even the noise of the migrating Canada Geese? Perhaps it is because, symbolically, the Caldwell First Nation people cannot be seen as authentically "local" even though they live in the local area. The CKCN defines the values and practices of their "local community" as necessarily distinct and separate from Indigenous culture. The report argues: "One cultural heritage should not be *sacrificed for the benefit of another.*" This notion that one culture is necessarily sacrificed for the survival (or benefit) of another indicates that they see no possibility of two or more cultures actually coexisting: one "community" means *one* culture. The singular definition of community used by CKCN, similar to the assertions of nation mobilized by UCE (discussed in the next chapter), explicitly define and limit "community" membership based on a notion of shared culture.

The CKCN's argument for the preservation of local non-Aboriginal cultural heritage demonstrates how anti-Indigenous groups now mobilize similar discourses about culture and heritage that many Indigenous groups have. Indigenous peoples often argue for the preservation of their endangered cultural heritage *as Indigenous people* who have been subject to laws of assimilation and cultural genocide. They also make arguments about their relationship to specific pieces of land, *as autochthonous peoples;* a framework that itself may have emerged from their need to make claims within modern legal/political contexts. Here, the CKCN makes a claim using a similar vocabulary about the value of their endangered culture, perhaps an example of active mimicry of Indigenous strategies about cultural preservation. However, without the historical backdrop of the documented state programs specifically designed and implemented to destroy Indigenous cultural practices (such as the Indian Act in Canada)—often called a form of cultural genocide—the CKCN proposal ends up defining Aboriginal people as the source of the threatening danger. By leaving out that history, the CKCN can claim that they are under threat. The strategies that they used to defend their expectations of continuity and certainty forced them to articulate a more precise definition of the characteristics of their community and culture, a culture that they have previously taken for granted and have therefore not needed to explicitly articulate. In doing so, they express a version of what I have previously called a dominant "Canadian-Canadian," white Anglophone culture that is "unmarked, and yet normative" (Mackey 2002).

As in the philosophies and practices discussed in the previous chapter, the settler project functions simultaneously on two interconnected registers: on an emotional register of settler agrarian culture and continuity, and on an economic and legal register that concerns ensuring certainty in land and economic competition. Although the version of community presented in the first part of the report to Indian Affairs is based on emotions and feelings and home and community, another pivotal way they expressed their concerns was by making the economic argument that a reserve would be a risk and danger to the economic health and development of their community.

A number of key concerns were raised in meetings and publications, which I outline below.

"Land use compatibility with areas of agricultural activity"
Given that the area is primarily made up of commercial farming enterprises, including hog farms, CKCN was concerned about whether the way in which the Caldwell would occupy their land might not be compatible with this intensive agricultural usage. If the Caldwell decided to have their land as primarily residential, it was assumed that farmers would likely have to change their farming practices. For example, as a result of specific Ontario zoning regulations, a hog farm must be a certain distance from areas zoned as residential. Therefore, what the Caldwell intended to do with their land could affect local farmers. What if the Caldwell wanted a casino, or a tourist operation? Would this incompatible zoning threaten their farms and livelihoods? Would the nearness of residents mean that there would be more stringent by-laws about the environment? They blamed the government for this situation.

"Stability of land prices, within the context
of values consistent with local market"
The concern here was that if the Caldwell were awarded a substantial settlement to buy land, they would then be able to "outbid" local farmers for land, buy up a "patchwork quilt" of farms, and then turn them into a reservation. The fear was that although the first non-Indigenous people who sold to the Caldwell might get a good price, the ones left behind, who did not sell to the Caldwell, would be left with devalued land that no one would want.[1] They blamed the government for this situation, arguing that it could destroy their long-standing, successful and productive agricultural community.

"Opportunity for future expansion and return
on investments of area farm operators"
This issue is related to how farming has become more and more mechanized in recent decades. One farmer told me that it was necessary to always keep buying land and expanding in order to keep ahead. This is in part because of the need for so much expensive machinery. He said that if the Caldwell could outbid him on the land, then he could not expand, could not invest in equipment for further farm growth, and his farm would be at risk.

"Maintenance of the integrity and functionality of the drainage systems"
This was one of the most repeated concerns expressed in my interviews with Chatham-Kent farmers. Many of the farms in the area have interconnected drainage systems, all leading out into Lake Erie. Therefore the farms are interdependent, because if a drain close to the lake is blocked, the connecting farms cannot drain their land. The CKCN was concerned that the Caldwell might not farm the land, and therefore would likely not take care of their drains, thus potentially blocking the drainage of other farms in the process.

Many of the above-mentioned problems boiled down to a question of whether, and if so, how, the First Nation would be required to follow provincial and municipal regulations and by-laws. CKCN members seemed to assume the Caldwell First Nation would not be required to follow those regulations. Although, as I discuss below, they had been informed that the Caldwell First Nation would be required to follow all by-laws and would have little autonomy, they spoke as if the Caldwell would have complete autonomy and control over their land, could do what they wanted with it, and would not be required to consult or be compatible with the people around them. They were angry at the government, saying that it had "dropped" the First Nation into the local community, and was then not going to deal with any of the problems and dangers that resulted—such as the ones mentioned above. CKCN members consistently painted the federal government as being against farmers—because it was "giving in" to the demands of Native people and abandoning farmers. They also argued that the federal government had introduced an unmanageable "4th level of government" into their community.

At the same time, members of these groups made other arguments about why the land claim and Indigenous rights more generally were wrong. It was in these conversations that the arguments against land claims moved into a different register, focusing less on specific economic arguments and more on fundamental questions and issues underlying land claims. In the process people began to draw on frameworks integral to *terra nullius* and state-of-nature philosophy, in which rights and ownership of land are increasingly based on hierarchical and stereotypical conceptions of Indigenous peoples, mobilized to define which collective groups are entitled to full personhood and inherited privilege and which are not.

FIRST POSSESSION? "WE WERE HERE FIRST"

When I began my interviews with members of CKCN, people often introduced themselves by telling me stories of how long their families had been in the area and what kind of hard work they had done to settle the land and build their homesteads; by introducing themselves in this way, they simultaneously located themselves *as* local and as attached to the land. Each person provided me with what I think of as a personalized settler genealogy of land possession and labour. Such narratives are understandable strategies, whether done consciously or not, to link people to specific pieces of land as well as to express their justifiable pride in their family history. Richard, for example, stressed both the longevity of his family's presence in the area and the hard work they did to succeed:

> So [my family is] in the 6th generation [here]. My brother's sons—my brother's on the farm with my parents—would be the 6th generation that started farming enterprises with their large families. It's tremendous. I'm one of four, my father's one of five, and my grandfather, I think, is one of about 15 or 16, and his father was one of about the same—I think 16 or 17 kids. Very large families; *lots of labour* to break the land … getting farms started.[2] (emphasis mine)

Many others also told stories about their large families doing hard labour in order to make the land theirs, to survive and prosper.

In some ways, these stories are told in a manner that implicitly communicates a kind of "evidence" demonstrating not only their emotional attachments to place, but also their sense of legitimate and rightful possession of the land. It is not only about purchasing land, but it is also about making it one's own through years of labour. As one person said, "This isn't just a farm, it's our *home*," which shows the deep attachments people have to specific pieces of land, and the pride they have in the work done to build their farms and lives. Such attachments are understandable and important. Yet, this sense of belonging and attachment to home, to the land, can also be mobilized to defend expectations of entitlement and certainty in settler possession of land and contribute to legitimizing Indigenous dispossession. Again, it is labour, in Locke's view, which turns wilderness into private property. By stressing the long years of labour that it took to make the land into their home, they implicitly make a claim of possession through labour.

Indeed, such arguments changed tenor when several people asserted that their families had been in Chatham-Kent *longer than* "Native people." Robert, a member of CKCN, was explicit in his claim that his family occupied the land before Caldwell First Nation as a way to argue against their land rights:

> In looking at Native land claims, what the government is trying to do is correct what they perceive as a wrong—that they displaced the people off the land and white people came in. The history of my family *dates back farther* than the Caldwells being in this area. The *Native people* that are here are *not indigenous peoples* in this area; they all came in with the British. (emphasis mine)

In a similar vein, Richard, the CKCN member who above mentions that his family has been farming in Chatham-Kent for six generations, explained his understanding of history. He said:

> There were no Indigenous Aboriginals in Southern Ontario when the whites got here. We were here first. Frankly, we were here first.

What connects these stories to the *terra nullius* and "state of nature" frameworks that I outlined earlier is how a story that begins about individual families occupying land can become transformed into a broader narrative about how a racialized category of people ("whites") were entitled to occupy and own land instead of another racialized category of people (Indigenous people). As discussed, while the original meanings of *terra nullius* and the Doctrine of Discovery (not the ones used by settler nations) were based on the notion of land that was actually unoccupied, the "unique twist" (Lindberg 2010) in how these doctrines were applied in settler nations meant that Indigenous lands were defined as "legally vacant," despite the presence of organized groups of people. It did not mean that the land was actually vacant or that white people were "here first." As I mentioned earlier, many people I have spoken to assume that *terra nullius* simple means "empty land," and they assume that this is also what the colonizers believed. It is significant that local people mobilize this common-sense, literal understanding of *terra nullius* to defend their sense of belonging and entitlement. In this way, even though people may not comprehend the complexities of colonial law, they do communicate an understanding of legal principles of "first possession," and that taking something belonging to someone else is ethically wrong.

Perhaps the fact that people might share the notion that taking land belonging to someone else is ethically suspect helps to understand why people end up creating a fictional, and impossible, narrative about the "white people" being on the land first. Similar to earlier colonizers, they might not feel that direct conquest is appropriate, and so they developed rationales and legitimating strategies for why they could take the land. These strategies, as discussed in the previous chapter, required racialized notions of Indigenous peoples as a whole as inferior, as we saw in the doctrines of Discovery and *terra nullius*. When Robert says "The *Native people* that are here are *not indigenous people* in this area," he refers to how members of *his family* occupied the land before a specific group of Native people. Here he is speaking about individuals. However, Richard's statement becomes racialized when he refers to more generalized collective categories of "whites" and "Aboriginals": he says, "*We* were here first" and "There were *no Indigenous Aboriginals* in Southern Ontario when the *whites* got here." Jim, another person I interviewed, explicitly used the term "white," saying: "When the white people came here, there were no Natives here."

Thus, one of the first ways the local people I interviewed created a link to the land and a sense of belonging was through a move that draws upon earlier colonial frameworks, even if incorrectly, a move that implicitly categorizes groups of people as having differential rights to land, but that also indicates that they share an ethical position about first possession.

NOMADS AND "WARRING TRIBES"

CKCN and UCE members used additional arguments to explain *why* and *how* the Caldwell "weren't there" or "did not exist" in the area. These arguments were based on talking about how the Indigenous people of the area (now making a "land claim") were nomadic, warring and "savage": they were violent, wandering, unsettled peoples. These ideas reverberate with Hobbes' and Locke's frameworks, articulated centuries before, in which Native people represent a "state of nature." Recall that, as I discussed in chapter 2, making Indigenous land available for settler appropriation, when it was not actually *empty land*, required a "unique twist"—a justifying rationale or "fantasy of entitlement"—that entailed defining Indigenous peoples as inferior and in a "state of nature." Indigenous people were constructed as unsettled, wandering people who did not engage in proper forms of agriculture by "subduing" and fencing the earth. This misrecognition of Indigenous relationships to land helped colonizers to define the lands as legally unowned, and legally vacant *(terra nullius)*.

The "unique twist" used by the CKCN is that they argue that the Caldwell First Nation was not actually Indigenous to the area, because if they were in the area they simply "happened to" be wandering through. After asserting that white people "were here first," Richard stresses both the nomadic and violent qualities of the Indigenous people:

> All of the original Native population in the area—the Neutrals—were *annihilated by Iroquois warring parties* back in the mid-1700s … The historical argument is that this was a group of Natives who represented several bands who *happened to be nomadic people* who were in the Pelee Island area when the War of 1812 broke out. They came together under a Colonel Caldwell and fought for the British … and were promised land. And I can tell you that there were white settlers in the area of South Chatham-Kent in 1812. *There were no Natives—they'd been annihilated by their own people.* (emphasis mine)

Here, the contradictory descriptions of tribal affiliations are revealing. On one hand, the earlier argument that the "whites" were in Chatham-Kent before the "natives" means Indigenous peoples are seen as one undifferentiated race. Yet the argument here depends on a marked differentiation between the Algonquin people and the warring bands of Iroquois. At the same time, however, the Algonquin were "annihilated by their *own people*." How can they be the Algonquins' "own people" if they were a completely different tribe? This claiming of "own people" only makes sense if Richard views the Indians as a race of people, not as separate bands or tribes. Yet, the phrase "annihilating their own people" conjures an image of almost cannibalistic savagery. Most significant here is the flexibility in these strategic arguments. They often depend, on one hand, on the kind of racialized assumptions we see here and, on the other hand, on apparently non-racial assertions of sameness and equality.

Another member of CKCN added to this story about the savage Iroquois and white occupation. Robert, who above said that his family's history in the area "dates back farther than the Caldwells," explains why this is so. He, like Richard, says that "The Indigenous peoples that had been here [were] called the Neutrals. And the Iroquois came through here and wiped them all out." Such tales of "savage Iroquois warriors" are consistently overstated to mythological levels in many historical and pseudo-historical texts.[3] In New York State I heard similar narratives, in which Indigenous peoples (in this case the Cayuga or "New York Iroquois") are represented as the source of the unjust dispossession of the "real" Indigenous inhabitants, the New York Algonquins. To use the term "New York Algonquins" is to confuse the word *Algonquins* with the word *Algonquians,* as in *"Algonquian-speaking"*:

> Anthropologists invented these two confusing terms, intending "Algonquin" to refer to one specific language and "Algonquian" to refer to all the languages related to the Algonquin language (just as Germanic languages are related to German). The Algonquin tribe call themselves Anishinabe, and they live in Canada…Algonquin people speak an Algonquian language, as do Chippewa and Cheyenne people. *Algonquian-speaking* groups in New York include the Mohican, Mohegan, and Munsee Delaware. (Native Languages of the Americas 2009)

The Algonquin people never occupied what is now New York, although *Algonquian-speaking* people did, and still do.

The construction of Indigenous peoples as savages can be considered part of broader "settler states of feeling," because not only do they mobilize colonial frameworks, they do so as part of a sense of entitlement to superintend Indigenous peoples, taking on a sense that they are entitled to assess whether Indigenous peoples even existed as legitimate "nations." They do so based on how they are seen to have occupied space and related to the land. The implicit assumption here, shared with earlier colonizers, is that they are qualified to assess and control Indigenous lives and relationships, based on their own culturally specific values.

Perhaps such narratives are strategically useful in versions of history that paint a picture of settler innocence and deny colonization. They deny the history of violence on which current "settled" relationships have been built. In doing so, such tales create happy endings in which (inferior) Iroquois savagery removes Native peoples from the land, leaving it for hard-working farming settler societies. In this specific case, the fantasy of entitlement imagines that the violent Iroquois wiped out the Neutrals and left an imaginary *terra nullius* in Chatham-Kent for today's settlers, a *terra nullius* that depends upon the construction of Indigenous peoples as existing in a "state of nature."

DEFINING LEGITIMATE SOVEREIGNTY

Members of CKCN and UCE also used the idea of "state of nature" in an additional way. Locke used "state of nature" to argue that even though Indigenous societies called themselves nations, they were not legitimate governments because they were disorganized and lacked sovereignty and a singular unified central authority, characteristics that were based on European structures and ideals. According to Locke, the territorial integrity of these societies did not conform to the law of nature and therefore did not merit respect. Bill, whom I interviewed in Chatham-Kent, mobilizes a set of ideas that evoke Locke's assessment of Indigenous social organization when he says the Caldwell Natives weren't really an "organised" band of Indians:

> That group of Natives [the Caldwell] *were not necessarily an Indian band. They were just individual Natives* that they had recruited. They were *from more than one tribe* … After the War of 1812 they decided to stay together as a group and call themselves the Caldwells. So no wonder they weren't represented in the treaty of 1790: *because they didn't exist.* (emphasis mine)

The declaration that *"they didn't exist"* is a powerful, present-day expression of what is at the core of *terra nullius* logic: Indigenous peoples may have lived in regions and wandered over the land, but they *did not exist as organized societies* because they were only a collection of individuals. As Bill says, they weren't an "Indian Band," they were "just *individual* Natives … from more than one tribe." For Locke, Indian peoples legally did *"not exist"* as legitimate competitors for land because they weren't *organized societies*. The land would therefore be seen as *terra nullius* and settlers could (legitimately, in their own eyes) claim it. The structure of Bob's argument is strikingly similar to that of Locke's, in that if the Caldwell Nation "did not exist" as an "organized band," as he says, the land claim would therefore also "not exist." The land could then continue to be owned by the rightful (settler) owners.

STATES OF NATURE: SUBSISTENCE HISTORIES IN THE MARGINS

Another example of how ideas about unsettled and nomadic Indigenous people were used to argue against land rights is evident in an "historical report" sponsored by Gerry Pickard, a former Member of Federal Parliament for Chatham-Kent, who at the time explicitly and fully supported the CKCN (Schwenger 1999). His assistant, Katherine Schwenger, an amateur historian, wrote her report as a response to the more authoritative Holmes Report, which was prepared by historians at the request of the Canadian government, and was used to make their decision about the legitimacy of the Caldwell claim (Holmes 1994). The Schwenger report consistently defines the Caldwell as nomadic and unsettled, implying that they were not inhabiting the land in such a way that they could legitimately claim previous occupation.

In interviews, many CKCN members mentioned the Shwenger report as an authoritative source for their interpretation of history. I contacted Mr. Pickard's office and his staff generously made me copies of both the Schwenger and the Holmes reports. The Holmes report is marked with handwritten comments in all the margins, which I assume were put there by Ms. Shwenger while she reviewed it in preparing her own. While the Holmes report documents the Caldwell First Nation's use of Point Pelee, the handwritten notes in the margins consistently and repeatedly comment that the occupation was "*seasonal*," that they did not engage in agriculture, and that the Caldwell were "not a defined band" but just "one of many groups that wandered in that area," an area full of *mobile* Aboriginal groups. Schwenger's report stresses repeatedly that Point Pelee had "tell-tale sign[s] of *seasonal occupation* by *migratory* Chippewas and Ottawas." Current First Nations oral traditions, she says, "still recall point Pelee as an area of *collective use* by all First Nations, and not the *exclusive domain* of any one individual or group" (Schwenger 1999, 21, emphasis mine).

Her use of the term "exclusive domain" recalls my discussion of first possession in Chapter 2, in which only some forms of possession are recognized as *legitimate possession*. Although Schwenger does not explicitly say that her report establishes that the Caldwell did not have full legitimate possession of the land, and therefore no basis for a land claim, her assumption in the report seems to be that the particular pieces of land that are claimed must necessarily have been *exclusive* to the band, must have had *constant year-round* occupation and be marked by particular forms of *agriculture and buildings*, in order for the Caldwell to make a legitimate claim for previous possession. Her report cites an "1858 Report to the Special Commissioners to Investigate Indian Affairs in Canada" that states that the Chippewas of Point Pelee:

are generally *dissipated and roving and unsettled in their habits* depending mainly as a means of support on the fish and wild fowl ... The clearings are small and poorly cultivated, Indian corn and potatoes are raised in small quantities. With the exception of the Chief, they live mostly in bark Shanties or wigwams and are poorly dressed. (cited in Schwenger 1999, 23)

It is not clear in the structure of her argument why this quote is included in her report. My reading is that it is included in order to bolster the idea that the Indigenous people were migratory and not properly settled in terms of recognizable (by Western standards) boundary marking, farming and habitation, in order to "plant" colonies (Seed 2006) and transform the land into secure private property.

Schwenger's report and comments also reproduce powerful assumptions about mobile people and agricultural labour, depending upon sedentarist-centric normative property assumptions. It thus misinterprets the legal basis of the claim. The Holmes Report (marked with Schwenger's handwritten notes) indicates that although the Chippewa mostly engaged in hunting and fishing, they also raised some crops and cattle (Holmes 1994, 8) and thus were involved in agriculture. This description of cultivation and husbandry activities engaged in by the Chippewa is interesting here, because it could indicate some "settlement" in Western terms (and therefore perhaps "legitimate" occupation according to Western logic because of their "civilized" labour). However, a comment in the margins of the Holmes report seems to indicate a desire to delegitimize such farming activities. The handwritten note on the margin beside that paragraph stresses "but at a bare subsistence level." Why would such a note about "bare subsistence" with regards to agriculture be there, if not intended to downplay the possibility of even minimal Chippewa agricultural activity, and therefore, according to settler logic, legitimate rights to ownership through their productive labour? Seed says that although Indigenous peoples did cultivate crops, most Indigenous people did not fence in or enclose their plots. This perceived "failure of most native Americans to use the fence to symbolize ownership" convinced English colonizers that "native plots did not create possession" (Seed 2006, 28, my emphasis).

Schwenger's interpretation regarding the legitimacy of the claim is incorrect. These particular criteria were not at issue in the claim, because, as I discussed earlier, it was a "specific claim." Specific claims "deal with past grievances of First Nations related to Canada's obligations under historic treaties" (INAC 2010). In this case, as I explained in the introduction to Part Two, the Caldwell had been excluded from the 1790 treaty signed in Detroit, and it is through this agreement that they were to become party to that treaty. Specific claims differ from comprehensive claims, which arise when there have not been legal arrangements or past treaties regarding Indigenous land rights. Many of the people arguing against the Caldwell claim treated it as if the criteria for accepting it as legitimate were similar to those required for "comprehensive claims," even though this was not legally at issue in the case. It is significant that the claim is interpreted in this way, because it shows that *even if* treaties were made in Canada, as they were in this case, these are discounted (as I argue in the introduction to Part Three) and more difficult, inherently racialized criteria that draw on the problematic assumptions of improvement in discovery doctrines, come into play.

The response to the Schwenger report[4] written by Indian Affairs clarifies that Schwenger's work is based on serious misunderstandings of law. The case does not, the letter says, depend on proof of "exclusive occupation," or on proof that the Caldwell had made a claim to Point Pelee at the time of the signing of the 1790 treaty. Nevertheless, I suggest that the consistent repetition of these concerns about nomadic versus sedentary use of the land indicates how powerful these age-old arguments continue to be, even if they are historically incorrect. The specific kinds of common-sense misinterpretations made in the Schwenger report, legitimated by Gerry Pickard and then taken up by CKCN members, indicate the powerful persistence and resilience of *terra nullius* and state-of-nature frameworks.

Significantly, similar themes of Indigenous nomadism and savagery also appear in the UCE official history of the area on their website. It says:

> The Cayuga Indians came to the area of New York in the 1500s, a *wandering nomadic tribe* that traveled around the northeast, *never having a permanent settlement*. They were known as *fierce warriors*, who forced the Hurons and the Algonquians, the original tribes of New York, out of this territory.... In 1807, [another] treaty included the sale of the last pieces of land the Cayuga Indians had in New York State. The Cayuga Indians accepted payment and moved away from the area, seeking new land and food sources *as is customary with nomadic tribes*. (UCE 1999, emphasis mine)

In the above statement it seems as if the Cayuga *chose* to leave their land because it was in their nature to do so as a *nomadic* people. The Cayuga were not nomadic. More importantly, there is no mention of the Sullivan Campaign of 1779, ordered by George Washington. He sent the Continental Army north to burn 43 Seneca and Cayuga villages, crops, fields and fruit tree orchards at the height of the Revolutionary War (Rossen 2008, 106). The soldiers' journals document the brutal destruction and murder of the Cayuga (Cook 2000 [1887]). The Sullivan Campaign drove most Cayuga people from the area, beginning more than two centuries of disconnection from their homeland and ancestors (Hansen and Rossen 2007).

In my interviews in New York State, Indigenous peoples were often seen as potentially archaic or uncivilized, caught in the past within a modern nation. In an interview, Betty Miller argued:

> This is 2002 and how far do you want to take your culture? Do you want to take it back to human sacrifices and cannibalism? [I read] a first-hand account of a French missionary and he talks about the Onondagas taking a Cayuga maiden as a sacrifice gift ... So, just how far back do you want to take your culture; what is that going to include? Do you get my drift? They say they want to practice their culture again? Well, it's fine to practice your beliefs, but just how far back? Do you want to do sacrifices again?

"INDIANS DON'T FARM LAND!"[5] DRAINAGE AND DOCTRINES

An additional way in which people communicated their self-evident beliefs about Indigenous characteristics related to entitlement to land had to do with agricultural labour, and who was seen to deserve the *quality* of land that the Caldwell were to purchase. Many people said that providing Indians with such *good* agricultural land in Chatham-Kent was a waste. Some argued that allowing Native people to have such high-producing land (always with the unspoken assumption that they would, of course, not farm it) was bad for the Canadian economy, and that letting them "use our" (Canadian taxpayers') money to pay elevated prices for that land was simply immoral. One farmer said:

> Here's the federal government turning around, coming into an established agricultural community—probably the best land in Southwestern Ontario ... This is the truth. This is land that's being used for tobacco and tomatoes. This is the best land you can get. I'm not saying they're not deserving of getting that; but they're using our dollars and paying twice what it's worth.

A similar example was Jackie Gladstone's response when, after the first meeting at the high school, Theresa Lalonde asked her on radio: "What do you think of when you think of a reserve? What vision comes to mind?" and Jackie replied, "Old junky cars out front. Their own rules. The laws don't apply to them sort of thing. *What are they going to do with that prime land*? That's my concern" (emphasis mine).

In this way, many earlier ideas about labour, individualism, civilization and the violent characteristics of Indigenous peoples resurged in these battles about land rights. UCE and CKCN members, in defending their right to the land, employ stereotypes about the characteristics of Indigenous personhood; these become normative judgments about the inferiority of Indigenous peoples and bolster the sense of entitlement to superintend Indigenous peoples. Similar to Lockean ideals, labour, particularly the assessment of agricultural "improving labour" as superior, is fundamental to these judgments.

SWAMPS, LABOUR, LAND AND JURISDICTION: THE DRAINAGE ISSUE

Members of CKCN and their supporters consistently and repeatedly brought up potential complications about drainage of their fields as one of their key objections to the Caldwell claim. This concern was repeated so often by different people, who all used almost the same phrases, that it began to seem almost scripted. The argument was obviously extremely compelling to people. The concern about drainage was based on the idea that *if* the Caldwell did finally get land, and that *if* they allowed it to lie fallow and undeveloped, the drains would become blocked, and that would adversely affect other local commercial farming operations. Ian, a local farmer who was showing me the computers and programs that assessed his land quality, drainage and productivity, explained his "problem" in this way:

> I: Well, if they were further downstream, and they wanted to establish some, a *swamp area*, or a *wildlife refuge*, which I can respect, I have nothing wrong with that, but it could have an *impact on upstream drainage*.
>
> E: If they had a wildlife refuge down there, how would that affect it? Does that mean there might not be as free drainage or something?
>
> I: Correct, the water could back up, and I could have trouble getting the water off of my land. … *Even if they use it for farmland*, sub-surface drainage in this land is almost a must. What access do I have to an outlet? … My water [has to] end up in Rondeau Bay. My land stops a few concessions from Rondeau Bay. So my water's gotta travel across somebody else's farm to get to the Bay. (emphasis mine)

The language used here presumes that Indigenous people would likely not engage in agriculture and, if they did, they would likely not care for their drainage areas. It is significant that Ian assumed that the Caldwell would allow or "establish" what he calls a "swamp," a term with negative connotations. Using the term "wetland" would have a different implication. These persistent, powerful and resilient assumptions were repeated to me often, and reflect deep-seated Western assumptions about the failure of Indigenous people to engage in productive, transforming, labour. It seemed self-evident to people that this would occur, and that therefore their land would be a "swamp" and, as in early Roman property law, "not under human control" (as discussed in Chapter 2). The implicit assumption is that the Indigenous people would wish to return the land to a "state of nature."

In Locke's conceptualization, people who exist in a "state of nature" are not seen to have rational and organized societies and governments. It seemed that this assessment of Indigenous governance was also adhered to by the people I interviewed, when, in subtle ways, the concern about drainage is revealed as a deep concern about jurisdiction and governance. The way it worked was that CKCN members consistently said that they had "never known" what the Caldwell intended to do with their land (so they just assumed it would be allowed to become a "swamp"). This not-knowing made them feel uncertain and angry. However, as John says above, "even if they use it for farmland" they were still worried, assuming the Caldwell would likely not care for and repair the drainage system. These concerns started to become clear when I found that CKCN members repeatedly argued that the Caldwell would follow *their own* rules, would not work with "the community," and would refuse to follow provincial regulations. The problem here is that the Caldwell had developed careful plans for their land, plans that were neither full-out capitalist farming nor wilderness conservation. These plans had been announced to the local non-Indigenous community in numerous ways, including letters to the newspaper before my interviews took place. However, during my interviews, when I asked people if they had heard anything specific and detailed about what the Caldwell planned to do with their land, none of them admitted to any knowledge. They kept repeating their problems with the drainage. John, for example, said that if his water "got plugged someplace, the municipality would come in and fix it. But if it was reserve, the municipality would have no authority to fix it. So if I'm up above, and the drain's blocked off, I can't get rid of that water." Why might it be that, despite information being provided by the Caldwell Nation, CKCN members persisted with the drainage issue? I think it was a matter of deep-seated anxiety about the question of jurisdiction. Let me explain.

The Caldwell clearly expressed their willingness to work with the local community on the issue of drainage on numerous occasions. Caldwell Chief Larry Johnson wrote a letter to the municipality regarding drainage issues in 1999, which appeared in the local paper and was also published on the Caldwell website. In the letter he assured locals that the Caldwell First Nation would respect all provincial and local drainage rules (something that had also been repeatedly stressed in all Government communication about the Agreement in Principle). The letter states:

> We recognize that drainage is an important issue in low-lying agricultural country. We are prepared to enter into an agreement with the municipal government to provide for the identification and management of existing drainage works and the construction or alteration of future drainage works. Basically, we should agree that existing drainage will be maintained—and that where drainage works on our reserve, the responsibility

for maintaining them is ours, financially as well as legislatively. Any proposed changes in drainage should be matters in which we would give each other notice, more or less as provided in the present provincial Drainage Act. We would like to see an effective, informal dispute resolution process, accessible to individuals as well as governments, as well as a clear environmental review of any proposed changes ... We believe that, with the proper facts and a clear understanding of our intention, we can deal with these issues. We hope that this letter will clarify our views and will provide the basis for an understanding between our two governments.

What is striking about the above letter is the crystal-clear willingness of the Caldwell to work with the local community to resolve any drainage issues. Also striking is the way that the Caldwell government takes responsibility for negotiating agreements with other governments. There is clear evidence of a willingness, and a promise, to negotiate with the municipality and make compromises. What is fascinating is that not a single CKCN member even once mentioned that letter or that promise to me, although there is no possible way they could not know about them. What was going on?

ONTOLOGICAL UNCERTAINTY AND THREATENED JURISDICTIONAL AUTHORITY

I began to wonder whether the underlying issue was something other than the actual drainage. After all, the CKCN could not have avoided knowing that in the agreement the Caldwell were *required* to negotiate with the municipality to deal with the drainage issue. Here, the question moves to issues of governance and force. I asked James about resolving the drainage issue.

> E In the case of drainage, wouldn't the reserve and the municipality make some kind of agreement?
>
> J: Who *enforces* it? If a reserve and a municipality reach an agreement, and the municipality violates that agreement, the natives can go to the provincial government and say "They're not living up to their agreement"—and force them to live up to it! But there's *nobody to force the natives* ... There's no clause that says if the natives don't negotiate in good faith "we'll come in and impose a settlement." So there's *no threat to the natives,* but there's *certainly a threat to the municipality*.

James' sense of threat that the government would not be able to control the Caldwell, despite all of the restrictions placed on the Caldwell by the government, exemplifies the sense of angry uncertainty expressed by many people I interviewed.

James seems to be fearful about not having control of Indigenous peoples and cannot trust their governments. Simply imagining an Indigenous nation, independent from settler governmental power to enforce control, seems to inspire powerful fears and provoke unknown dangers, even though, considering how land agreements limit autonomy, such independence *is* largely imaginary. Similar sentiments are expressed by Ian. It is here where anxiety and anger about a perceived loss of ontological certainty about the future begins to emerge more explicitly. Ian says:

> I: There are *no clear-cut rules* ... Nothing has been spelled out as to *what the future holds*. I just know that they can *operate independently...*
>
> E: So in other words, they would have their own by-laws, etc.?
>
> I: The way a reservation is defined now ... If we're looking at a *new-age reservation* where they incorporate things like the provincial drainage act...and provincial land use regulation, then I don't have a problem with it.

The dilemma here is that a Caldwell reserve *already would* necessarily be the kind of "new-age reservation" that Ian says that he would not have a problem with. The land first purchased by the Caldwell would be under the Provincial Drainage Act (because it would be purchased in "fee simple," and thus it is like land purchased by anyone). The Agreement in Principle already incorporated the requirement for negotiations with the municipality about drainage (as well as loss of taxes and payment for services such as roads) as part of the process of turning land into a reserve. The CKCN would know this.

One possible way to comprehend such persistent—and seemingly deliberate—refusal to accept the agreement in principle might be based on a deep mistrust CKCN members had of both the federal government and the Caldwell First Nation. Indeed, when I later asked CKCN members about the Caldwell chief's letter and the federal requirements, they admitted that they had actually known about what they called his "*supposed* willingness" to compromise. However, they said, the drainage rules and the Chief's promise would not make any difference to them. They said this was because *even if* they made an agreement with *this* chief, Larry Johnson, everything "might change" with a different chief. There was no security or certainty in dealing with a Native band. Ian argued that "It *could be* that you would be able to reach a settlement with them and live side by side. Very good. *Could be*. But *could be* the *exact opposite*."

In my view, their expressions of fear about possible futures indicate, first, that they are unable to see the Caldwell First Nation as a recognized and legitimate government that has authority to negotiate to make (and keep) agreements and follow rules and regulations. This presumed inability mirrors Locke's theorizations that Indigenous nations are not recognizable as proper governments that can have sovereignty over land.

Another possible way to understand the strange logic of what I call CKCN's fearful concerns over drainage is evident in their response to the letter from the Chief. The Chief's letter ends like this:

> Our Council is a government, one that is recognized in Canadian federal legislation as well as in the Canadian constitution. We have the authority to make laws for our people and our land. We intend to do so—and we intend to do so in a way that also respects the rights of our neighbours.

This letter makes it clear that the Caldwell First Nation, even as they negotiate and compromise, also assert autonomy as a separate government "recognized in Canadian federal legislation as well as in the Canadian constitution." The Caldwell Nation takes on the authority of a government, stating that they "have the authority to make laws for our people and our land." The way in which the letter expresses willingness to compromise, but does not give away authority or autonomy, is perhaps the underlying problem for CKCN members. What they experience as the problem, I suggest, is *not* the actual drainage itself, but is instead the broader question of what they sense may be changing relations of power and jurisdictional authority. The problem is actually *who* controls the situation and who has the authority to do so. Those who have previously had unquestioned authority to decide how Chatham-Kent will be run are confronted with a chief who does not promise to forever in the future be subordinate and follow their rules. He asserts the authority of running a legitimate and recognized government that will negotiate relationships. If jurisdiction is the "power to speak law" (Pasternak 2014, 148), Chief Johnson is doing just that. Whether or not Canadian law recognizes his authority to do so is not the issue here; in fact, Agreements in Principle and Canadian law stipulate the terms of such negotiation and limit the jurisdictional authority of Indigenous governments. Instead, I suggest the idea of recognizing the jurisdictional authority of an Indigenous government elicits a deep ontological uncertainty because it unsettles expectations of certain entitlement to control the relationships between Indigenous and settler peoples. It is the nature of any negotiation between (equal) parties that the results and the future are never guaranteed. However, Ian said that this approach is not acceptable, because within it "There are *no clear-cut rules* … Nothing has been spelled out as to *what the future holds.*"

In terms of the issue of jurisdiction, it is also important to note that CKCN members constantly refused to trust the ability of the federal government to protect their future interests and shield them from the dangerous uncertainties of Indigenous land rights. Many people complained that the government would pull out and leave "the community" to deal with the "mess" it left behind. In order to protect themselves in a manner that they did not expect the government would, and to ensure the certainty of their ownership and futures, members of CKCN took it upon themselves to start the South Kent Property Development Corporation. The corporation signs agreements with people guaranteeing that if they sell their land, they will provide the corporation with the "first right of refusal." One of the key participants in the corporation explained it in this way:

> The intention was that—like, once this thing hit the news, everyone was in a panic state, saying, I don't want to leave this area but I don't want to be the last one here, either, because then my property won't be worth anything by that time. And so we formed a property development company and took right of first refusal on 20,000 acres. So that, collectively—you see, if the intention is to blockbust, property values go down over time, because if a property comes up for sale, if my neighbour's farm comes up for sale, I could say 'Well, I'll maybe buy that to protect my own assets.' And I may be willing to pay even a little more than market value for it to do that. But the trouble is, if I buy that piece, this piece will be up for sale tomorrow; that piece the next day—how long can I stand this as an individual? So that what we've done is we have this private development company that can buy land; and it is *all of us* buying land ... And if we take a loss on it, we all take a loss—not just one person.
>
> This company is in the business of buying land. What we do with it is our business. And how much we pay for it is our business. But, we're not bidding against the Natives. But if anybody makes an offer to purchase any of this land, we can step in front of it and take the deal ourselves. [We have signed on] 20,000 acres.

This collective project is designed to protect their certainty of ownership and expansion in the future, something they thought the government should be doing. Significantly, it is designed to protect the property rights of a specific group of people against another group, and both groups are implicitly racially and culturally defined. Another member, Paul, said,

> If you get an offer and you're *uncomfortable with that offer*, or you're not sure if the offer's fair or you don't know who the potential buyer is, you can go to this property development company and they will match that offer. You know you're *selling it* to people who are *in the community who have—put down roots.*

As discussed earlier in the chapter, clearly "the community" does not include the

Caldwell First Nation. To say they would make sure you sell to people "in the community" and to people who have "put down roots" is a way of saying that they will not sell to Indigenous peoples who wish to start a reserve.

In this chapter I have explored how local people's uncertainty and anger around land rights becomes embodied in particular actions and languages. Their defensive strategies illustrate aspects of contemporary "settler states of feeling" because, as I have shown, they reflect and/or reproduce foundational conceptual frameworks that are essential to settler colonial and national projects. I have shown that *how* they argue that they are entitled to the ownership of Indigenous territories draws on key aspects of settler colonial philosophy discussed in Chapter 2, including the racialized frameworks of the doctrines of Discovery and *terra nullius* and their underlying assumptions that Indigenous lifeways and relationships to land and each other are necessarily inferior. I have also shown that their powerful feelings of home and the "community" of their "culture," based on agricultural labour, are mobilized to exclude Indigenous people from belonging, and to devalue their relationships to each other and to their territories based on culturally specific notions of the value of certain kinds of improvement. I also identified a pattern of a self-identified "community" of non-Indigenous people working together to ensure they can block Indigenous peoples from purchasing land, and literally blocking Indigenous peoples' ability to compete with them for good, productive land. This, as discussed, was one of the purposes of the earlier *terra nullius* and "state of nature" frameworks and the laws that emerged from them: in effect the goal (or result) was to cut out competition from Indigenous peoples, so that settlers could prosper. The key to this process was not only to conceptualize and try to materialize Indigenous peoples as inferior, but also to encompass their independent nations within the "domestic" jurisdiction of the nation-state, and thus be able to superintend and control them. Settler structures of feeling, in this way, draw on older frameworks to continue to justify and reproduce the settler state's fantasy of authority to "superintend Native peoples" and their lands (Rifkin 2011, 342), now and into the future.

The discussion of jurisdiction, I have argued, played out specifically in the issue of anxiety about drainage. The question of jurisdiction is the question of "who has the power to speak the law" (Pasternak 2014, 148), and I showed how people reacted with "settler anxiety" when Chief Johnson took authority to "speak the law" and challenge pivotal settled expectations that non-Native governments and people naturally should have authority over Indigenous politics and peoples. The people that I interviewed ended up defending their certainty that Indigenous territories and peoples are, and should remain, enclosed in the "jurisdictional imaginary" (Rifkin 2009) of the settler state. I now move on to how the jurisdictional imaginary of the settler nation makes its way, in more explicit and complex ways, into how people mobilize against Indigenous land rights.

Notes

1   One man I interviewed said: "It's kind of like the blockbusting that occurred in Detroit, where you go in and you pay very inflated prices for the first piece of land, you make it so uncomfortable for the rest of the neighbours that they eventually sell at a discount to get the hell out of the way of the development. That's how some farmers in the area have characterized what would happen to property values in the area if the chief was to get this large influx of money."

2   The patrilineal nature of land ownership is apparent here in that only "fathers," "brothers," and "sons" are mentioned.

3   Stereotypical histories tend to "paint a picture of the Five Nations as ferocious warriors if not 'bloodthirsty savages.' But the Iroquois were very much like their Iroquoian-speaking neighbours: the Wendat, Tionnontatehronnon, Erie, Neutral and Susquehannock ... agrarian people residing in villages, with similar political structures and many common cultural customs. Traditionally, warfare was a relatively low-level affair with seasonal raids on enemy villages in search of revenge for past attacks and killings by the other side" (Innisfil Public Library 2009).

4   In response to the report, the office of Robert Nault, then Minister of Indian Affairs, provided a detailed 21-page critique, saying in part that the report "demonstrates a lack of understanding of government policy, the Specific Claims process, appropriate legal principles and case law" (Minister of Indian Affairs and Northern Development 1999: 1).

5   A quotation from Willman and Biehl (2005, 152).

Chapter 4

SETTLER JURISDICTIONAL IMAGINARIES IN PRACTICE

Equality, Law, Race
and Multiculturalism

A letter to the editor of the *Ridgetown Independent* newspaper in Chatham-Kent, Ontario, Canada, published in 1999, exemplifies many of the complex fears, concerns and angers I found during fieldwork. The author introduces his letter as a "clarification" of why readers should not be "troubled" by the "NOT FOR SALE" signs of the Chatham-Kent Community Network that were ubiquitous in the area at the time. He explains what he calls "the true meaning" behind them:

> First, I would like to ask [a previous letter-writer who was troubled by the signs] if he/she is living beside a Canadian. Does this Canadian have to follow the same bylaws as you do regarding fire safety, building codes, firearms, access to property or any other bylaws that help ensure that you as his/her neighbour can continue living as you do now? After all, that's what bylaws are for—to ensure that everyone in a community, neighbour-to-neighbour, has equal status and follows the same rules...
>
> Now, let's talk about what those "NOT FOR SALE" signs really mean to those people who have put them out on their property. What's "NOT FOR SALE"?

    i) Their land to another country;

    ii) Their right to have neighbours who follow the same laws they do;

    iii) Their right to purchase land at fair market rates;

    iv) Their family history, which is being totally disregarded because someone else can claim they were here even earlier;

    v) The future of their families to continue building on that land; and

    vi) Their memories, not only of good times, but also of hard work that made that land what it is today.

Finally, the people who have those "NOT FOR SALE" signs up are certainly not racist—in fact they are very proud of this country and all the nationalities of people that have blended together to make it what it is today. The First Nations people are very welcome to buy land and live in south Chatham-Kent with the rest of the Canadians who reside there now (whether they are Irish-Canadian, Dutch-Canadian, African-Canadian or any other Canadians). But the fact is that we are all of one country—working together, living together, being part of this one country together. That kind of loyalty to your country should not be ridiculed. After all, when the Americans came knocking on our borders during the War of 1812, the British, the natives and the United Empire Loyalists together said "NOT FOR SALE"—and that is why we are lucky enough to be here today—*as one country.* (*Ridgetown Independent* March 11, 1999)

The letter is revealing because it endeavours to detail what were previously "settled expectations" within the nation. It seems that the land rights action has challenged arrangements previously seen as settled.

The last three numbered points, above, reveal anxious and vulnerable feelings about the potential loss of "family history" and "memories." Land rights are felt to threaten and "completely disregard" longstanding personal and familial settler identity narratives of "good times" and "hard work." As discussed, such feelings may be understandable, considering how they are central to broader settler narratives of belonging. However, they are still "settler states of feeling" that legitimize ongoing colonialism because they pivot on a sense of entitlement to Indigenous land. Because such narratives work by linking the "hard work" performed by settlers to making the "land what it is today," they mobilize the idea that productive labour provides entitlement to land in the past, present and future ("the future of their families to continue building on that land"). In this way they implicitly mirror John Locke's "labour theory of value," a theory foundational to legitimizing colonial concepts of *terra nullius* and the Doctrine of Discovery. In response, the letter maps a normative world in which being and acting as a specific kind of loyal *Canadian* is the key to appropriate, acceptable and *expected* behaviour.

The letter maps a jurisdictional imaginary of the settler nation-state, within which "territorial, sovereign space is projected as a discrete, non-overlapping, absolute domain of space" (Pasternak 2014, 153), enclosed by fixed territorial boundaries. But the jurisdictional imaginary is more than territorial: it is also juridical and cultural. The assertion of Canada as "*one* country" based on liberal frameworks of supposedly "equal status" and "the same rules" outlines the expectations of law and national belonging within those boundaries. Within this juridical jurisdiction, nationhood is based on liberal ideals, according to which the role of governments is to guarantee a specific version of what is seen as "equality" by protecting property and ensuring that a singular legal jurisdiction applies throughout its territory. The letter shows that expectations about the continuity (and certainty) of these "rules"—laws within these boundaries—are important and assumed. The author of the letter moves back and forth between national and local community legal and cultural norms (represented in laws, property ownership and labour) that, she/he argues, need to be defended. In this jurisdiction "the First Nations people" are "very welcome" and offered an invitation to join "the rest of Canadians." However, the price of admission is that they must follow the rules of "one country" and assimilate into the territorial jurisdiction, as well as into the political and cultural imaginary of the settler nation.

A similar letter to the editor of the Syracuse *Post-Standard*, written by Sally and Robert Roehr (1999) from Union Springs, New York, carries the headline "Cayuga's success would create a house divided." The letter says:

> The Declaration of Independence states that "All men are created equal." Are we now saying that some men are created more equal than others? This new sovereign nation [the Cayuga Nation][1] will not have to observe any of our laws. No hunting or fishing regulations will apply. All property will be taken off the tax rolls and the Cayugas will pay no local, state and federal taxes....
>
> The Cayugas say they want a large reservation to maintain their cultural identity, yet historically reservations have been a social disaster. They have encouraged dependency on a hierarchical tribal government. There are numerous other ways to preserve cultural identity—one only has to see the beautiful Amish and Mennonite communities in the land claim area. These people maintain their traditions—while working diligently, paying taxes and observing the laws of the land...We believe in the equality of all races. *We are all native Americans* and welcome the Native Americans of the Cayuga tribe into our community to buy land, work beside us, pay taxes and observe our local, state, and federal laws (Roehr 1999)

This letter also maps out expectations about appropriate behaviour of citizens within singular sovereign nations, stressing the importance of equality, the same laws, hard work and taxes. Both letters propose that everyone within the nation must be equal, and this means following the same laws. The authors represent the singular, legally homogeneous nation and community as natural, reasonable and necessarily *indivisible*. Both letters also propose that being against Indigenous land rights is egalitarian and patriotic, and is definitely not based on race. Other "tribal" sovereignties ("nations" within the nation) are, on the other hand, seen to promote divisiveness, inequality and destructive hierarchies. Many members of UCE spoke to me in interviews and expressed views similar to this letter, speaking of the American ideals of equality and their acceptance of "other cultures" as evidence that the people who accuse them of being "racist" against the "Natives" are wrong.

This chapter begins with these letters as a starting point to explore how settler states of feeling and expectations about jurisdiction inflect these conflicts. I continue to explore how particular frameworks and vocabularies of belonging and property are activated and mobilized to defend past and ongoing settler sovereignty and to refuse Indigenous sovereignty. Here, I specifically explore what I call self-evident "One Nation" discourses, in which a singular sovereign settler-national jurisdiction is felt to be the only reasonable and acceptable form of governance and source of loyalty. Although most nations do not actually have entire populations that share a singular national identity, the dream of indivisibility is still a powerful fantasy and productive desire within most forms of nationhood (see Mackey 2002; Handler 1988), one that is reproduced continually in rituals of patriotism and everyday actions of the state and its citizens. I suggest that these sentiments reflect settler structures of feeling because they assume, defend and reproduce, in complex ways, the foundational settler colonial fantasy that Indigenous territory is always-already encompassed within the domestic space of what they see as the superior jurisdiction of the nation (Mackey 2014). In other words, they assume that Indigenous polities are, or should be, subordinated to the "jurisdictional imaginary" (Rifkin 2011) of the settler state.

The condition of possibility for the anger people feel about uncertainty, I argue, is based on their expectations that settlement is now settled, and that settler-state jurisdiction and law over space and people is, and should be, fixed and certain. However, as I am arguing in this book (see especially Chapter 2), this sense of certainty is based on a long and complex "fantasy of entitlement and expectation," which in turn is based on legal *fictions* and the creation of a settler "jurisdictional imaginary." As discussed in Chapter 2, jurisdiction of spaces and peoples can, in theory, be quite flexible and overlapping (Pasternak 2014). Indeed, they were more flexible before the emergence of late European imperial systems of modern state sovereignty and the emergence of settler nation-states (Pasternak 2014, 151), within which the ideology and practice was to try to create an "empire of uniformity" and "perfect settler sovereignty," a supposedly unified singular jurisdiction that would legally obliterate Indigenous customary laws (Pasternak 2014, 149). Those living within settler nation-states "are already presumed to exist within a particular body of law. But this picture of legal authority that holds us captive, and is repeated to us inexorably in the language of modern territorial sovereignty," tries to erase "the multiplicity of Indigenous legal orders exercised daily across the land" (Pasternak 2014, 149). In practice, of course, jurisdictions still overlap, and Indigenous jurisdictions have not been erased. As Onondaga Chief Irving Powless pointed out to me as we walked over the fields of Cayuga traditional territory in 1999, the Haudenosaunee already *are* sovereign nations, and have been for thousands of years. If they did not have "inherent sovereignty," they would not be negotiating land rights with the federal government. It is not, Chief Powless said calmly, up to American citizens to decide on the lives or governments of the Haudenosaunee or any other nations. The confidence with which Chief Powless speaks of these matters indicates the degree to which such settler feelings of entitlement are based on fantasies of certainty, a certainty that is unsettled by unapologetic assertions of Indigenous sovereignty.

A pivotal element in the power of the fantasy is how it enables people to draw on ideologies of settler nationhood and thus mobilize particular versions of equality, culture and race in ways that allow them to see themselves as both victims and generous benefactors, all the while protecting settled expectations and reasserting settler sovereignty as superior. Framed as love for the community and nation, these letters do not explicitly propose a singular *identity* or race for all people within the nation, requiring everyone to have the same cultural *values*. Instead, as I show below, these letters and interviews map out a "jurisdictional imaginary" of the nation which mobilizes notions of racial equality, tolerance and multiculturalism to define the appropriate and rightful place and behaviour of all citizens within it. At the same time, I argue, these ideas draw on self-evident racialized notions of culture, labour and personhood to discount Indigenous peoples and land rights. This is a modern "multicultural" version of the nation-state that is nevertheless in keeping with both Locke's and Hobbes' liberal political philosophies outlining the social contract and defining civil society. The relatively recent, yet ubiquitous, Western notion of the individual has at its root the idea of the *indivisible*. Such notions of indivisibility also inform "modern nationalism's foundational premises of possessive individualism,[2] bounded political sovereignty, and singular national identity" (Handler 1988; Turner-Strong and Van Winkle 1993, 10). The idea of indivisibility also, as discussed, informs Western notions of property.

In this chapter we see settlers working hard to force Indigenous peoples conceptually into the singular (yet "multicultural") jurisdictional imaginary of the nation, and I examine how concepts such as equality, race, multiculturalism and taxes are mobilized in this task.[3] Even though this jurisdictional imaginary on one hand seems coherent—and has a logic that is linked to earlier philosophical conceptions about the relations between property, personhood and sovereignty—it also reveals ruptures and contradictions that indicate how it is mobilized flexibly (and often anxiously) in an attempt to render whole and rational the problematic fantasies of entitlement and possession that underpin it. Although hundreds of years of Indigenous resistance have made it clear that these arrangements have never been settled, the re-emergence of land rights challenges, as "contact zones" of the tensions within the settler project, reveal the anxiety underpinning the "unfinished project" of "perfecting" and finalizing "settler colonial sovereignty claims" (Pasternak 2014, 237).

ONE NATION DISCOURSES

Opponents of land claims in Ontario and New York use strategies that often appear distinct from one another, yet are based on similar axiomatic assumptions that consistently delegitimize Indigenous peoples and their claims. Both use what I call "One Nation" discourses. This powerful fantasy of singular nationhood is repeated time and again in UCE protest signs and interview statements. Many of these signs mimic a quintessential American ritual of patriotism, the U.S. pledge of allegiance, saying "One nation indivisible," "ONE people with liberty and justice for all," or simply "One nation."

Other UCE signs focus on the notion of equality, often represented as sameness in laws, rights and responsibilities. Such signs read "Equality under the law: One nation indivisible," or "One set of laws for all. One nation. Equality." Such signs might be read as referring to the declaration of independence, liberal understandings of "the law," the pledge of allegiance, as well as the enlightenment models of nationhood described above. These ideas are deeply embedded in people's subjectivities, in part through repeated rituals of patriotism that are institutionalized and carried out throughout lifetimes. Each and every Upstate Citizens for Equality meeting I attended began with: "I pledge allegiance to the flag of the United States of America ... One nation, under God, indivisible, with liberty and justice for all."

Many UCE members framed their resistance to land claims in terms of their "rights" and responsibilities as *Americans*, and authorized it by referring to the pledge of allegiance, a patriotic ritual that promises "loyalty" to one sovereign nation, the U.S. Ron and Helen, two UCE members said, for example:

> Ron: You've got to be all one, with the same rules and regulations for everybody.
> Helen: Like the pledge of the allegiance says: "One nation under God, indivisible."

> Ron: We've said that ever since we were [children]. Seventy-seven
> years, *Now has that been wrong all those years? I don't think so.*" (emphasis
> mine)

The belief in singular and indivisible nationhood is deeply felt, and deeply socialized into people as an axiomatic truth. For Ron it cannot, and could not, be experienced as "wrong all those [77] years," given an entire childhood and adult life spent repeating it. Thus, quotidian repetition makes a "truth" so self-evident that it is not questioned. The ritual itself becomes irrefutable evidence that there can only be singular nationhood. Ron and Helen told me a story to further illustrate their point. They talked about attending an event at the chiropractic college in Seneca Falls, organized by UCE to discuss the Cayuga land claim. Ron said,

> There were some Indians there that night ... some Indian girls; students ...
> from Cayuga College. When they had to pledge allegiance before the
> meeting started, those two girls sat next to Alan and I and neither one of
> them raised their butt off that chair the whole time. They sat right still.
> Now see, that's not right. I mean, if they want to be in America and they
> want to be like the rest of us, [they should] do like we do.

Ron's frustration with the "Indian girls" not standing up for the pledge of allegiance is framed as a concern with them being like "the rest of us" and doing "like we do." It reflects a deep inability to imagine how others might experience different, even competing, forms of loyalty or nationhood. A key reason for this is, of course, the self-evident nature of One Nation discourses, and how they have been embodied in daily rituals. However, it is also important to see that underlying his frustration is that, in his view, the geographic terrain is *always-already defined* as U.S. national space. Thus it is difficult to comprehend that Indigenous people might have historical and ongoing rationales to resist dominant forms of American nationalism, an inability that is prevalent because of the ubiquity and power of the common-sense jurisdictional imaginary. In Ron's view there is no choice: when in the geographically defined America, one *must* want to be American and behave as an American. To me, it also simplistically reflects popular anti-immigrant sentiments, such as, " if they don't like it, they should just go back where they came from." This is the ahistorical yet mythologized jurisdictional imaginary in action: Indigenous nations are always-already domesticated into U.S. jurisdiction.

Significantly, several other UCE members also mentioned the same "Indian girls" who did not stand for the pledge. As I saw, for the UCE, collective attention to whether and how people participated in the pledge became a form of disciplinary surveillance, a test of patriotic loyalty. The young women's actions were turned into an example of how unacceptable and improper multiple loyalties (and multiple governments) are to the nation. The expectation that Indigenous peoples should naturally become enveloped (some might say "caged") within the national jurisdiction and imaginary was common during my fieldwork. It was most often expressed, as it is here, as the most logical and natural state of affairs, and emerges from the foundational fantasy of entitlement to define land and others that I have discussed in previous chapters. The unselfconsciousness with which such a view is held and expressed demonstrates the power of quotidian common sense. At the same time, it shows how such settler senses of entitlement allow their proponents to feel deeply certain of the logic that bolsters their relative privilege. The sense of righteous entitlement means that they fail to understand that the settler project is not complete, and that many Indigenous people do not share the common-sense logic of the jurisdictional imaginary because they continue to be members of sovereign nations.

WE "CERTAINLY AREN'T RACIST": CULTURAL PLURALISM, RACE AND SETTLER INNOCENCE

One striking characteristic of the letters at the beginning of this chapter is how both mention other "minority" cultural communities strategically, as a way to assert that their opposition to land rights is "not racist," or that their key interest is in the "equality of all races." Such assertions were common in my interviews. Indigenous people making land claims are told they would be welcome if only they would behave appropriately. Instead of making claims for land and sovereignty, they should behave like "Irish-Canadian, Dutch-Canadian, African-Canadian or any other Canadians" in Chatham-Kent, or be like "the beautiful Amish and Mennonite communities in the land claim area" in New York. These communities are acceptable and welcome, say the letters (and many of the people I interviewed), because they behave as if we "are all of one country—working together, living together, being part of this one country together." Although they "maintain their cultural identity," they are seen to behave properly by "working diligently, paying taxes and observing the laws of the land."

These statements condense a bundle of interconnected assumptions making up a shared settler logic. Similar to the frameworks I discussed, the underlying assumptions are: that the nation is and should be the primary allegiance; that non-Indigenous people have the right to superintend and control the behaviour of Indigenous people; and that the nation had, and continues to have, superior sovereignty and jurisdiction. I will now explore how ideas about race, culture and sovereignty intersect to produce specific versions of racialized exclusion of Indigenous people based on their claims to land and sovereignty. My analysis also reveals the complex interplay of how non-Indigenous minority cultures can be used as a cudgel to delegitimize Indigenous peoples, governments and cultures.

The claim that anti–land claim activists are innocent of racism (and that they support "racial equality") here depends upon proposing that they cannot be *racist* because they accept *cultural* differences within the nation and community. These kinds of discourses, twinned as they are with assertions of tolerance, are familiar from my earlier analysis of the cultural politics of multiculturalism in Canada (Mackey 2002), and represent a complex politics of recognition (Simpson 2014; Coulthard 2007). There I examined similar assertions of liberal tolerance for cultural difference twinned with assertions of the need for singular nationhood, discourses that are mobilized to superintend and limit "multicultural others" and Indigenous people. I argued that nation building does not only proceed by erasing difference, as proposed by some scholars, but that the most important issue for the settler national project was to maintain the white settler's unquestioned right—and expectation—to define and manage the nation, its right to decide when and how minorities are allowed both their similarities *and* their differences (Mackey 2002). I argued that official multicultural policy and identity abduct minority cultures and the mythologized "tolerance" for cultural differences, and use them for the national project without promoting genuine respect or equality. In that analysis, I specifically explored the flexible use of multicultural "others" to manage the nation-state and discount Québec nationalism and Indigenous rights. Here we see representations of settler tolerance for more recent immigrants' (seen as "cultural minorities") cultures being used to discount Indigenous peoples, land rights and sovereignty. The case of Indigenous peoples, specifically in relation to territorial rights, indicates a different kind of difference that elicits settler anxieties and defensive strategies that are informed by particular kinds of racialized settler imaginaries.

The assertions reflected in the letters and my interviews imply that people who defend against Indigenous land rights are not racist because they accept and even celebrate all the diverse cultures and communities, such as Amish, Mennonites and so on. They are "very proud" of this country and "all the nationalities of people that have blended together to make it what it is today." Such assertions are proposed as signs of tolerance and cultural inclusivity. The letters argue for one set of *laws*, and appear to say that it is not necessary to have one singular *culture*, thus feeding into the notion that they are not racist because they respect different *cultures*. They also say that they respect Indigenous *cultural* heritage. Yet these frameworks also limit and define tolerable forms of such "multicultural" difference in precise, clearly defined ways. These communities are acceptable because by "*working* diligently, *paying taxes* and observing the *laws* of the land" they can be encompassed within the unity (and legal jurisdiction) of the nation, in ways they think Indigenous land rights and sovereignty cannot. The argument here implies that Indigenous people should be equivalent to, and behave in the same way as, other minority groups. They invite Indigenous people into their communities, as long as they behave appropriately and "buy land, work beside us, pay taxes and observe our local, state, and federal laws." In Chatham-Kent, they welcome First Nations people "to buy land and live with the rest of the Canadians who reside there now"—as long as it is clear that the nation is primary. They should, in short, behave like loyal national and local subjects.

The essence of this demand is that Indigenous people must, like other minority populations, "melt" into the supposedly unified "mosaic" or "melting pot" of the multicultural jurisdictional imaginary of the nation. In Canada, "while earlier national narratives alluded to the racial superiority of 'white' Canadians and their hand in subjugating/civilizing Indigenous populations, in recent decades it has become far less fashionable to insinuate such things. Canada has thus consistently drawn on the multiculturalist rhetoric of equality as a framework for narrating Canadian-Indigenous relations" (Adese 2012a, 480).

This multicultural "logic" works in complex ways. First, the claim of tolerance to, and recognition of, cultural difference provides the alibi to produce a claim of settler innocence of racism. Although regimes of recognition "are seen as invariably virtuous" they are a "technique of settler governance." Recognition is made out to be a transcendental, universal value, and generous desire to include cultural differences is a "gift." Yet it is ultimately "a political antidote to historical wrongdoing," seeming to "salve the wounds of settler colonialism" (Simpson 2014, 20). Adese (2012a, 484) argues that "multiculturalism can be understood as a tool through which the nation has sought to conceal its intolerance ... while reinventing itself free of its colonialist past."

Important here, in the multicultural management of populations, is that focusing on *culture* vacates Indigenous and settler realities and histories, as if land rights and sovereignty are only about *cultural preservation*, and not, as they are, also based on historical material processes related to competing claims for territory and sovereignty. Such assertions attempt to produce Indigenous peoples as equivalent to other minority cultures within a multicultural model that limits "ethnic" cultures to non-threatening relics, preserved within the modern nation-building project. They reveal a push to discipline Indigenous people to assimilate into a liberal version of tolerance for (limited) cultural differences, acceptable because they do not challenge unmarked settler dominance in the nation-state (Mackey 2002). "Recognition is the gentler form, perhaps, or the least corporeally violent way of managing Indians and their difference, a multicultural solution to the settlers' Indian problem" (Simpson 2014, 20). In this chapter we see settlers trying to force Indigenous peoples into the (multicultural) jurisdictional imaginary of the nation. Such pressure enacts a "tricky benevolence that actually may extend forms of settlement through the language and practices of, at times, nearly impossible but seemingly democratic inclusion" (Simpson 2014, 20). Such "recognition" of culture promises to "reproduce the very configurations of colonial power that Indigenous demands for recognition have historically sought to transcend" (Coulthard 2007, 437). Adese (2012a, 484) suggests that the "refusal of Indigenous peoples to succumb to multiculturalism" is based principally on the assertion, implicit within multiculturalism, that "we are not sovereign nations that Canada must negotiate with on a nation-to-nation basis."

These discourses are therefore also evidence of peoples' inability (or unwillingness) to understand the specific historical relationships and sovereignty of Indigenous people and that nation-to-nation relationship. They, like many government discourses, forget or deny the history of Indigenous and non-Indigenous relationships, in which the appropriation of Indigenous land and the attempted destruction of Indigenous cultural and territorial relationships with their homelands (and the production of the singular nation-state now seen as natural) was essential to the settler project. The fixation on cultural difference and tolerance "occludes indigenous sovereignty" (Simpson 2014, 20).

Focusing on "recognizing" culture instead of sovereignty "is a tricky move, as sovereignty has not been eliminated. It resides in the consciousness of Indigenous peoples, [and] in the treaties and agreements they entered into between themselves and others" (Simpson 2014, 20). As we see here, national boundaries and jurisdictions are contentious, because Indigenous peoples' ongoing presence and their resistance have both challenged the "founding myths of settler nationhood" and resisted being subsumed within multiculturalism, a policy intended to turn Indigenous people into "ethnic minorities." However, the irony is, as Rifkin (2011, 342) points out, that the difference between Indigenous peoples and other ethnic or minority groups is precisely "their indigeneity—their occupancy as polities on the land currently claimed by the United States [and Canada] prior to the extension of Euro-authority over it." Audra Simpson writes:

> The state did not want Indians to remember, let alone act upon, other political traditions and authorities…This was not the "culture" that multiculturalism sought to protect and preserve. This, rather, was sovereignty and nationhood, something that was and still is an uneasy fit within a state that wishes to be singular…. Precontact nations are not "confederatable," as settlement requires a new political tableau or one made of parts that can be assimilated. (Simpson 2014, 159)

Indigenous people should not be forced into the containment categories of the multicultural imaginary because of this specific history, and because of cultural and political traditions that are not assimilable into settler multicultural jurisdictional imaginaries.

Indeed, the problem of racism for many non-Indigenous people of colour is often framed as *exclusion* from the nation-state as full subjects. In this anti-racist configuration the nation-state becomes the horizon of possibility—what is "given" and "settled." An awareness of settler-colonial forms of racialization and territorial jurisdiction indicate that for Indigenous peoples the problem is not exclusion from the nation, but forced enclosure and domestification within it. Rifkin, writing about the U.S. context, argues that the primary issue that "frames US-Indian relations, then, is not racist exclusion from citizenship but forced incorporation into the state" (Rifkin 2011, 350). Proposing inclusion in the nation (as just another jurisdiction-ally assimilable national "ethnic group") is not a generous gift (although it is, like in the examples here, continually presented as one). Forced citizenship, also known as enfranchisement, has a long and brutal history, and many Indigenous peoples continue a politics of refusal (Simpson 2011, 2014) in which they "are members of their own first nations, first. And for some, only" (Simpson 2011).

The important concern, then, for analysis, should not be only tracking the *exclusion* of Indigenous peoples from the nation-state, but also the politics of how threatening and dangerous differences are disciplined, "contained, controlled, and normalized" (Mackey 2002, 6) through discourses of cultural recognition, inclusion, and tolerance, as we see here. So this move, in which Indigenous people's claims for land and sovereignty are "disciplined" by equating them with other minority groups, is a move to push more threatening material and cultural claims to the strictly (multi-) "cultural" realm, proposing that tolerance for different cultures makes its proponents innocent of racism. In this case, Indigenous claims to land are threatening to the very core of the settler project to appropriate (and keep) land, and eliminate Indigenous people *as Indigenous peoples* who can assert sovereignty as nations. Here settler "multicultural" logic attempts to contain and define Indigenous peoples as domestic.

Domesticating Indigenous polities (materially *and* culturally) into colonial and national projects and settler jurisdictional imaginaries has always depended (and continues to depend) upon racialized thinking and practice, even if framed as "multicultural." The assumptions underlying the doctrines of *terra nullius* and Discovery that legitimized and continue to underpin this singular jurisdiction depend upon the erasure of Indigenous sovereignty and the dehumanization of Indigenous peoples and governments. The fantasies of entitlement that naturalized settler national sovereignty still depend upon that categorization of Indigenous peoples and governments as naturally inferior. Thus, the conditions of possibility for the settler nation are necessarily infused with profoundly racialized thinking and practice. Even if the anti–land right activists see themselves as not "racist" individuals, the structures that enable their nations and private property are. So are they "racists" or not?

If we conceptualize these desires to encompass Indigenous people within the settler jurisdictional imaginary as "structures of feeling," they are not only or fundamentally *individual* attitudes and emotions. As historically and structurally produced structures of feeling, they emerge from a long history of settler ideology and practice in which they have been, and continue to be, naturalized. Thus, if these people are "racist," settler nation-states are racist too. All of us who defend settler nation-states' jurisdictional imaginaries depend upon these racialized structures and ideas.

The settler project has meant that settlers feel empowered to define the terms of inclusion in the nation-state, as if the settler state always-already has legitimate and singular sovereignty, and can therefore define the terms of inclusion and exclusion of all populations, especially Indigenous peoples. It has historically been the white settler majority's unquestioned right—and expectation—to define and manage the nation, its right to decide when and how minorities are allowed both their similarities *and* their differences (Mackey 2002). Tolerance, recognition and the "specific technique that is multicultural policy are but an elaboration of an older sequence of attitudes towards 'the problem' of cultural difference on acquired, some might argue, *seized*, territories" (Simpson 2014, 21). Such techniques move "Indigenous peoples and their polities in the settler imaginary from Nations, to people, to populations—categories that have shifted through time and in relation to land and its dispossession," setting Indigenous peoples up for governmental regulation (Simpson 2014, 21). In this way, assertions of equality also depend on racialized frameworks integral to foundational narratives of settlement. The claim that "*We are all native Americans* and welcome the Native Americans of the Cayuga tribe into our community" can only exist through delegitimizing Indigenous sovereignty, governance and personhood. These assertions of equality twinned with invitations to belong and join the national project and jurisdictional imaginary form part of the "fulcrum of settlement's labor (and its imaginary)" that continues to "sustain dispossession and occupation" (Simpson 2014, 20).

CULTURE, BLOOD AND TAXES

Despite the claims of tolerance for cultural diversity explored above, intolerance and disdain for Indigenous *culture* also emerge in these discourses, drawing on long-standing racialized settler conceptions of Indigenous people. The letter from New York (above) asserts that "The Cayugas say they want a large reservation to maintain their cultural identity," as if this is the main reason for the land claim. In fact, the Cayuga do not frame "cultural identity" as the reason for their land rights action, nor do they declare that the desire for a "reservation" is its goal. The claim is based, as I discussed earlier, on long-standing agreements and treaties and the fact that the "people of the Cayuga Nation have called the land surrounding Cayuga Lake their homeland for hundreds of years" (Cayuga Nation 2014). The letter continues: "yet historically reservations have been a social disaster. They have encouraged dependency on a hierarchical tribal government." Although there may be truth to the claim that reservations have been a "disaster," the reasons for the problems with reservations are much more complex and quite different from the reason proclaimed here. The statement condenses a number of self-evident liberal, individualist and neoliberal judgments about culture and governance. More importantly, the reservation culture of "dependency" and "hierarchy" is produced here as the primary and *only* culture of Indigenous people. This again vacates Indigenous cultures and nations of histories, traditions and other forms of governance and authority beyond those imposed by settler governments (such as the Indian Act in Canada). Further, this dependent culture is produced as "bad culture" when twinned, as it is, with the alternative: the good culture of "the beautiful Amish and Mennonite communities in the land claim area," who offer "numerous other ways to preserve cultural identity." These people supply a positive example of "maintaining traditions" because they behave as good citizens while "working diligently, paying taxes and observing the laws of the land." They are also white and perceived to share "family values." The message here is that Indigenous people do not behave as good citizens, and that this is inherent in the reservation culture of Indigenous people. Thus, the professed tolerance for different cultures only goes so far, especially if the culture is framed as essentially "dependent" and "hierarchical," as opposed to the acceptable culture of the Amish or Mennonites, which is seen to produce hardworking, taxpaying, law-biding, loyal citizens.

The notion that Indigenous people were not "good citizens" who pay their taxes, work hard and behave lawfully, recurred often in my interviews. Such normative judgments about labour and contribution to society, and by extension the value of their personhood, were commonly evoked as an often implicitly racialized means to discredit Indigenous cultures and claims for land. These Lockean ideas about labour and taxes are particularly evident in an interview I had with UCE members James and Betty Miller in Cayuga County, New York. I sat with the Millers in their large, bright and recently renovated kitchen, drinking coffee and gazing onto their pleasant pond and luminous green farmland. James, a tall, tanned, plain-spoken farmer in his 60s, and Betty, his vibrant wife, had come into the area from another U.S. state several years before. They now owned substantial property in the claim area. Often in my interviews with people who opposed Indigenous land rights, I would come to a point at which I would propose that Indigenous people might see history a bit differently than they do, and that Indigenous people might argue that *they* were here first and that *their* land was taken against their will. This, I said to the Millers, is what many Indigenous people argue is the basis of land rights. I asked them how they would respond to such an argument.

Betty began: "If *they* think this is really ... what they call it? Their 'homeland'?" James added, with a shake of his head. "*Their* 'homeland?" as if the thought was unfathomable. James argued: "There are none here, none here at all. Now there're [Indian] people here ... Harry has Indian blood in him and we have a lot of friends that have Indian blood, but they're not [out] to get a free [ride]."

> B: They don't want anything for nothing, they want to be like the rest of us; they pay taxes.
>
> J: They pay taxes and they work for a living ... They shouldn't have a reservation and be tax-free. I don't think that's fair.
>
> B: And really, why do they have anything more than the rest of us do? We work for a living, they should work for a living too. Our family probably lost things too over the years, but it wasn't us who were fighting these Indians, it was our ancestors and probably not even our ancestors ... It was all history, it's over.

James first mentions friends of theirs who have "Indian blood" yet are different from other "Native people" because "they're not [out] to get a free [ride]." In this way, the example of the "good Indian" is used to communicate what behaviour is unacceptable in the more general category of "Indians." The point here seems to be that even if a person has "Indian Blood," it is possible and desirable to act "like everyone else," *despite* their Indian blood. It is possible and necessary, it implies, to *overcome* the *inherent qualities* of "Indian blood" and become a good, responsible, American citizen by paying taxes and acting "like the rest of us." Of course, understandings of being "Indian" based on blood should not be surprising. They are self-evident to many, emerging as they do from long-standing racial ideologies and U.S. and Canadian policies that have based "Indian" status and rights on "blood quantum," in the U.S., and a covert yet de facto blood quantum in Canada, through the Indian Act and other state practices (Lawrence 2004, Morse 2002).

Yet, for James, being "like the rest of us" depends on history being "over." When I suggest to James in the interview that Indigenous nations argue they have land rights because they were independent nations before the American nation was formed, he responds:

> I don't know, history is history, and as I understand it the white man beat the Indians. There was a war and we won this land. We won the war, and why the Indians feel that they should have everything back that they had before the war, that doesn't make any sense. If you go to war with Japan

or something and you win the war you've got your land; that's part of the United States, or Canada, or any other county. And the Indians got beat. That's the way I understand it.… It's all history. It's over.

The above conversation with the Millers is similar to many of the interviews I had with members of the UCE in New York and the CKCN in Ontario,[4] and illustrates the way that numerous contradictory settler narratives of entitlement are flexibly combined. Here, James first says history is over and is not important, and then he uses his incorrect version of history to make a more general argument that "Native Americans" were conquered. Since the Haudenosaunee were never conquered, this statement illustrates how easily history can be revised to justify ongoing inequality. It also demonstrates how history is used in contradictory ways: it is first ejected from the argument when it does not suit his goals ("history is history") and then resurrected when it bolsters his argument ("They were conquered"). In addition, here we see an explicit "conquest narrative" in which it is proposed that military might created unequivocal victors and victims. This use of the "conquest narrative" differs from most of the frameworks I have discussed, in which land rights are discounted based on narratives of settlement and improvement (or "improvement narratives"). These differences indicate that such discourses are not a totalizing, homogeneous and consistent "settler logic," but are instead flexible and often inconsistent. Despite such incongruity, however, both "improvement" and "conquest" narratives are mobilized in ways that conceptualize Indigenous people and societies as ideally and rightfully contained within settler jurisdiction.

TAXES AND NATIONS:
DELEGITIMIZING INDIGENOUS SOVEREIGNTY

Others who talked about the need for one nation and one set of rules also tended to make derogatory judgments about Indigenous peoples' contributions to society, constructing them as freeloaders who want special rights. Such discourses express a deep sense of entitlement to define and police the norms of acceptable behaviour in North America. They also, however, do not simply attack individual Indigenous people, but work to characterize Indigenous nations as illegitimate political entities. Paul, for example, begins with his discomfort with "special rights" and ends by arguing that Native people, in his view, are simply *not* separate nations.

> I don't agree with groups of people, whether they're raised based on race, colour, creed, religion, I don't believe that anybody should have special privileges or rights or whatever based on any of that stuff … I just disagree with the whole thing that Natives should have separate nations … it shouldn't be that way.…

> If you're being funded by the federal government you're not a separate nation, and most Native people in this area, though they live in their separate nations, they work in our nation. And then they don't contribute to our nation at all, they don't pay taxes or none of that stuff. How do they consider themselves to be an independent or separate nation, or whatever it is?

Another CKCN supporter, Mitch, agrees with Paul, saying says First Nations aren't "real nation[s]" mirroring the underlying assumptions of the philosophies and jurisprudence discussed above, in which settler sovereignty is necessarily superior because Indigenous societies are not "real" nations.

Ronald, a local schoolteacher, similarly cannot understand the idea of Native people as a separate nation. He argues that a reserve is unacceptable because it means special privileges and rights for some people within Canada.

> I don't want a reserve here…. Not because I don't want Native people, I have no problems with them living here. I have problems with the reserve: it's a special government, a special right or privilege … I think reservations are wrong right from the get go…
>
> I just can't understand how they would want to live like that, being singled out within Canada … Long term, that's what I hope will come out of CKCN: political reform of the whole Indian relations act or whatever the hell it's called.

Ronald is not simply against a reserve in his area, but has a broader goal of changing Indigenous-state relations to ensure there will be no competing Indigenous sovereignties within the nation.

The goal here, even though it is framed as equality, is ultimately political assimilation. Many of the CKCN supporters I interviewed also expressed the self-evident assumption that Indigenous peoples and lands are, and should continue to be, encapsulated and assimilated into national boundaries, jurisdiction and laws in the name of equality, fairness and economic efficiency. These examples illustrate how assumptions emerging from *terra nullius* and "state of nature" frameworks are informed by the settler jurisdictional imaginary, and augmented by liberal ideologies of equality and entitlement. These frameworks are tied together through concepts of improving labour and paying taxes as actions which entitle people to ownership of land. It is through these actions that people are seen to become legitimate citizens of sovereign nation-states.

The issue of taxation is also contradictory. As I have discussed, much anti–land claim discourse is framed as anti-government, and thus against what they see to be too much taxation. Yet here, in apparent contradiction, paying taxes is seen as an essential indication of patriotic loyalty. Since paying taxes is a marker of a particular relationship between citizens and the state, these assertions illustrate that, despite opposition to taxes on one hand, people appear to see taxation relationships with the state as essential to producing the national community, on the other. At the same time, a lack of such relationships with the state appears to put people outside of that national community.

In contradictory ways, these logics are similar to the neoliberal discourses of citizenship promoted in Canada, discourses that divide "deserving" and "undeserving" citizens (Brodie 1998, 31). Although neoliberal governments work endlessly, they say, to reduce taxes, "deserving" citizens must also fit the neoliberal model of self-reliant, entrepreneurial, market-oriented, and most importantly, independent citizens who do not drain the resources of the state. Such discourses have been applied to divide "deserving" and "undeserving" immigrants (Arat-Koc 1999), refugees (Pratt and Valverde 2002), welfare recipients (Chunn and Gavigan 2004) and others, based on normative ideals of neoliberal citizenship. Similarly, Indigenous peoples are, as we see here, constructed as undeserving freeloaders demanding special rights, in part because they are perceived, incorrectly, as a collective that is exempt from paying taxes.

Finally, when Paul slips seamlessly from his discourse against "special rights" based on race, into saying that he does not think Indigenous people should have separate nations, he presents Indigenous sovereignty as a "special right" based on race. This idea also underpins a remarkable quotation from Ron, a CKCN member:

> I have some Scottish ancestry. Many people were kicked off their land in Scotland, and wound up here. Unjustly kicked off. Now if I go back to Scotland and say, "You owe me because of what you did to my great, great, great, great grandfather," what are people going to say to me? They'd laugh me out of the country. So why are *they* [Native people] any different? Because their skin's a little different colour, that's all. The Welsh, in England, they might say, "Our country's been stolen from us; we've been crowded into the poorest part of the island. And all the rest of you people should leave because this is our island." …This isn't unique to Canada; this has happened all over the world. It's only now that, because in certain areas in the world—and Canada's not the only one that's got problems, Australia's got problems, New Zealand's got problems, Africa's got problems—but their skin's a little bit different colour than the people that came, so they can distinguish each other better.
>
> You take a native person—how much native blood do you have to have in you to be a native today? One sixteenth or something? One thirty-second or something? So here I've got someone way back in my

history that was a native, and I may be one sixteenth native so the rest of the country owes me. *How much does that fifteen sixteenths of me owe to myself?* (emphasis mine)

Ron's discussion of ancestry, land rights and restitution is fascinating, because he ultimately transforms his own individual body into a microcosm of a nation-state to illustrate his point. Ron's final image of parts of his own body owing other parts is rich with significance, illustrating how liberal nation-state logic is based on the ideal of a unified "collective individual" as defined by C.B. MacPherson (discussed in Chapter 2). Ron's image of his own body *as* the nation is also poignant because it naturalizes his blood-based understanding of the indivisibility of the nation. In other words, when he talks about one part of himself owing the other parts, it naturally seems ludicrous, impossible and completely irrational that one part of a body could owe another part anything, because a body is a singular, bounded, unified object, much like his idea of what a nation is. In this way, Ron naturalizes the idea that competing loyalties or claims are divisive and will destroy the unified singular ideal nation (his body). Because bodies (and thus nations) are seen as always-already singular and unified (which we know is not the case with nations), Indigenous rights and sovereignty within settler nation-states are made to appear unnatural and simply not possible.

Ron's embodied argument about indivisibility also depends on transforming Indigenous rights into a claim for special treatment based on race, and not an ethical demand for justice based on the colonization and appropriation of the land of sovereign Indigenous nations. Ron's argument is that it is racist for Indigenous people to have specific rights: "Because their skin's a little different colour, that's all." The ubiquity of such interpretations of Indigenous sovereignty as essentially race-based and "racist" is another example of how compelling liberal nationalist settler narratives are, and how difficult it is for people to even think outside the box of "one nation"—a nation normatively composed of minority and majority cultures and one set of laws (see Mackey 2002). CKCN members are unable to understand that land rights are based on histories of sovereignty and overlapping, fluid jurisdictions between peoples, histories that predate nation-states as singular, jurisdictional entities, and in which relationships were negotiated *between* independent Indigenous and colonizing nations and powers.

Indigenous nations negotiate relationships with Canada today on the basis of forms of sovereignty and self-determination that existed *before* the nation-states that exist in their territories today, even if such sovereignty is not the same as Western national sovereignty. Treaties, therefore, were not originally domestic (inside the nation) issues. Were it not for the "state of nature" and *terra nullius* frameworks that were fundamental in redefining sovereign Indigenous nations as inferior, and therefore not sovereign, treaties would not continue to be considered domestic issues but would be part of international law. From this perspective, debates about land rights are not about the place of minority cultures within singular nations. They are instead debates about how to work out a relationship between separate, sovereign nations.

In addition, despite the brutal racism of settler states' treatment of Indigenous peoples, land rights are not *racial* rights. They are not asserted based on the "race" of Indigenous peoples, or claimed with the primary purpose of ameliorating racism and making Indigenous peoples "equal" to other citizens. Indigenous nations were not founded as "races" and are not a "race," despite the long process in which the settler state racialized them. Settler states institutionalized the official *racialization* of Indigenous peoples with laws such as the Indian Act in Canada, which created and violently implemented bureaucratic categories of "Indian," "half-breed" and Metis," brutally defining Indigenous peoples in terms of race and blood. Many official members of First Nations are white, mixed race and black, and many non-Indigenous people have married into First Nations communities and have full citizenship status. Other so-called "full-blood" Indigenous peoples have, through the same process, been disenfranchised from their nations and land through the process of forced "enfranchisement" into nation-states (Lawrence 2004). Indigenous rights emerge from membership in historically recognized cultural, legal and political entities that had, and continue to have, their own authority and sovereignty (whether recognized by settler state or not) to negotiate relationships.

The above comments by UCE and CKCN members and supporters indicate that axiomatic views of the nation as singular, indivisible and a "collective individual" are very resilient and powerful, and that they emerge—increasingly rigid and inflexible on one hand, and yet flexible and contradictory on the other—especially in moments of crisis, when peoples' settled expectations are threatened. Framed in the language of modernity, progress and equality, these are nevertheless "settler states of feeling" because they are underpinned by the assumption that the Crown and the nation-state naturally have superior underlying title to Indigenous lands, and that Indigenous peoples, governments and territories should naturally be encompassed by, assimilated into and managed within a singular unified settler project. These discourses juxtapose culture, race, territory and jurisdiction in ways that draw on older racialized frameworks of colonial entitlement and also defend and reproduce contemporary dispossession in complex and flexible ways. Attempts to manage Indigenous peoples and nations—through discourses and practices that reproduce the jurisdictional imaginary of the unified settler nation such as recognition, multiculturalism, conquest or cultural and racial inferiority—are more than individual efforts to try to erase and make invisible that which will not go away: Indigenous sovereignty.

This chapter has traced how the people I talked with in local communities work strategically to try to shove Indigenous people and their governments (back) into settler-state jurisdiction so that they can feel certain about settler futures, cultures and their own ownership of land. However, the settler project is not settled and certain, and settled expectations of entitlement are not guaranteed.

These efforts at jurisdiction over Indigenous lives and governments make profound sense within the broader context of centuries of settler colonial and national bolstering of key assumptions and frameworks of settler entitlement and superior sovereignty. The powerful, ubiquitous and axiomatic nature of these fantasies of entitlement makes it understandable that they are used in this way, and it is not a matter of blaming individuals for these foundational (to settler colonialism) ideas. They embody the dilemma and the reproductive labour at the heart of the settler project. However, if what is at stake is imagining or building a decolonized relationship between Indigenous and settler peoples and governments, these are precisely the kinds of ideas I argue need to be shifted and unsettled, because of their effects. They close down the possibility of people even beginning to recognize that Indigenous nations are sovereign nations that may have different, yet equally valuable, ontologies and epistemologies of sociality and property. They deny the possibility, and the need, to imagine and build a decolonized space within which one might recognize and negotiate differences, interconnections and autonomies.

CONCLUDING THOUGHTS ON PART TWO

So far in this book I have argued that the feelings of anger and uncertainty expressed by the people I interviewed represent more than individual emotions. Instead, my analysis of longstanding ideas and practices of settled expectations and certainty reveals that similar ideas have become normalized and naturalized through law, and thus make sense as characteristics of "settler structures of feeling." They communicate "settled expectations" of certainty over land and control of Indigenous peoples that have long been built into colonial and settler projects. The ubiquitous and axiomatic nature of these assumptions makes it understandable that they are used in this way. These are legal and philosophical logics of settler colonialism that come alive as "settler structures of feeling." They make sense within the broader context of how centuries of settler colonial and national culture and law have bolstered their key assumptions and frameworks. My question now becomes, What might this normalization of certainty mean for decolonization?

Theorizations about how to decolonize settler colonialism are complex, complicated and emergent. Although the topic is a site of passionate debate, no one pretends to have the full authoritative answer of how to decolonize. What is clear is that decolonization entails uncertainty, since it will be a "messy, dynamic, and

... contradictory process" that cannot be authoritatively "codified or defined" in advance (Sium, Desai and Ritskes 2012, ii). I suggest that denaturalizing settler beliefs and authoritative practices based on supposedly self-evident certainties about the primacy of settler-state sovereignty over Indigenous lands and peoples is important, both in terms of law and public policy and also for settler subjects and national cultures. If the construction and defence of certainty is at the core of ongoing settler colonialism, then settler *uncertainty* may actually be necessary for decolonization. Living without the entitlement to know everything (and therefore be certain) will likely lead to settler discomfort, a discomfort that may need to be embraced instead of resisted in order to participate in the difficult work of decolonization. In the next section of the book, I explore how it might be possible to do so.

Notes

1   That the author calls the Cayuga Nation a "*new* sovereign nation" is significant, as if the Nation's sovereignty only exists because it is recognized by the United States. The Haudenosaunee Confederacy, of which the Cayuga Nation is a member, have been sovereign nations for thousands of years and, as discussed in this chapter and throughout Part Three, have never stopped asserting this sovereignty.

2   "Possessive individual" discussed in Chapter 2.

3   Immigration and forms of "multiculturalism" often become essential to settler nations, because in the process of nation-building over Indigenous lands, the nation needs immigrants to help build it and populate it. "Multiculturalism" is often later employed as an ideology and practice to build a regenerated national identity characterized by so-called tolerance and equality (Mackey 2002). The new "multicultural" identity works to erase Indigenous sovereignty, although it may happily include (appropriate) Indigenous cultures as part of the "heritage" of the nation (Mackey 2002).

4   There were also many differences between U.S. and Canadian responses. For a more detailed account see Mackey 2005.

Part Three

IMAGINING OTHERWISE: EMBRACING SETTLER UNCERTAINTY

INTRODUCTION
Treaty as a Verb

The act of *turning round*, of shifting one's orientation and redirecting the momentum by which one previously was impelled, offers possibilities for perceiving differently, for seeing and engaging in ways that less take for granted the jurisdictional matrix of the state and ... compels a reconceptualization of the terms of occupancy for everyone. (Rifkin 2013, 336)

The theft of land has enabled our incredible achievements, and also our dreadful mistakes. It is up to us to reclaim our responsibilities as Settlers — as world makers, as dreamers and builders, and people who can work together despite our differences to achieve great things — and to use our powers, privileges, and skills differently. We built this world, we built the nations of Canada and America, but we did it by trying to destroy many other nations as part of the process. It's time to reverse this process. (Barker 2013)

Over 40 years ago, in his book *The Fourth World: An Indian Reality*, George Manuel, Secwepemc chief, addressed what was necessary to change "Indian-European relations":

When we come to a new fork in an old road we continue to follow the route with which we are familiar, even though wholly different, even better avenues might open up before us. The failure to heed (the) plea for a new approach to Indian- European relations is a failure of imagination. The greatest barrier to recognition of Aboriginal rights does not lie with the courts, the law, or even the present administration. Such recognition necessitates the re-evaluation of assumptions; both about Canada and its history and about Indian people and our culture... Real recognition of our presence and humanity would require a genuine reconsideration of so many people's role in North American society that it would amount to a genuine leap of imagination. (Manuel and Posluns 1974, cited in Regan 2005, 3)

Manuel's words continue to have a chilling power today, despite over 40 years of what many see as "improvement" or "progress" in the recognition of Indigenous rights. Deep, persistent and flexible epistemologies have developed over centuries, and have produced deep-seated settler self-evident certainty in entitlement. Although such ideas have shifted and changed flexibly over time and in different contexts, one consistency is that they have persistently constructed settler entitlement, jurisdiction and control of Indigenous people as natural. This has entailed perceiving Indigenous lifeways as inferior, undeserving and unacceptable, and sovereignty and land rights as unreasonable, unnatural and dangerous. In doing so, they have also repeatedly denied even the possibility of substantive Indigenous sovereignty and autonomy. Given the persistence of such frameworks, how might it be possible to imagine decolonized relationships between Indigenous and settler people in settler nations? If, as I have argued, the production and defence of settler certainty and settler futurity have been central to the ongoing colonial process, where do we go from here?

Theorizations about how to decolonize settler nation-states are being passionately debated, and no one pretends to know in advance what will be required. The process is necessarily uncertain. Sium, Desai and Ritskes (2012, 1) say that despite their "certainty that decolonization centers Indigenous methods, peoples, and lands," decolonization cannot be pre-visioned; it cannot be certain. Decolonization cannot affirm "settler futurity" (Tuck and Yang 2012, 1–3). The "settled expectations" and "fantasies of entitlement" I have explored here represent an example of how "Eurocentric thought has dreamed imaginary societies that generate our cognitive prisons" (Henderson 2002a, 14). These axiomatic assumptions are the "cognitive prisons" of settler peoples, and they need to be unsettled. I suggest that denaturalizing settler beliefs and authoritative practices based on supposedly self-evident certainties about the primacy of settler-state sovereignty over Indigenous lands and peoples is important, both in terms of law and public policy, and also for settler subjects and national cultures.

In addition, because, as I have been arguing in this book, settler colonialism is a complex and singular social formation concerned with the appropriation of Indigenous land, decolonization must also be a material process. Tuck and Yang argue that decolonization must "involve the repatriation of land simultaneous to the recognition of how land and relations to land have always-already been differently understood and enacted; that is, *all* of the land, and not just symbolically" (Tuck and Yang 2012, 7). In this third part of the book I argue that to even be able to imagine the possibilities of such material change and conceptual re-imagining will require what I call an "epistemological shift" towards a stance of settler uncertainty and openness, as a starting point to imagine and practice otherwise.

EPISTEMOLOGICAL SHIFTS

What do I mean by epistemological shift? So far in this book I have discussed particular Western epistemological frameworks and explored how land, relationships to land, concepts of nationhood and categories of persons have been framed within them. One epistemological problem addressed in most land rights cases is how we determine to whom the lands of North America belong. How one goes about formulating an answer depends on one's epistemologies. Within the Western epistemologies I have discussed, the answer to that question assumes a number of foundational relationships and concepts. These include the ideas that: things, in particular land, can actually be "owned"; people are individual sovereign subjects essentially separated from each other and nature; the highest value in human relationships with land and the natural world is based on particular kinds of labour perceived as "improvement"; specific kinds of improvement can make a human being into the owner and master of land and nature; and that other kinds of relationships with land preclude that ownership. Finally, all of these assumptions intersect with the notion that those who "improve" land are naturally and essentially superior to those who don't, and that they are thus naturally entitled to the privileges they reap. All of these interconnected beliefs are integral to the supposedly obvious argument, embedded in law, that settler governments have legitimate title to the land of the nation-state, and that the nation-state may then "give" Indigenous people, or "allow" Indigenous people to have, specific limited, or bare, "land rights" and/or sometimes possession.

Western philosophical theory has told us a great deal about epistemologies and power in recent decades. Theory, therefore, has an important place in imagining and practicing such shifts in epistemological frameworks. But what kind of theory? Scholars and activists in North America and around the world have been arguing for years that we need different ways of thinking about relationships between Indigenous and non-Indigenous peoples, and that a first step is to recognize and value Indigenous world views, and not subsume Indigenous lifeways into Western and national frameworks of superiority (see Asch and Macklem 1991; Asch 1992a, 1992b, 2002; Bell and Asch 1997; Alfred 1999; Monture-Angus 1998; Harris 2002; Nadasdy 2003; Mohawk 2000; Tully 1995; Turner 2006).

However, doing so in an appropriate manner is neither easy nor common sense. What are the roadblocks to this process? Many of the settler premises of and assumptions about colonialism I analyze in this book are precisely the ones that I argue need to be re-examined, re-opened and regarded as contingent, arbitrary and replaceable in order to decolonize. In doing so it might be possible to reinvent, alter and renegotiate how we experience and negotiate relationships, so that we move away from colonialism. However, to do so requires first that we as settlers recognize that our self-evident epistemological and ontological assumptions are specific and not universal. It also requires persistent willingness and motivation to understand, or at least respect, that there are equally valid epistemological and ontological alternatives. Such processes have a multitude of possible dangers if not carried out in mindful and self-critical ways, because disengaged (or possessive) curiosity *about* the "other" can easily become both fetishizing and objectifying. Audra Simpson (2007) has called on Native Studies scholars to refuse to fetishize Indigenous culture and engage in acts of "ethnographic refusal." Learning *about* Indigenous people can also be used as a way to appropriate knowledge or to invent a fantasy of "becoming indigenous" (Mackey 2005) for settlers. Settler states and citizens have rarely found it difficult to enjoy and appropriate colourful aspects of Indigenous cultures and traditions, and have made a habit of mobilizing Indigenous imagery and ritual to legitimate settler nations and events, rituals and paternalistic programs (Mackey 2002). Curiosity without mindful engagement can similarly result in self-referential and narcissistic settler identifications with, and projections onto, Indigenous peoples that involve objectifying Indigenous peoples into precisely the limited stereotypes discussed here. Tuck and Yang argue that the "metaphorization of decolonization makes possible a set of evasions, or 'settler moves to innocence,' that problematically attempt to reconcile settler guilt and complicity, and rescue settler futurity" (Tuck and Yang 2012, 1).

It has been, and will be, more difficult to respectfully listen to, comprehend, and respect the authority of the more challenging knowledge and wisdom of Indigenous peoples. This would represent an epistemological shift. As Dale Turner, Anishnabe philosopher, points out,

> By and large, the non-Aboriginal legal and political academic community does not recognize Indigenous intellectual traditions as valuable sources of knowledge (never mind wisdom). Our "tribal secrets" are of anthropological or historical interest only — most non-Aboriginal academics are still more interested in generating a discourse *about* Aboriginal peoples than in defending, say, the epistemological value of Indigenous ways of knowing. (Turner 2006, 90)

Indigenous traditions and knowledge developed in the work of Indigenous scholars are powerful, vital and absolutely necessary sources for theorizing how to (re)conceptualize and (re)build such non-colonizing visions and practices. Concepts and practices of treaty, as defined and critiqued by many Indigenous scholars and activists, offer important epistemological models of relationality that unsettle the bounded, binary oppositions central to the epistemologies and practices of mastery and entitlement that we have seen repeated throughout this book. They also mark out an important space — a necessary space, yet also a limited space — for *non-Indigenous* people in the process of creating such relationships.

WHO DECOLONIZES? AND HOW?

How does one respond appropriately as a settler Canadian or U.S. citizen in the 21st century to the explicit and subtle violence that is embodied in the past, present and future of our nations' relationships with the Indigenous peoples who lived here before we did, and that continue to live here? What roles can and should non-Indigenous people play in decolonizing processes? I know many well-intentioned settler people who will happily rush headlong into "helping" Indigenous people, assuming they know what the problems are and how to solve them. Such an approach, even if framed in terms that are more supportive of Indigenous land rights, may often reproduce coloniality by imposing normative and often unconscious settler standards, appropriating Indigenous world views or spirituality, or engaging in a myriad of other destructive, albeit well-intentioned and "charitable," acts resulting from an ingrained sense of entitlement. One key problem here is that so often it is Indigenous people who are seen as "the problem," not settler ideologies and practices. Other, equally well-meaning non-Indigenous people — deeply concerned and wanting to avoid participating in the reproduction of colonial relations — may decide that they should stay out of the way of Indigenous people's autonomy and self-government. Are these really the only two choices? Who will take care of the difficult and necessary work of decolonizing relationships? Who will deal with the "settler problem?"

As I have documented throughout this book, some of the main roadblocks to imagining and practicing decolonization[1] are axiomatic settler frameworks and their entangled practices. Thus, it makes sense that we, as settler descendants, should take responsibility to engage in learning how to participate in this process. Fortunately, Indigenous traditions and theorizing have opened an important, indeed a central, place for non-Indigenous people in the decolonizing process. For example, Dale Turner argues:

> Abolishing colonialism is the goal of many Indigenous and non-Indigenous peoples; finding a way to do it is the great dilemma. If a just political

relationship *has to be dialogical* in nature, *Indigenous peoples will not* be able to secure a *"post-colonial"* political relationship *without the help of non-Indigenous peoples.* (Turner 2006, 109, emphasis mine)

But exactly what form should this "help" take? Based on the experience of past "help" that settler states and citizens have provided to (and forced upon) Indigenous peoples — such as agricultural training, residential schools, forced adoption and other forms of assimilation — how is it possible to rethink and practice "helping" in such a way that it does not reproduce patronizing coloniality, but instead promotes the unsettling of relations of domination?[2]

A first step, as I have suggested so far, is beginning to see ourselves as already "living within Indigenous sovereignty" (Nicoll 2004b, 17). Part of this process entails engaging seriously with diverse Indigenous perspectives on foundational relationships regarding treaty. The concept of settler involvement in decolonization is elaborated upon in the Report of the Canadian Royal Commission on Aboriginal Peoples (RCAP).[3] The Royal Commission was established in 1991, in the wake of the 1990 violent confrontation at "The Pines" in Oka, Québec, between the government of Québec, the Québec provincial police, the Canadian military and the Mohawks of Kanesatake and their supporters. The Commission's six-volume Report (RCAP 1996) examined the relationship between Indigenous peoples, the Government of Canada and Canadian society as a whole, and drew on extensive research and community consultation. Overall, the report argued for a fundamental restructuring of Crown-Aboriginal relationships. The report is deeply critical of Aboriginal–non-Aboriginal relations as they have existed, and opens up space for — and even requires — non-Aboriginal peoples' involvement, because we are, both Indigenous *and* non-Indigenous, all "treaty peoples":

> From an Aboriginal treaty perspective, European rights in the Americas — to the use of lands and resources, for example — did not derive legitimately from international law precepts such as the doctrine of discovery or from European political and legal traditions. Rather, the historical basis of *such rights came about through treaties made with Aboriginal nations.* In this view, the terms of the treaties define the rights and responsibilities of *both* parties. It is as a result of the treaties that *Canadians have,* over time, *inherited the wealth generated by Aboriginal lands* and resources that Aboriginal nations *shared so generously with them.* Thus, although the term "treaty Indians" is commonly (if somewhat misleadingly) used to refer to members of Indian nations whose ancestors signed treaties, *Canadians* generally can equally be considered *participants in the treaty process,* through the actions of their ancestors and as the contemporary

beneficiaries of the treaties that gave the Crown access to Aboriginal lands and resources. (RCAP 1996, 56, emphasis mine)

Thus, despite the failure to recognize their necessary involvement, settler peoples *already are* participants in, and beneficiaries of, treaties. Non-Aboriginal Canadians are therefore invited (indeed urged) by RCAP to take an active role in creating decolonizing relations.[4] At the same time, it is important to point out that in fact treaties were not made in all parts of Canada (especially in British Columbia). However, even if we are not "all treaty people," in that the specific territories we as individuals may live upon are not under treaty, Canada as a settler nation could not exist without treaty relations. Further, as Lowman and Barker (2015, 67–68) argue, "claiming status as a treaty person" cannot be a "panacea for Settler Canadian uncertainty, discomfort, or guilt." My point here is that, as settlers, working to see ourselves as treaty peoples, and learning to think and behave like responsible treaty partners, can be a fruitful way to begin to imagine respectful co-existence.

But how do we begin to think like responsible treaty partners? Susan Hill talks about a quotation that she read in which an author says that historians need to put on a "cultural lens" when they're examining Indigenous histories. Her reaction to that was:

> We don't need you to try to … *think like an Indian* … What we need *you to do is to find out what your responsibilities* are to us…. Because everyone in this room has treaty rights. *If you didn't you couldn't be here. Canada wouldn't exist…*
>
> And so when you're looking at *our issues, what you call our issues,* I'm asking you to remember that *they're your issues too.*
>
> And it's not just about what's good for the Indian, or what they want. It's about *how can we live together in this place* under that agreement of *peace and respect and friendship that our ancestors promised each other.* (Cited in Indigenous Knowledge Forum 2004, emphasis mine)

Thus, the idea of settler peoples' responsibilities for treaty agreements is central to decolonization. It does not, I agree, mean learning to "think like an Indian," but it does involve difficult and sometimes frightening *re*-thinking and re-experiencing one's place in the world and thus one's relationships to others. The epistemologies and "logics" of settler colonialism I have discussed throughout this book are so deeply axiomatic and flexible that seeing Indigenous issues as "our" issues, and thinking about our responsibilities in treaty relationships requires major epistemological shifts. It requires that settlers first unsettle the myriad epistemological certainties that have been instilled in us for centuries, based as they are on axiomatic assumptions about proper and acceptable relations between peoples, property and personhood. Only then might it be possible to actually see and listen in new ways, and then be able to imagine new relationships that are not based on coloniality. This is what I mean by the necessity of unsettling epistemologies of mastery in order to participate in decolonization.

In other words, participation needs to be attentive and critically self-reflexive. *How* treaty is conceptualized is important. The Crown saw, and often continues to see, treaty in very different ways from Indigenous peoples. Many Canadians, including the anti–land claim activists I spoke with, still "regard treaties as an extinguishment of rights, and acceptance of the supremacy of the crown, and a generous gift of land to the Indians so they might have land of their own" (Government of Canada 1983, cited in Valaskakis 2005, 77). As discussed, the underlying assumption of Canadian law regarding Indigenous peoples' sovereignty is that Crown sovereignty always trumps Indigenous sovereignty. Many governments and settler citizens thus see treaties as contained, completed and bounded objects that are not relevant anymore, and certainly not pivotal to an ongoing process of negotiating equal relationships between nations. Treaties are seen as past strategic performances, now delineated in time and in a manner expedient for nation-building. They are conceptualized with a kind of temporal fixity, reflecting perhaps ideas about the fixity and certainty of property entitlement in western property regimes. Work by Borrows (1997), Mills (2010), Lindberg (2010) and others show that Indigenous views of treaty differed greatly from how they have been interpreted by settler governments since. In a recent book discussing treaty relationships, Michael Asch (2014, ix and especially Chapter 5) makes the cautious argument that, with regard to at least some treaties in Canada, Indigenous interpretations of their meanings and terms were actually "shared understandings" with the settlers who made them at the time. He (Asch 2014, ix) writes that "there is at least the case to be made for the proposition that there were those who acted in good faith in the past," and that therefore acting on the basis of Indigenous understandings of treaties, now and in the future, would not be a break with the past, but consistent with it. Nevertheless, complex Indigenous meanings of treaty — and thus the building of ongoing relationships of mutuality and respect — have most often been occluded in assertions of superior Crown sovereignty.

Is it possible to move beyond such understandings? In this final section of the book, I argue that to do so will require learning how to listen differently and to embrace particular forms of critical uncertainty: to allow preconceptions to become unsettled. The importance of an epistemological shift is, for me, about developing new frameworks that allow settler-subjects to see, hear and thus know and act differently, frameworks that are not exclusive and exclusionary, that do not require the taming or discrediting of other ways of knowing in order to meet settled expectations and maintain fragile ontological certainty. In short, I argue that many of the foundations of settler identities and practices need to be unsettled so that we can learn to live with, and even embrace, the uncertainty that is necessary in order to learn how to imagine and build decolonized relationships. Here I am not suggesting that such uncertainty replicate the so-called "resilience," "flexibility" and "privatization of risk" celebrated and promoted by neoliberalism (Calhoun 2006). Instead, I am imagining a principled, historically aware stance of self-conscious refusal to mobilize axiomatic knowledge and action that have emerged from settler entitlement and certainty. This kind of refusal may open space for genuine attention to alternative frameworks and seed possibilities for creative and engaged relationships and collective projects. Settler colonialism implicates everyone and its decolonization is, and should be, unsettling (Tuck and Yang 2012, 7) because it requires major material and conceptual changes. It requires, as Nicoll argues, "falling out of perspective" — specifically, out of a "white know it all perspective" that assumes an "omniscient position" above Indigenous understandings of sovereignty (Nicoll 2004b, 21). How can we listen to others if we already *know*? First of all, it helps to understand Indigenous theorizations of treaty relationships.

THEORIZING TREATY RELATIONSHIPS

A poster advertising a "settler treaty card," published by Briarpatch magazine (see <briarpatchmagazine.com/settlertreatycard>), outlines the privileges and responsibilities of settlers. It has a shock value that works precisely because it turns common-sense settler understandings on their heads. The poster states:

> Introducing the Settler Treaty Card™
> "You can't live here without it!"
> With your Settler Treaty Card™, YOU get access to countless privileges that your ancestors' representatives signed on for in perpetuity — privileges like settler self-government and access to the land.[5]

Turning such understandings on their heads may be one important way to unsettle deep-seated ontological certainty, a certainty which has, as I have argued, become naturalized. As such, the attainment of the ontological certainty of some has been secured at great costs to others, through relations of domination and oppression. This process has impacted both those defined as dominant and those defined as inferior in very different ways. For those defined as dominant, who have learned to expect ontological certainty, one of the effects has been an inability to see, hear, comprehend and thus fully respect epistemologies that do not fit within their settled expectations. In the following chapters I explore alternative epistemologies aimed at mutuality and relationality through difference rather than mastery of one over the other, of alliance without subjugation rather than equality as sameness.

Learning to understand and even experience such an epistemology might allow settler citizens to see and hear differently, and learn to develop decolonized relationships. In the next chapter, when I move to a discussion of how the Onondaga Nation diplomatically enter and yet unsettle a New York courtroom, I offer an illustration of the struggle between these competing epistemologies, and of the potential of imagining otherwise.

Because the notion of all of settlers as "treaty peoples" uses existing historical agreements that should be everyone's shared responsibility as their foundation, it can be seen as a potential invitation to non-Indigenous people to develop new relationships with Indigenous peoples. Treaties, as conceptualized in Indigenous theory, offer a legal and moral rationale for sharing decolonizing labour. Indigenous versions of treaties and sovereignty are also theories: they have epistemologies embedded and elaborated within them and embody important and sophisticated theorizations of how to know, understand and live in the world. They provide, as I document in the following chapters, visions that help people trying to enact the kinds of transformations or "epistemological shifts" necessary in order to decolonize. These theorizations are not invitations to become Indigenous, or to see like an Indigenous person. They are invitations to be(come) responsible, by learning how to listen and respond appropriately as partners in particular treaty relationships.

One of the main characteristics of the settler epistemologies and practices I have discussed so far in this book is that they consistently construct and naturalize dualistic and binary models of home, belonging, identity and property: land is either owned fully as individual property, not owned at all, or belongs to the crown who as a recognized state can own land in common; identities are bounded and homogenous, fixed and non-negotiable, one either is or isn't American; homes are perceived as either completely safe because they contain no difference or conflict, or they are seen as deeply threatened by differences that cannot be assimilated. Such oppositions and boundaries animate judgments of superior and inferior labour and personhood. Clear fences and borders mark the ideal inside and dangerous outside of properties and identities, fixing the characteristics of those entitled to define others and appropriate land, as well as those who are deemed naturally un-entitled and undeserving. Such epistemologies of mastery offer no window to imagine a shared project of building relationships within homelands that can account for complex and often violent, but sometimes fruitful, overlapping histories, or the resulting similarities *and* differences between settler and Indigenous peoples. This is the epistemology of mastery underlying what I have called the settler "fantasy of entitlement." Decolonization will require moving away from such epistemologies in order to imagine and build different relationships.

The philosophies and practices of "living treaty," as enacted in the specific cases I discuss here, offer the potential to move beyond such rigid binary understandings of relationships, without losing sight of the important political differences and incommensurability that are important to maintain (Jones with Jenkins 2008; Wolfe 2013; Tuck and Yang 2012). They offer ways to think about key epistemological shifts that contribute toward, and are necessary for, decolonization practices in a number of ways. It is not that Indigenous people (or non-Indigenous people, for that matter) expect this to be an easy process. But it is a necessary one. As Borrows points out:

> Bravery requires us to face the complexities of our relationship to Canada. While different First Nations have different traditions in this regard, I am trying to highlight that even peoples who consider themselves independent from Canada would still find themselves in a relationship with others in their territories. We might need to work with others from time to time, even as we pursue different objectives from them. Working in and outside "the system" does not have to be a dichotomous contradiction … Thus, I believe bravery is directed towards goodness if it contains hope that change and healing can occur … I think it is brave to believe we can be reconciled to those who have hurt us, and that we can make a new and better world together (as imperfect as that world will be). (Borrows 2008 19–20)

The question, then, is how do we begin to do so? How can we begin to imagine otherwise?

TREATY AS A VERB — THE SPACES BETWEEN THE ROWS

One of the most famous and much-discussed treaties, the Covenant Chain, recorded in the Two Row Wampum, or Guswentha, was made between the Haudenosaunee and the Dutch in 1613. It is understood by the Haudenosaunee as the basis on which all subsequent treaties were made and as a model of relationships between peoples. The wampum itself is a white shell belt with two purple rows. The Ganondagan web site provides the following description:

> Haudenosaunee tradition records the following as the Haudenosaunee reply to the initial Dutch treaty proposal: You say that you are our Father and I am your son. We say, We will not be like Father and Son, but like Brothers. This wampum belt confirms our words. These two rows will symbolize two paths or two vessels, traveling down the same river together. One, a birch bark canoe, will be for the Indian People, their laws, their customs and their ways. The other, a ship, will be for the white people and their laws, their customs and their ways. We shall each travel

the river together, side by side, but in our boat. Neither of us will make compulsory laws nor interfere in the internal affairs of the other. Neither of us will try to steer the other's vessel. The agreement has been kept by the Iroquois to this date. (Friends of Ganondagan 2010)

The Two Row is often simply interpreted in terms of the autonomy and *separation* of the two separate rows, vessels, or nations, as may seem apparent from the text: "*These two rows will symbolize two paths or two vessels ... Neither of us will make compulsory laws or interfere in the internal affairs of the other. Neither of us will try to steer the other's vessel.*"

It is often seen as an image of separation and non-interference. However, nuanced analyses undertaken by a number of Indigenous scholars provide a provocative interpretation based on a slight yet significant shift of focus: they theorize the significance of the *shared* river, of the path *between* the rows. Susan Hill says:

Within the oral record of the Haudenosaunee, it is noted that the relationship was to be as two vessels travelling down the river — the river of life — side by side, never crossing paths, never interfering in the other's internal matters. However, the *path between them,* symbolized by three rows of ... beads, was to be *a constant of respect, trust and friendship. Some might say this is what kept the two vessels apart, but in fact, it is what kept them connected to each other.* Without those three principles, the two vessels could drift apart and potentially be washed onto the bank (or crash into rocks). This agreement was meant to provide security for both sides ... The premise of non-interference, *within the concept of brotherhood, demonstrates the desire to be allies rather than to have one side be subjects of the other.* (Hill 2008, 30, emphasis mine)

Similarly, Leroy Little Bear describes the Guswentha, pointing out that while the parallel lines mean that people would never cross paths, "at the same time, we're *bound together* by three rows of white wampum that join it into one belt. And I've been taught that those three rows represent peace, friendship and mutual respect" (cited in Indigenous Knowledge Forum 2004).

The point about being *bound together and also independent* that Susan Hill and Leroy Little Bear allude to here is pursued in detail by Dale Turner (2006) in his book *This Is Not a Peace Pipe,* offering non-Indigenous people an important lesson in treaty interpretation. He discusses how non-Indigenous academics, even if they do account seriously for Indigenous philosophy such as the Two Row Wampum, or Guswentha, tend to misinterpret it. It is often seen as parallelism based on a clear and permanent separation of the nations. He cites Allan Cairns (2000), non-Aboriginal author of the book *Citizens Plus,* who says,

> The two-row wampum model so frequently proposed as the arrange-
> ment that will fit our needs, stresses the permanence of difference. As
> an image it postulates different paths that never converge. The image is
> coexistence with little traffic between the solitudes. It does not suggest
> shared endeavours for a common purpose….Parallelism — the two-row
> wampum — does not address the reality of our interdependence, and our
> intermingling. (Cairns 2000, 92 cited in Turner 2006, 45)

Turner (2006, 45) argues that Cairns misinterprets the Two Row Wampum because
he fails to recognize the sophistication and "depth of Iroquoian philosophical
thought." Turner then explores the complex meanings of the Guswentha and reveals
the powerful significance of its political vision of autonomy and interdependence
within Haudenosaunee political philosophy.

Turner points out that Cairns fails to mention the three rows *in between* the
two purple rows. These three beads that *bridge the parallel rows* represent peace,
respect and friendship. He argues that missing the meaning of the beads is a serious oversight. It is through exploring the significance of the three beads, Turner
suggests, that one can begin to understand what the Haudenosaunee meant by
a "just political relationship" (Turner 2006, 48). The Guswentha, guided by the
Great Law of Peace, embodies a set of powerful embedded principles of behaviour:
respect, reciprocity and renewal. These principles are central to understanding
Haudenosaunee political thinking about how to maintain political relationships in
practice. These principles both define and make sense of the "*relationship between
the two purple rows*" (my emphasis, also see Asch 2014). The "two participants
in the political relationship — Europeans and Iroquois — can share the same
space and travel into the future, yet neither can steer the other's vessel." However,
he continues,

> Because they share the same space they are inextricably entwined in a
> relationship of interdependence — *but they remain distinct political entities.*
> Cairns fails to understand this because he omits an important part of the
> political relationship: the three beads of respect, peace and friendship that
> bind the two rows *together but as independent nations.* Respect, peace and
> friendship are pivotal to *maintaining* the relationship, not to establishing
> it. (Turner 2006, 54, emphasis in original)

In other words, while Cairns sees these lines as representing what keeps people
apart, according to Turner, Hill and Little Bear, they are actually what keep peoples
who are distinct from one another *together* over time. They define their relationship
so that they walk *beside each other* with respect, entwined *and* independent, as equal
brothers rather than as father and son. Borrows concurs with this interpretation,

saying, "our treaties were intended to accomplish *alliance without subjugation*" (Borrows 2008, 19–20).

It is significant that the idea of building complex relationships of interdependence and autonomy between Indigenous and non-Indigenous peoples is not something members of UCE or CKCN brought up or even gestured towards. They proposed dualistic and oppositional models of relationships: either equality (defined as sameness and assimilation) or separation (which they saw as inequality). The Guswentha model allows for simultaneous distinction and interdependence through what Asch (2014, 130) calls "linking." It idealizes neither separation nor sameness, and thus refuses paternalistic notions of settlers "helping" Indigenous peoples to progress, if progress means becoming like settlers, or of settlers becoming Indigenous.

This kind of relationship is not a matter of having power over another, but of negotiating both autonomy *and* relationship simultaneously. These are not dualistic relationships based on subordination *or* equality, superiority *or* inferiority, freedom *or* slavery, or autonomy *versus* interconnection. Instead, the two-row wampum represents a more complex negotiation around autonomy *and* interdependence. Cairns and many other non-Indigenous scholars might find this kind of image difficult because of deep-seated axiomatic Western enlightenment property-based assumptions about autonomy, freedom and property as boundedness and separation. Western frameworks conceive of autonomy in terms of one nation, one community and singular peoples with clear boundaries and fences in-between: in some ways, autonomy is seen as a kind of property. We imagine that we "own" our selves, communities and nations, and this means that we are independent, autonomous, bounded and safe. If we are attached to such a view of autonomy we cannot help but assume the two rows are there to keep the parties apart. In Turners' view, the Haudenosaunee have sophisticated theorizations and practices regarding *the relationships between* the parties represented by the two lines. Thus, treaty is about negotiating differences *and* autonomy, *within* the context of appropriate relationships and interconnections.

RECONCILING AUTONOMY

As a non-Indigenous person, I have tried to find ways to visualize and imagine this way of thinking about treaty relationships. One of my goals is to work to understand such frameworks, but not to do so by trying to "see" or "be" "like" an Indigenous person (not to put on a specific cultural lens). Instead I try to listen to and hear what my Indigenous partners in treaty say, and learn to make sense of it by examining and unsettling my own taken-for-granted frameworks. I have found that a vibrant body of discussion in feminist theory about the concept of "relational autonomy"[6] has helped me to understand and visualize Haudenosaunee theories of relationality, and to do so, I hope, without forcing Indigenous ways of knowing into preconceived settler frameworks. I have some hesitation in using feminist approaches to try to understand Indigenous–non-Indigenous relations, mainly because of the problematic history and present of some versions of feminism and Indigenous peoples. As Margaret Jacobs (2009) so revealingly argues in her book *White Mother to a Dark Race*, a women's movement of white "maternalists" in the U.S. and Australia played a powerful role in supporting the removal and education of Indigenous youth for assimilation from 1880 to 1940. She explores how attitudes proposing the deficiency of Indigenous mothers and Indigenous families, and then proposing white maternal feminists as the logical caregivers, ultimately supported child removal and residential school policies (Jacobs 2009; see also Lawrence 2004). There are many other more recent examples of problematic versions of feminism, in which white feminist notions of "global sisterhood" have reproduced colonial relations (see Mohanty 2003). On the other hand, because feminism is not monolithic, it is possible to draw on some provocative analyses that can help unsettle axiomatic assumptions of personhood and relationships.

Feminist philosophers have critiqued how human relationships are seen within liberal philosophical frameworks that have historically valorized ideals of boundedness and independence from others, specifically Macpherson's "possessive individualism," which is foundational to liberal theory. Dean suggests that this possessive "individual is not understood as part of something larger, as fundamentally interconnected with others ... Rather, it is a proprietor of capacities engaging other proprietors" (Dean 2013, 69–88). Many feminists argue that the concept of autonomy should not mean individualism, self-sufficiency and "free" will.[7] Instead, it should be seen to be facilitated by and embedded within relationships. Many have thus re-theorized autonomy as "relational autonomy" to render it compatible with lived realities of social interdependence, capable of recognizing and supporting deep commitments to others and to collectivities.[8]

The concept of relational autonomy, as defined by Catriona Mackenzie and Natalie Stoljar, focuses on "the implications of the intersubjective and social dimensions of selfhood and identity for conceptions of individual autonomy and moral and political agency" (Mackenzie and Stoljar 2000, 4). A key concept in the notion of relational autonomy is the idea of the "constitutionally social self." An idea that is familiar to feminists, this means that "the identity of the self is constituted by various social attachments" and that the "context of the self's ends are social," in the sense that they represent not just individual ends but also shared ends and goals (Barclay 2000, 61). Lorraine Code's project of revisioning the self-in-relation is relevant here, specifically because she develops ecologically modelled epistemologies and notions of "Epistemic Responsibility" that she argues can disrupt the "hegemonic social imaginary for which domination and control are overriding theoretical-practical goals" (Code 1991, 2000, 2006).

Another approach differentiates between static autonomy and dynamic autonomy. Mackenzie and Stoljer say that for Fox Keller, dynamic autonomy is a "kind of competence that promotes an enhanced sense of self," as differentiated from static autonomy that is competence pursued in interests of domination and defensiveness. Static autonomy "arises from seeing others as a threat to the self, from insecurity about the self, and from fears of dependence and loss of self control, leading to patterns of domination/control over others" (Mackenzie and Stoljer 2000, 9–10). This is helpful because we might say that the opponents of land rights defend their "settled expectations" with static, bounded and defended versions of autonomy, personhood, community and nation. Dynamic autonomy, on the other hand, "promotes a sense of agency in a world of 'interacting and interpersonal' agents and a sense of others 'as subjects with whom one shares enough to allow for a recognition of their independent interests and feelings — in short, for a recognition of them as other subjects'" (Mackenzie and Stoljer 2000, 9–10). This kind of an understudying of autonomy, which potentially disrupts the modern liberal epistemologies of mastery and boundedness discussed in this book so far, allows for connection as well as enough distance to allow for mutual respect. Such feminist theorizations help me to better understand the political relationships theorized in the Guswentha, as well as the specific kinds of alliance-building I discuss later.

RENEWAL: TREATY AS A VERB

Part of the sophistication of the concept of the Guswentha and other treaties is the notion of renewal, which emerges from and is necessitated by a focus on attending to the lived and changing relationships symbolized by the spaces between the rows. Such renewal is theorized as "polishing the Covenant Chain." *The Encyclopedia of New York State* (Brandão 2010) describes the "Covenant Chain as integral to" the alliance and treaty system between the "Iroquois and English."

> From 1677 to 1777 the Iroquois and their allies met almost annually in Albany with the English … to renew the terms of the alliance.
>
> The Covenant Chain grew out of the governing practices of the Iroquois Confederacy and diplomatic relations between the Europeans and American Indians living in New York …. For these reasons, alliances — a form of group decision making — needed to be carefully monitored. The terms of alliance and the duties of each party needed to be repeated and reaffirmed; any breaches needed to be explained and amends made for them…
>
> European negotiators quickly learned the protocols of councils and

adapted to the Iroquois way. Used to formal written treaties, Europeans tried to follow their own protocols and kept extensive written records of meetings ... But Europeans learned to view matters in Iroquois terms and soon were involved in the series of at least annual negotiations to work out trade relationships and military alliances. Although Europeans may have come to North America with ethnocentric notions of their superiority, of their "right" to native land, and of natives as "subjects" of European crowns, the actions of the Dutch and English governments of New Netherland and New York Colony belie that arrogance. Their participation in alliances with the Iroquois showed that they viewed the Iroquois as nations with rights to negotiate treaties. (Brandão 2010)

This concept of renewing treaty and polishing the "rust from the chain" is so central because it ensures that all participants — at regular intervals — must be aware that the relationship is not new, that it is not beginning now; it has roots deep in the past and it changes over time. It is also significant that colonizers appeared to be able *at that time* to see Indigenous nations *as* nations and participate in the protocols of polishing the chain, even if, as we know, such participation did not continue to the present.

The Covenant Chain indicates that the collective past of relationships must be recognized and dealt with in order to imagine and build ongoing relationships. Treaty means that participants should meet at appropriate intervals to assess, discuss and "polish" the ongoing relationship to make sure it is still strong. Thus, the treaty is a vibrant, supple, responsive, ongoing interactional process that requires regular injections of human creativity and relationality in order to ensure the viability of the ongoing relationship, focusing on what lives between the wampum rows. The Haudenosaunee have not given up on such treaty practices. Organizers of the Canandaigua treaty commemoration continue to invite Presidents of the United States to come and meet to "polish the rust from the chain" (Jemison and Schein 2000).

It is notable that Western models are decidedly more static and less participatory. Today's inhabitants are assumed to have consented to Hobbes' social contract retroactively. The original settler contract had a "fictional permanence"[9] that projected consent for its terms into the future. This is distinctly different from "polishing the chain," which is a ritualized process of periodic return to (re)negotiating consent and agreement, a renewal of the "covenant" that can be (re)lived, and (re)experienced by people today.

For many Indigenous peoples, treaty was and is a sacred covenant made between sovereign nations in which they agree to *ongoing* relationships of respect, friendship and peace, and thus recognition of the *ongoing nationhood, autonomy,* and *rights* of

Indigenous nations. "Treaty," seen in this way, potentially disrupts settler senses of entitlement to land because seeing all of us as "treaty peoples" brings material and social aspects of colonial pasts into the present in a manner that recognizes the ongoing autonomy of Indigenous peoples and the ongoing treaty relationships in which the settler nation-state participates as one party to (and beneficiary of) past land agreements, not as the assumed unilateral sovereign.

As I mentioned, many settler governments and citizens see treaty as an object, not a process. Rather than brothers or sisters travelling side-by-side in the same river of life, the Crown (or the Republic or State in the U.S.) has entitled itself to be the powerful parent and deemed Indigenous nations as dependent children. Indigenous meanings of treaty have often been silenced in this process, although they have also been persistently asserted.

Therefore, instead of seeing treaty as an object — a noun — I think that one way to begin to decolonize is to learn to conceptualize and experience treaty-making as a verb.[10] It is an historical and ongoing, exploratory and often uncertain process of building relationships for which non-Indigenous people must also take responsibility and in which they must engage. In other words, we need to think about how "we treaty," and how to behave responsibly if "we treaty together" or "make treaty" together. It is a relationship that we *build over time*. Like all good relationships, there are rules of respect and autonomy, but there can be no pre-planned and decided trajectory because a treaty is relational and interactive. Relationships are by their nature *uncertain*: they require seeing, listening, and responding creatively to an "other" who is autonomous and also connected to us. Treaties are not generic and fixed in time. They are *sui generis*, one of a kind, unique. They must be worked out in specific contexts, accounting for specific histories and trajectories of relationships. Even if you don't like the people you "treaty with," you have a responsibility to keep your word and fulfill your promises. If we carefully examine Indigenous notions of treaty, we see that treaty has a sophisticated and complex set of meanings and instructions that are tied to the careful nurturing of ongoing relationships through time. Treaty is a participatory verb.

In the next two chapters I discuss two case studies of Indigenous views of treaty in action. First, I explore how the Onondaga Nation mobilizes such treaty epistemologies in a New York State Courtroom, then I look at two examples of what I call "alliances of relationality" that I encountered during my fieldwork. These cases of Indigenous and non-Indigenous collaboration — the Onondaga Nation and NOON (Neighbours of the Onondaga Nation), and the Cayuga Nation and SHARE (Strengthening Haudenosaunee-American Relations through Education) — allow me to gesture towards how Indigenous and non-Indigenous groups are working outside of the courtroom, in face-to face encounters, towards creating alternative and non-colonizing visions and practices.

I do not offer these case studies in order to propose a general, universally applicable framework that encapsulates a model of decolonization.[11] My account of these processes teases out important and provocative elements that are "good to think" with, and may offer entry points that others may consider, and/or use, in order to develop their own relationships in different moments and contexts. What I hope these case studies show is that it is possible to hear, see and think differently, and that unsettling ontological certainty by rejecting epistemologies of mastery may often require what seems like terrifying risk-taking, but that it need not be disturbing or unsettling in a *damaging* way. Unsettling old patterns and risking new ways of seeing and of forming relationships between Indigenous and settler people may in fact sometimes be exhilarating, even liberating, as settler-subjects learn to turn sedimented ontological cages and epistemologies of mastery on their heads.

Notes

1   Although I do not draw on it extensively here, the field of education (and pedagogy more generally) is one area in which the question of how to build decolonizing relationships between Indigenous and non-Indigenous peoples, as well as racialized and non-racialized peoples, is being addressed in complex ways (Jones and Jenkins 2008; Dei 2002; Biermann 2011; Battiste and Henderson 2009; Tejeda 2008; Kuokkanen 2010; Iseke-Barnes 2008; Boler 1999; Zembylas and Boler 2002; Smith 1999; Simon, Rosenberg and Eppert 2000. One key issue in this work is how it highlights self-questioning as essential for moving beyond our own sedimented frameworks in order to be able to decolonize. Paulette Regan's book, she says, is "a pedagogical strategy for designing decolonizing truth-telling and reconciliation processes. On a deeper level it is about learning to live in truth, envisioning reconciliation as a liberatory, non-violent form of resistance" (Regan 2010, 214).

2   This discussion has a developing body of work I am unable to address here. Examples include: Regan (2010); Snelgrove, Dhamoon and Corntassel (2014); the open access issue of the journal *Decolonization: Indigeneity, Education and Society* 3, 3 (2014) on "Indigenous Land-Based Education," guest edited by Matthew Wildcat, Stephanie Irlbacher-Fox, Glen Coulthard and Mandee McDonald, available at <decolonization.org/index.php/des/issue/view/1584/showToc>; Ritskes (2013); Morgensen (2011); Barker (2013).

3   The majority of the recommendations of the RCAP report were simply shelved by the Crown. The recent report of the Truth and Reconciliation Commission says: "In 1996, the Royal Commission on Aboriginal Peoples (RCAP) put forward a bold and comprehensive vision of reconciliation. The RCAP report observed that if Canada was to thrive in the future, the relationship between Aboriginal peoples and the Crown must be transformed. The report concluded that the policy of assimilation was a complete failure and that Canada must look to the historical Treaty relationship to establish a new relationship between Aboriginal and non-Aboriginal peoples, based on the principles of mutual recognition, mutual respect, sharing, and mutual responsibility" (Truth and Reconciliation Commission 2015, 240).

4 Also see Asch, especially 2014.

5 The fine print on the poster states: "Settler Treaty membership entitles the card-holder to: share this territory (except reserves) with First Nations people and move freely throughout it; freedom of religion; freedom to engage in economic activities and to use the land for the purposes of agriculture; the right to self-government (including trade and taxation, determination of citizenship, social services such as child welfare, health and education); and peace and goodwill. Card holders are required to recognize the reciprocal treaty rights of First Nations, including: freedom of movement throughout this shared land as well as those territories reserved for the exclusive use of First Nations; freedom of religion; freedom to engage in economic activities and assurance to a right to a livelihood as well as assistance in times of need; self-government (including trade and taxation, determination of citizenship, and social services; and peace and goodwill. All rights of both settlers and First Nations are further delimited by our shared responsibilities to maintain good relations and to be good stewards of the land."

The even smaller print states: "Some restrictions apply. The Settler Treaty Card is not valid in most areas of British Columbia. Treaties entitle settlers to use the land for agricultural purposes to the depth of a plow. The underlying title to sub-surface resources, forests and waters remains with First Nations. The information presented here is based upon an oral understanding of the settler/First Nations relationships defined through the numbered treaties of the Prairies, and some local variance in the treaty relationship may apply. Settlers and settler descendants are advised to consult with local First Nations treaty elders regarding the oral understanding of treaties in your area, as well as any unresolved land claims requiring restitution."

6 Asch (2014, 125–133) uses Levi-Strauss' reflections on the role of marriage in linking families as a provocative and interesting way to conceptualize what I am visualizing as "relational autonomy."

7 Rifkin (2013, 336), working in the field of Queer Indigenous Studies, also confronts selfhood. He writes: "Becoming conscious of the everyday enactment of settlement involves relinquishing the notion of an autonomous, extra-political selfhood existing in a place apart."

8 This is a vibrant and developing literature, strongly related to feminist re-visioning of the subject. Sources include Barclay 2000; Code 1991, 2000, 2006; Lloyd 2000; Mackenzie and Stoljar 2000; Nedelsky 1989, 1990, 1994; Young 2001. For an interesting take on autonomy that is not explicitly feminist, yet deals with native-settler relations, see Colloredo-Mansfeld 2002.

9 Thank you to Jennifer Henderson for her comments on Hobbes and the term "fictional permanence."

10 am indebted here to the work of Brian Street (1993) and Susan Wright (1998), who discuss "culture as a verb."

11 Indeed, the specific case studies I discuss do not in any way generate universally applicable approaches, given that there are, of course, many different cases and kinds of conflict over land rights. Indigenous peoples may assert sovereignty in a less relational and more oppositional manner that the Onondaga Nation case I describe in the next chapter. Indigenous peoples may also, and often do, mobilize conceptions of sovereignty that are more conceptually similar to, or even competing with, Lockean-based Western notions

of national sovereignty. Based on my specific case studies, I have distinguished between settler and Indigenous epistemologies, emphasizing the ways in which Indigenous politics may not conform to settler expectations and imperatives. In doing so, I may at times err too much on the side of highlighting how Indigenous epistemologies *differ from* dominant settler epistemologies. I use the term "sovereignty" "to indicate a parallel version of established community and sociality that is as equally valid, yet distinct from, Western state sovereignty," and I explore how the Onondaga seek to achieve recognition of a form of title that does not conform to the conventional parameters of property and jurisdiction. However, in doing so I am not arguing that only Indigenous assertions of sovereignty based on *difference from* Western epistemologies are worthy of respect and recognition. Nor am I saying that such epistemological differences are *the source* of settler uncertainty. My goal in exploring the differences between western and Indigenous epistemologies is to suggest that awareness of profoundly different political epistemologies may allow settlers to unsettle the self-evident nature of their certainty and to suggest other possibilities of relationality, not that Indigenous *difference* in terms of conceptual and political frameworks is essential or that it is Indigenous difference that creates settler ontological uncertainty. Instead, I would suggest that it is the very fact of Indigenous assertions of entitlement to land and sovereignty — of self-determination and expectations of Indigenous control — that make settlers uncertain, unsettling certainty in their sense of unquestioned settler entitlement and control (as we saw in Part Two). It is important to note that I am not suggesting that Indigenous modes of placemaking, peoplehood and sovereignty must necessarily be at odds with U.S. and Canadian modes of sovereignty in order to recognized and respected *as Indigenous*. I am decidedly not arguing that Indigenous epistemologies need to be different from those of Lockean property in order for there to be an ethical imperative to acknowledge and engage them. My point here is not that Indigenous epistemological difference is the basis for why settlers need to recognize and respond to Indigenous sovereignty. All Indigenous claims are political claims, and as I argue here, should be seen by settlers from a stance of alert vulnerability and embracing uncertainty of their entitlement.

Chapter 5

"TURNING THE DOCTRINE OF DISCOVERY ON ITS HEAD"

The Onondaga Land Rights Action

There is no such thing as the First Nations land claims. There is no such thing as an Indian land claim[s]. He's got nothing to claim. We own the territory. It should have been called "White land claims." (Frank Calder, in an interview at a conference about the 30th anniversary of the Calder decision, cited in Asch 2007, 53)

In March 2005, the Onondaga Nation asserted its rights to a wide stretch of New York State. The difference between this and many other "land claims" is that the Onondaga did not frame it as a land *claim*, but as a "land rights action" in which they explicitly sought to work with other people in the community to improve human and environmental relations. The Complaint for Declaratory Judgment begins with an inclusive and relational approach: "The Onondaga people wish to bring about a healing between themselves and all others who live in this region that has been the homeland of the Onondaga nation since the dawn of time" (Onondaga Nation 2005b, 1–2). It continues: "We want justice. New York State took our land illegally and needs to acknowledge this injustice and our rights to the land. But we will not displace any of our neighbors — the Onondaga know all too well the pain of being forced to leave our homes and do not wish that on anyone" (Onondaga

Nation 2005a). Here land rights are mobilized for historical justice and rights, but also as a mode of healing relationships between people within shared spaces, of building alliances to protect the land and those relationships.

The Onondaga land rights action explicitly works against the oppositional pattern described in Part One of this book, in which settlers and Indigenous peoples are seen to compete for bounded plots of land within a Western property paradigm. The Onondaga want recognition of their title, but they do not wish to posses or own the land in the Western sense of property. Their aim is neither to control nor subdue the land. They do not, however, present their view of property as a rejection of settler peoples or lands. They present their land rights action as something which can *secure* their own and their neighbours' relationships with the land and each other for the present and future. They therefore reject the way in which the settler contract defines relationships between Indigenous and non-Indigenous people, without "threatening" or "unsettling" other aspects of the settler contract. They simply live the reality that multiple autonomies exist, as in the Guswentha.

In this chapter I discuss the Onondaga Nation land rights action, focusing specifically on one day in Federal Court in 2007. I use these events a lens through which to document and understand how the Onondaga practice "treaty as a verb" or what I call "treatying." By exploring how the Onondaga behave in the courtroom it is possible to see how they subtly yet decisively work to turn many sedimented colonial understandings and connected practices on their heads. I use this phrase of "turning on their heads" as a metaphor because in the courtroom the lawyers for the State of New York (who were countering the land rights case) accused the Onondaga Nation of trying to turn "the ancient Doctrine of Discovery on its head." This statement implied that the Onondaga's argument for their land rights went against the very basis of U.S. sovereignty, implying that the Onondaga nation, instead of the "discoverers" (now the government), has underlying title to the land.

From the outset of their legal action, the Onondaga refused Western legal concepts of property in which people own land individually and as an object: "The Nation and its people have a unique spiritual, cultural, and historic relationship with the land, which is embodied in Gayanashagowa, the Great Law of Peace. This relationship *goes far beyond federal and state legal concepts of ownership, possession, or other legal rights.* The people are one with the land and consider themselves stewards of it" (Onondaga Nation 2005b, 1–2, emphasis mine). This notion of land differs from the Western concepts of property discussed in Chapter 2, in which fixed and bounded property is the basis of a range of foundational settler logics related to settler fantasies of entitlement and certainty. The Onondaga communicate their autonomy and sovereignty when they say that their relational concept of property goes "far beyond" U.S. legal concepts. Although the Onondaga do not count on obtaining justice within the U.S. legal system, after many years of deliberation, they did finally enter into the U.S. Court system. The nation's goals in doing so are relational, responsible and inclusive, as they specifically refer to all the people and the land of central New York. A broad collaborative project emerges from this relationship to the land in which the Onondaga have an important role: "It is the duty of the Nation's leaders to work for a healing of this land, to protect it, and to pass it on to future generations. The Onondaga Nation brings this action on behalf of its people in the hope that it may hasten the process of reconciliation and bring lasting justice, peace, and respect among all who inhabit this area" (Onondaga Nation 2005b).[1]

Long before entering into court, the Onondaga built alliances with their neighbours. They aligned themselves with problems they share with other local people, such as unemployment and pollution. A major problem around Syracuse, N.Y., is the prevalence of toxic remains of industrial development concentrated in Lake Onondaga, remains that large factories left behind as they moved to other sites in the global economy, where labour and resources are cheaper. Onondaga Lake is one of the most polluted lakes in the world, and also the most sacred site of the Onondaga. Perhaps one of the most unusual strategies of the Onondaga is that they include large corporations in the claim. The suit names as defendants: the State of New York, the City of Syracuse, Onondaga County and five other corporations who are named for their environmental damage, including Honeywell International, Hansen Aggregates, Clark Concrete Company and Valley Realty (Onondaga Nation 2005b).

Further, their approach is not legalistic, nor do they wait for the state to offer legal solutions. As we have seen, waiting for the state to solve land rights cases can be a futile exercise that may have dubious results. Hill, addressing non-Indigenous people, says:

> If we are successful in our legal action, there will be a court decision that your leaders will have to recognize. We are hopeful of success, but uncertain whether the Onondaga Nation can obtain justice in your legal system. But we know that acknowledgment which produces justice is essential for healing.
>
> We are not waiting on a court schedule to dictate healing with our neighbors and the environment. (Hill 2006a)

The Onondaga offer a sophisticated and relational approach that also makes clear they have their own versions of justice that are distinct from Western legal frameworks, and that invoke shared responsibility. The nation thus invokes and enacts their sovereignty despite entering into relations with the United States.

Although the Onondaga finally made their legal claim to the U.S. courts for their land in 2005, it was not a decision that emerged lightly for numerous reasons, primarily because they are a sovereign nation that "does not ordinarily seek justice in the United States court system" (Onondaga Nation 2007a) because it is a foreign system. In other words, their land rights are not a "domestic" issue, but one between two nations. They therefore question the jurisdictional and juridical imaginary of the settler nation-state, arguing that although the Haudenosaunee are "physically situated within the territorial limits of the United States," they "retain their status as sovereign nations."

The Onondaga were never conquered. They have always had autonomy and nationhood. Thus, Onondaga sovereignty (as they define it) *and* their ongoing relationship with colonial and now national and state governments are firmly embedded in a sense of continuity over time and in different circumstances, as in the discussions in the previous chapter about the Covenant Chain and treaty as a verb. The Onondaga have consistently worked to build relationships of mutuality with their neighbours. At the same time, nation-state institutions and courts lack legitimacy amongst the Onondaga, as a result of their failure — both historically and in the present — to fulfill mutual obligations as set out in earlier treaties and agreements. In terms of reclaiming their land and finding justice, the Onondaga Nation did not trust that it could find justice in the courts.

This meant that although the legal action was one part of their strategy, they decided to do much of their work outside of the courtroom and within their local community. They continued to work, as they had done for decades, on building their relationships with, creating understandings of alliance and cooperation with, other local citizens. These collaborative practices emerge from long-standing Onondaga traditional beliefs and roles, enacted within a 21st century context. It is also significant that they created these alliances long before making the legally framed land rights action. This approach turns the logic of many property-based oppositional land rights patterns on their heads. The Indian Law Resource Center said:

> [The] Onondaga case is remarkable because the suit asks only for a declaratory judgment that the land was illegally taken from the Nation and that the Nation continues to have legal title to the land. It does not ask for possession of the land or for compensation. The Nation is primarily interested in demanding clean-up of the many Superfund sites in the area around Syracuse, especially Onondaga Lake. (Indian Law Resource Center 2010)

The words of the Onondaga Declaratory Judgment in their land rights case thus indicate that they propose different models of relationships, of autonomy and of jurisdiction. They say they want justice and recognition of their title, and yet they will not displace any neighbours because they wish to heal the land for all people (Onondaga Nation 2005a). The sources for the Onondaga's approach emerge from long-standing Haudenosaunee and Onondaga belief systems such as the Great Law of Peace and the Two Row Wampum, as well as the special historical and contemporary role of the Onondaga as the "Fire Keepers" or central council fire of the Haudenosaunee (Onondaga Nation 2007c). Further, the Onondaga have watched and waited for many years before making their claim, learning all the while how to do so following their traditional frameworks, traditions not frozen in time but necessarily flexible within changing political, economic and social contexts.

The Onondaga refused to engage with New York State's preferred compensation for land rights: casino deals. In doing so, they averted the violent backlash and divisiveness that other land rights actions had already elicited in New York. As Kimmerer points out, "in other land claims around the country, some tribes have negotiated for cash, land, and casino deals, reaching for relief from grinding poverty on the last shreds of their territories. But the Onondaga envision a radically different solution that honours their ancestral land and their spiritual responsibilities to it" (Kimmerer 2008). Tadodaho Sid Hill said, "the Onondaga will not settle for methods used to resolve other Native American nations' land rights actions." This refusal of casinos is because, "Our values do not allow for the harm that casino gambling can cause. We want this action resolved in a way that preserves, not disrupts, the social fabric of our Nation as well as that of our neighbors," Hill said (Onondaga Nation 2005c). By refusing casino gambling on these grounds, they subtly undercut the potential objections of the Upstate Citizens for Equality, an organization that started by opposing another Haudenosaunee land claim and casino settlement, the Oneida Nation (Turning Stone Casino). The Onondaga's opposition to casino deals conceptually transforms their potential opponents into neighbours, by including them in their geographic and moral universe and by refusing the binary oppositions that have characterized Indigenous-settler relations. In this context, it is significant that UCE have not vocally opposed the Onondaga land rights action, despite their pitched battle against the Oneida Nation.

The Tadodaho's description of what healing entails includes not only the Onondaga peoples, but also the environment. In an article published in the *Syracuse Post-Standard*, he writes: "No one is happy when they do not understand those around them. No one can live in peace when the waters are poisoned, the land contaminated, fish too toxic to eat, and the air too polluted to breathe" (Hill 2006a). It also expands to include a relational healing, including repairing the lack of understanding and knowledge robbed of the non-Indigenous neighbours of the Onondaga. Again, speaking inclusively of his non-Indigenous neighbours, he says:

Our neighbors were also wounded by actions that most of those living nearby today have no knowledge of. You were robbed of the chance to live side-by-side in harmony with a culture that is different from your own; a culture that understood and cared for this land for centuries before your ancestors arrived. And we were all robbed of the opportunity to learn and grow together. (Hill 2006a)

Tadodaho completes his letter by inviting people to enter into a shared project. "By working together to heal Mother Earth, we are working to heal each other. You, too, are invited to join the healing" (Hill 2006a). He speaks directly to non-Indigenous people ("you") and evokes a vision of a future that includes all. At the same time, he speaks from a position of Onondaga sovereignty, thus implicitly creating an image of them, and inviting them to see themselves as neighbours, "living within Indigenous sovereignty" (Nicoll 2004b).

The Onondaga have developed and communicated a notion of shared responsibility for the future and for human relationships within specific geographical spaces and with overlapping histories and futures. This notion of shared responsibility is based upon a contemporary strategy that draws on Indigenous notions of treaty as based on sharing the land (Lindberg 2010; Asch 2014). Within this response-ability (ability to respond appropriately) people do not act out of models of individual personhood, but instead find versions of relatedness that are not about sameness or so-called "equality." The image presented by the Onondaga is of healing and reconciliation between people who *share* territory, but do not compromise their autonomy. If we visualize the Guswentha that I discussed in the previous chapter, this is a way in which the Onondaga stay in their autonomous canoe — within the parallel lines — yet also focus on the interaction between the rows. They foster respect, peace and friendship in the name of caring for the shared earth — the earth here symbolized by the bed of white beads that both parallel rows are embedded within and must share. They are living the relationships that are embodied in the Guswentha.

THE LEGAL CONTEXT: *SHERRILL V. ONEIDA*

The Onondaga Nation officially filed its Complaint for Declaratory Judgment in its land rights action in March 2005. Over the next two years, before the day in court that I describe below, there were a number of pivotal court decisions that dramatically altered the legal landscape for Indigenous land rights in New York and in the U.S. more generally.

The precedent-setting, and now infamous, decision made in 2005 in the case of *City of Sherrill V. Oneida Indian Nation of N. Y.* (03-855) 544 U.S. 197, is seen by many legal critics as a watershed case, "directly at odds with the federal policies of the last three decades" (Krakoff 2005, 5), because it means a "shuttering of the courthouse door to Indian claimants" (Berkey 2005–6, 382). The specifics of the case are that the Oneida Nation had purchased land within their traditional territory on the open market and wished to have this land declared "Indian Country,"[2] or reservation land, and removed from the tax rolls of Sherrill County. The court decided for Sherrill County and New York State, who opposed the Oneida claim.

Sherrill marked a major shift because the court argued, on the basis of a rarely used legal term called "laches," that the Oneida had waited too long to make their claim and that it was, therefore, ineligible. Further, using language that reveals a powerful sense of settler entitlement, the court was unwilling to disrupt what it called the "settled expectations" and "justifiable expectations" of the current non-Indian occupants of the land. The decision reads, in part: "When a party belatedly asserts a right to present and future sovereign control over territory, longstanding observances and settled expectations are prime considerations" (Supreme Court of the United States 2005). Krakoff (2005, 6) argues that in this case, the Court embraced "an apologist stand toward the many instances of immoral and illegal governmental actions against the tribe…ultimately suggesting that the passage of time renders that history irrelevant, indeed even unmentionable."[3]

More significant in the context of the Onondaga land rights action is that the court in Sherrill, according to some commentators, went far beyond its usual judicial role.

> The Court stepped outside its traditional function of deciding questions of law on a factual record compiled by the court below, in accordance with conventional notions of due process, the rules of civil procedure and the rules of evidence…. The Court's unorthodox approach doomed the Oneidas from the outset. Having recast the case as one about the passage of time, the Court's result was largely foreordained. (Berkey 2005-6, 377)

Wandres notes that the Court undertook "judicial activism" and imposed a "power which is explicitly reserved to Congress" when it "took a broad step towards extinguishing tribal sovereignty" in Sherrill (Wandres 2006–7, 140). Berkey argues that "shorn of its doctrinal trappings, Sherrill can be viewed as a kind of judicial blaming the victim" (Berkey 2005–6, 383).

Fort (2008–9, 5–6) says the opinion on the case is "full of contradiction, introducing the equitable defenses of laches, acquiescence, and impossibility into an area where courts had almost always barred them from being used as a defense." The case has "serious doctrinal problems" that are well documented.[4] She (2008-9, 3–5) argues that it would be more accurate to label this defense the "new laches."

> New laches barely resembles the traditional defense of laches that has been used with relative consistency since the fourteenth century [in

common law] … Laches is rarely used outside of some narrow areas of common law, and had been all but barred from federal Indian law cases. The Supreme Court's decision in *City of Sherrill v. Oneida Indian Nation*, however, injected this new equitable defense into the area of federal Indian law to be used by state and local government defendants to eliminate land claims before they begin…. It would be more accurate to label this defense "new laches," a defense created from a combination and (mis) understanding of laches, acquiescence and impossibility, applicable *only* against Indian claims. Rather that being based solely upon the length of time from the original wrong to its arrival in federal court, the new laches defense is based upon the disruption a successful claim may cause to the "settled expectations" of state and local government defendants.

Fort (2011, 405) calls the "New Laches" a "pernicious defense not properly called 'equitable'" but instead "something else — a defense of the majority for the wrongs it never made right" (Fort 2011, 405). She suggests that the courts, "at least in the Second Circuit, feel that they have found the magic bullet to automatically eliminate all land claims" (Fort 2008-9, 54). Significantly, the assessment of the potential fallout from Sherrill is devastating for Indigenous nations in that it is "likely to end all Indian land claim cases and settlement efforts currently pending" in New York and "throughout the nation" (Wandres 2006–7, 142).

In 2005, on the basis of the problematic Sherrill decision, a request to re-hear the claim of the Cayuga Nation was also rejected by the Courts. In that case, the Court of Appeals for the Second Circuit "interpreted the Sherrill decision as precluding the tribe's disruptive possessory land claim … and applied the doctrine of laches to bar both ejectment and damages claims" (Wandres 2006–7, 142). Attorney General Eliot Spitzer's brief against the Cayuga claim echoes historical arguments for dispossessing Indigenous peoples through the valuing of transformative labour, saying that "subsequent landowners developed the land from an empty wilderness to the many towns, villages, and improvements in the region" (cited in Adams 2006). The issue of "disruption" is primary in the "new Laches" emerging from Sherrill. In short, the courts "created a defense that changed the definition of laches and created a new theoretical, procedural, and doctrinal defense" (Fort 2011, 395). Land claims would now be "considered disruptive if they may upset the settled expectations of current landowners" (Fort 2011, 395).

Furthermore, the implementation of any remedy which is disruptive is impossible, and therefore the claim must be dismissed. Importantly, the level of disruption needed to dismiss the claim under new laches was set at the lowest bar, making it possible for states and counties to argue any

> remedy is disruptive, even if the remedy is monetary and would come
> from state coffers, not from individual landowners. (Fort 2011, 395)

Again, as we saw in these arguments in Chapter 2, the "settled expectations" of land ownership should not be disrupted. The decision unequivocally defends and institutionalizes colonial settler ideologies and entitlement in a brutal and explicit manner, even citing the Doctrine of Discovery to deny the land claim. Settled expectations could now not be "disrupted."

The Onondaga Nation, therefore, was required to make its argument in a new legal context, within which any possessory or so-called "disruptive" claim could be thrown out on the basis of Sherrill. Another significant result of the Oneida and Cayuga decisions is that claiming of monetary damages became one of the few allowable forms of relief in land rights cases, because it was seen as less "disruptive." In other words, it did not challenge the "settled expectations" of landowners. The Onondaga did not, however, want money. As their lawyer said in court, the "Onondaga Nation will never accept money in exchange for land rights. It's morally repugnant to them; they simply would not do it and be regarded as selling their mother" (Onondaga v. New York 2007, 19).

On one level the Onondaga had no alternative but to argue a non-possessory claim. However, even before Sherrill, theirs was always a non-possessory land rights action. As Sid Hill says in his brief to the court regarding the State's motion to dismiss the case on the basis of Sherrill and Cayuga, "Our instructions to begin this legal action in this healing, non-disruptive manner were given well before either the Sherrill decision by the Supreme Court, or the dismissal of the Cayuga Nation's land claim by the Second Circuit" (Hill 2006b, 8–13). Thus, although it was impossible to know how the Court would define a "possessory" or "disruptive" claim in the post-Sherrill, post-Cayuga legal context, the Onondaga had already framed their land rights action in a manner that would not threaten existing settler occupation. It was not, I suggest, primarily a legal strategy.

I want to be clear that I am not discussing the hearing as a lawyer might, to analyze the efficacy of the Onondaga legal strategy *as* a legal strategy within the legal system of the United States. Nor do I wish to examine why the nation may have used specific legal arguments and not others. The legal context is contradictory and complex, making no sense even to many law commentators (see above). Instead, I explore their powerful and subtle arguments within the court, and suggest that they are deeply significant for a different reason. I discuss them because, within the context of this book, the arguments made demonstrate precisely the kinds of epistemological shifts — the actions of turning common-sense colonial ideas and practices "on their heads," and thus unsettling the ontological certainty of settler colonialism — that I suggest are essential to decolonization processes in settler nations. The arguments made by the Onondaga in court carefully enact an "epistemological shift" in a number of complex ways, beginning with their assertion that they have title to the land, *even if* they do not want possession or "ownership" of it in the Western sense.

TREATYING IN COURT

In October of 2007 I received email messages that the Onondaga were trying to mobilize support for people to attend their first court hearing, which centred on the State's motion to dismiss their land rights action on the basis of the Sherrill decision. So, on October 11, 2007, I drove from Ottawa, Ontario (Canada), to Albany, New York, to attend the Court. On arrival, crowds of people stood outside the courtroom, many with signs supporting the Onondaga. Long line-ups of people were waiting to go through security and enter the courthouse. The crowd included many Haudenosaunee people as well as their NOON and SHARE supporters.

When we finally managed to enter the large, stately courtroom, it was absolutely packed with people of all ages. I recognized many of the Onondaga and Haudenosaunee Elders, Clan Mothers and community members, who were dressed in Haudenosaunee regalia. One could sense the intensity and seriousness in the room: the Onondaga people had been waiting for over 200 years for some form of justice from the colonial government. Because of lack of space, many of us stood at the side of the room. Large numbers of lawyers in dark suits occupied the tables at the front of the courtroom. Finally, Federal Justice Judge Kahn entered in his judicial robes and the room went quiet with expectation. Then the case, "Onondaga Nation versus the State of New York, et al, Case Number 05-CV-3134," began. All indented passages below, preceded by the name of the speaker (e.g., "THE COURT," "MR. COULTER"), are from the transcript of the hearing.

The hearing began with the lawyers introducing themselves: They were David Roberts, Assistant Attorney General, appearing on behalf of the State of New York, and Mark Puzella from Goodwin, Proctor, appearing on behalf of the non-state defendants (the corporations). The lawyers for the Onondaga Nation were Robert Tim Coulter, Curtis Berkey and Joe Heath. The judge asked the New York State attorney, David Roberts, to start. He began his remarks by defining the Onondaga case as "clearly a disruptive possessory land claim," thereby dismissing the case on the basis of the Sherrill and Cayuga decisions, and arguing that there was consequently no need for a trial. The case, he said, "raises a claim that was void at its inception" (Onondaga v. New York 2007, 8).

When Mr. Coulter stood to argue on behalf of the Onondaga, he immediately changed the terms of the debate so that the question at hand was not focused on formal procedures, but instead on the court's willingness or refusal to listen to the

Onondaga. He said "the large issue today is whether the Onondaga Nation, having been excluded from the federal court and the state courts for more than 185 years, will ever be allowed to proceed with its land rights case" (Onondaga v. New York 2007, 8). Coulter continued to reframe the terms of the discussion, redirecting attention from the settled (and legal, according to Sherrill and the New York lawyer) expectations of settler entitlement to the land to questions of justice and history.

> The Nation has suffered enormously for well over 200 years because of very blatant, straightforward and wilful violations of the federal law by the State of New York in acquiring the Onondaga land. The State did that, not only in violation of the federal laws and the federal Constitution, but in violation of New York State's own laws and Constitution, and in violation of the treaties that have been made with the Haudenosaunee and the Onondaga Nation. And that was all done with just a pittance of token compensation to the Nation. (Onondaga v. New York 2007, 9–10)

Coulter explained that the defendants contended "because all that happened so long ago, that the Nation shouldn't be allowed to proceed with its case at all." However, he argued, the "proposition that the mere passage of time is sufficient to bar a suit such as this [has] … never been accepted in federal law." Thus, rather than accept the framework of laches proposed by the State, Coulter argued that its approach is based on a misinterpretation of the law. The Onondaga case could not, therefore, reasonably be forced to fit within such a framework because, as he argued, the Onondaga case is neither possessory nor destructive (Onondaga v. New York 2007, 10). As we see below, Onondaga Nation's case rejects the usual expectations of land rights cases, which tend to focus on getting monetary "relief" for the Indigenous Nations. Here, the Onondaga's main focus was to clarify that they *did not want* money or possessive ownership of land as "declaratory relief."

This was when the concept of property became central to the hearing. Coulter's arguments seemed to elicit a sense of confusion and wonder in the courtroom, as Judge Kahn clearly strived to understand title as something other than possessive ownership. He struggled, in other words, to hear and understand the terms of an unfamiliar property regime.

> THE COURT: Well, what are you seeking as declaratory relief? In other words, you're not seeking the lands, am I correct about that?
> MR. COULTER: That's correct.
> THE COURT: And you're not seeking money?
> MR. COULTER: That's correct.
> THE COURT: So what are you asking the Court to do?
> MR. COULTER: Solely for a declaratory judgment. The declaratory

judgment would require nothing of any party... would not constitute any form of coercive relief, and would not lead to any indirect results that would be coercive or disruptive. Now, the Nation has not in this case asserted any possessory right at all ... The Nation also hasn't asserted a right to any relief that's based on a right of possession. And I also want to make clear ... that the Nation does not want to accomplish an eviction or an ejectment indirectly ... The Nation doesn't want that. That is not what we request. And we would at every stage want to be sure that a declaratory judgment doesn't do that. That would be tantamount to an eviction; the Nation does not intend to do that and will not do that. (Onondaga v. New York 2007, 11)

Sitting in the courtroom, one could not help but get a sense that Coulter, speaking for the Onondaga, was speaking a foreign language to the court. If land is not property and a commodity, then what is it? How is it possible to relate to land other than in terms of ownership and control? The judge, therefore, seemed uncertain of what he was being asked to declare, if not that the Onondaga fully own and control the land.

THE COURT: But what would you want this Court to do? If you were the Court, what would you want me to declare?

Explaining that the "essence" of the declaration would be that the State of New York's method of obtaining the land went against U.S. law and consequently, the Onondaga were asking the court to declare that they still have title to the land, Coulter then clarified that the Onondaga want *title* but *not* possession.

The Nation would like a declaration that title is still in the Nation. But that does not mean that the Nation intends to invalidate the deeds and documents of title held by present day landowners. No, because that would ... in effect, throw them off their lands, throw them out of their homes. We don't want that. And we want to be absolutely clear about that. (Onondaga v. New York 2007, 12)

The judge, in response, again seemed to want to clarify that they are requesting something outside of familiar frameworks. He asked the lawyer to ensure that he had heard correctly, that he was not confused.

THE COURT: So if I heard you right, you're asking the Court, among other things, or whatever you're asking, to award title to the tribe with the understanding that everything would stay the same but they have title? (Onondaga v. New York 2007, 12)

What the judge was having trouble understanding was how title can exist without ownership, and how land can be something other than a possession or a commodity. According to settled law, title to land as *possession* would lead to legal "relief" in terms of compensation in land and, therefore, eviction or a change in current residents' ownership. Title to land as *commodity* would likely lead to legal "relief" in terms of financial compensation, which the Onondaga refused.

The Onondaga, through Coulter, argued against the expectations of a liberal property regime within a capitalist economy in which liberal philosophical principles and capitalist economic principles are co-constitutive of legal frameworks. Coulter had to establish, therefore, that a concept of title without ownership exists.

> MR. COULTER: This is an action for title, but the only relief we're requesting is a declaratory judgment. And we believe that any declaratory judgment in a case such as this should be one that does protect against unfair or unjust outcomes for present day land holders. So when we say a declaratory judgment about title, we do not mean something that would have the effect, direct or indirectly, of throwing people off their land or out of their homes. That is not what we want. We're speaking of a title that is more abstract, more general than that; a title that does not carry with it possessory interests. That is possible. That concept of title is well known.
>
> THE COURT: Is that a concept of law? Does that exist in the law?
>
> MR. COULTER: Oh, yes.
>
> THE COURT: …gives people title without any right to do anything to the land or evict or to change possession forever? (Onondaga v. New York 2007, 13)

How, the Judge seemed to be asking, is it possible to have title without the power to control the land or other people? At this moment, I would suggest that the judge is being compelled to confront a property regime and a relationship with, and understanding of, land which appears not to make sense in Western law. Coulter in response tried to provide a framework for the judge that does not fall too far outside of his ontological expectations, a framework that might unsettle such expectations but not go so far as to threaten or completely delegitimize them.

He thus began to explain that such a concept of "bare title" does exist, citing a number of cases in which it is discussed. He explained that "bare title" is "title that does not necessarily carry with it any beneficial interests as such. That concept exists." He continued with the comment, "Sadly, we have only one word to cover all those different concepts, we always say title, that [sic] that means so many different things" (Onondaga v. New York 2007, 14).

We might view Coulter's approach as enacting the values of the Guswentha, of understanding treaty as a verb, and of feminist frameworks of relational autonomy, in that he works to communicate and respect across difference, asserting both autonomy and relationality. His approach is indicative of a complex and nuanced approach to the relationship between the Onondaga and U.S. law: he defers to the Court by his use of legal precedent, yet at the same time he makes a subtle critique of the limits of Western law. He suggests implicitly that the law, as it exists, is not sophisticated enough because it has only one term, "title," to contain a possible myriad of relationships to land, implying perhaps that this notion of a supposedly universal Western property regime is also built on, or reflected within, a flawed linguistic foundation. In this way, speaking for the Onondaga, he implicitly questioned Western legal property regimes and ontologies, but did so within the confines of making an argument within a Western courtroom.

By stressing the Onondaga desire not to disturb the possession of current owners; Coulter emphasizes the important legal point that the Onondaga land rights action is *not* the same as the Oneida claim, the one that was refused in the Sherrill decision. It is not, as David Roberts had called it, a "disruptive claim." In addition, his strategic statement, "We do not want to disturb the possession or expectations of present day landowners" (Onondaga v. New York 2007, 14), uses terminology (the term "expectations") that evokes the Sherrill case, specifically the importance it grants to the "settled expectations" of residents.

Although the arguments made by Coulter were of course strategic within the rules of the game as defined by U.S. law, he also communicated how the Onondaga land rights action involves a form of deep recognition of their neighbours. To invalidate someone's deed, he says, "can be eviction by another name."

> The Nation has said that's unfair. The Nation itself has been thrown off its lands, and it doesn't want to do that to anyone else. It knows how that feels. And the Nation has foresworn that, both in this lawsuit and publicly; they do not want that. (Onondaga v. New York 2007, 14)

This passage reveals a powerful strategy of relational autonomy through its explicit *emotional and experiential* linkage between the Onondaga nation — as a singular yet collective subject ("it knows how that feels") — and its potential opponents. In this way, the Onondaga assert some similarity of experience and a form of empathy, but not sameness.

We have seen throughout this book that in such situations of conflict, opponents of land rights have often used collective subject positions ("we" own the land, or "we" were here first), but usually have done so to create a dividing line between themselves and the Indigenous peoples claiming land rights. That is to say, such subject positions often create essentialized divisions and binary oppositions between parties. The Onondaga strategy does not create such binary oppositions. Instead, they may be mobilizing the image of "understanding how it feels" to build the possibility of reciprocal empathy and respect between parties that have often been opposed. First, they are saying they hear and understand the concerns of their neighbours and are responding to them, that they hear and respect their fears. By "understanding" the fear of eviction, they also potentially build retrospective empathy[5] for their own past evictions: implicitly saying "if you feel horrible now, imagine how we felt when it happened to us. Wasn't it unjust?"

If we think of the Two Row Wampum as a metaphor, the Onondaga here actively "polish the chain," refusing to stay isolated in the image of two separate and opposed parallel rows, and shifting the focus of the relationship to the middle beads of ongoing relationships of respect and friendship. Instead of fostering conflict between parties or depending on abstract notions of rights to make their case, they carefully turn the symbolic battle on its head. Coulter continues:

> The Nation also has felt enormous pain for generations, knowing and seeing that the legal system of this country and the legal system of this state has been unwilling to provide any redress, has been unwilling to acknowledge in any way that a very blatant violation of the law took place to deprive the Nation of its lands. They rightfully have felt that they're not being accorded equality before the law. It's understandable that they feel marginalized and discriminated against. And a declaratory judgment in this case would go very far toward healing that wound. It would also go far toward wiping away the stain of what has been done, a stain on the honor of this country and a stain on the history of the state.
>
> That's why we've asked for a declaratory judgment. That's what the Nation wants. We do not want anything that's going to disrupt the neighbors of the nation....We want them to live comfortably and well with the Nation, just as they do now. (Onondaga v. New York 2007, 16–17)

Here he describes the Onondaga as a singular collective subject that can feel emotions, while also simultaneously drawing persuasively (and strategically) on U.S. discourses of patriotism to argue for the importance of redress. The Onondaga in this way mobilize a non-confrontational discourse of relationality, in which they find a sometimes victimized, yet agentive, empathetic and communicative voice.

However, they do not accomplish this complex task through taking a subject position of dependence or subordination; they do not relinquish their autonomy or their interpretation of history. This is the treaty goal of "alliance without subordination" (Borrows 2008, 19–20), embedded in a complex understanding of intertwined histories. Coulter explains that "we" (the Onondaga) began by approaching the conflict in a way they felt was appropriate: they tried to negotiate nation-to-nation with the United States and with the State of New York, as they should do as a sovereign nation. Because New York would not negotiate without the Onondaga going to court first, the Onondaga are in court (even though it is inappropriate, according to its beliefs). This compromise is a manner of working between the rows of the wampum: asserting autonomy *and* interdependence. Similar to the letter to the Municipality of Chatham-Kent written by the Chief of the Caldwell First Nation, discussed in Chapter 6, the Onondaga assert their autonomy as a government — a sovereign nation that should be negotiating with another government. Like the Caldwell, Onondaga assertions of sovereignty are combined with declarations of its respect and desire for peace with its neighbours. In this way they demonstrate respect for a foreign legal process, yet simultaneously change the terms of the debate embedded within that process. They do so by maintaining their sovereignty and relationality while pursuing justice rather than formal legal measures usually defined by abstract rights.

The response of the New York State Attorney, Mr. Roberts, shows an unwillingness and/or inability to understand or hear anything other than the expected liberal property regime of possessive ownership. He focuses on reasserting the danger of the claim to the people of New York.

> MR. ROBERTS: Mr. Coulter stands up and says that they don't seek to disrupt present day owners of fee title that live within the claim area. That's completely inconsistent with the relief that's sought in this case. It's inherently disruptive. What they seek is a declaration that the ancient treaties by which title passed from the Onondagas to the State and ultimately through generations to the current people that live in a swath that runs 10 to 40 miles wide from the Canadian border down to the Pennsylvania border, bisecting the State of New York, they're asking this Court to issue an order that would say that the plaintiffs in this case hold fee title to that swath of land. There are a couple of very strange aspects of their assertion that that would not be disruptive to the people in the claim area. (Onondaga v. New York 2007, 20–23)

Roberts thereby upheld his arguments that interpret title in one manner only: as fee simple title.[6] For New York State, just as for the UCE and CKCN, fee simple is the only understandable and reasonable arrangement of title and property. In their view, it necessarily requires — or leads to — full possession, full control and clear competition and division between historic claims and current holders of title.

Judge Kahn's response to such a simplistic argument was striking. He challenged Roberts, injecting: "I don't think he said he did want fee title. I don't think he used the word 'fee.' It was more abstract" (Onondaga v. New York 2007, 23). The judge's assertion that he had understood a different meaning of title from Mr. Coulter resulted in the following evocative response from Roberts, a response which explicitly placed the Doctrine of Discovery as the authoritative source of ownership.

> MR. ROBERTS: It's definitely abstract. But if you look in their briefs, they actually say they want fee title. And the thing that's strange about this contention is that it turns the *ancient doctrine of discovery on its head.* As the Court fully knows, the doctrine of discovery would hold that the crown holds fee title to lands in the country that's being colonized, and that remains subject to the possessory Aboriginal right of the natives that live there. And that's the title, the Aboriginal title that was extinguished in the treaties that were entered into in this case.
>
> THE COURT: Legally extinguished?
>
> MR. ROBERTS: Pardon me?
>
> THE COURT: Is it legally extinguished?
>
> MR. ROBERTS: Yes, sir. And the thing that's strange about the argument you're hearing here today from the plaintiffs is that they're asking this Court as a remedy for its ancient transfer of an exclusively possessory interest in the lands ... So what they're asking for is a role reversal ... It's a very confounding ... sort of title that the plaintiffs are asking for in this case.... And the reason they go through all those gymnastics is because they're trying to find some way of wiggling around clear precedent[s] ... that spell doom to their claim. (Onondaga v. New York 2007, 23–25)

For Roberts here, any challenge to the settled expectations of the property regime is "gymnastics" and "wiggling around precedents," not a legal argument and not reasonable at all. In treaty terms, it suggests a clear refusal to "walk side by side" and an insistence on power-laden colonial relations of father above son.

The judge, however, interrupted Mr. Roberts again, and brought the concept of justice back into the discussion. He said that the Onondaga are "trying to find some way to get justice" (Onondaga v. New York 2007, 25). There was suddenly a brief but pregnant silence in the courtroom: the Onondaga later said they found the judge's statement about justice important, perhaps even indicating recognition of their viewpoint. Yet Mr. Roberts responded by repeating his argument in more explicit terms, again suggesting that the claim is somehow destructive.

That the judge could and did take a more probing and questioning stance than the lawyer for the State in some ways reflects the structure of courts and legal reasoning. While the judge's questions and interventions may reflect a willingness to hear unfamiliar epistemologies and an openness to the Onondaga case, it also reflects his institutional role. He is institutionally empowered with the entitlement to weigh and judge sides, as distinct from Roberts and the other lawyers, who must take and argue specific sides. Indeed, Western legal systems and structures are adversarial, which means that Roberts, unlike the judge, could not, even if he wished to, say to the Onondaga, "Please explain to me. I don't understand." He is required by the structures of the law to demonstrate that their argument is flawed. He is necessarily defending the legality of settler entitlement, and the irrationality of the Onondaga case.

When the Court then asked Mr. Coulter if he had a brief surrebuttal, he recapped his key arguments based on United States law and, again, switched the terms of the debate to whether the Onondaga will be heard and will be entitled to any form of relief. His purpose was to defeat the motion by New York (that the case should be rejected before being heard) and make sure the case could be fully argued in the Court. The judge, however, was still trying to pinpoint what "relief" might look like if it wasn't to be land or money, and kept pushing Coulter to clarify. He said: "You're asking the Court to use its own creativity. Shouldn't you spell out what you think the Court should do? ...What specifically, instead of abstractly, would you like this Court to grant in terms of relief?" (Onondaga v. New York 2007, 28). Coulter responded by suggesting that they want, as they have requested, a declaratory judgment, so that the specifics can be discussed in full in court. He states that:

The Onondaga Nation isn't asking for some form of title that would secretly carry with it a right of possession that would somehow indirectly result in dispossession of the Nation's neighbors ... It's not needed. We haven't asked for it. (Onondaga v. New York 2007, 29)

In this way, Coulter stresses the Onondaga desire for non-possessory title, a concept that the opposition does not recognize and that the judge seemed to find puzzling, although interesting.

In this chapter I have explored how the Onondaga, inside and outside of court, enact "treaty as a verb." Their approach demonstrates how, if we use the metaphor of the Guswentha, they went about negotiating the rows in between and working on polishing the beads of respect, friendship and peace, while also asserting and maintaining their autonomy. Their approach both respects the court and also proposes an alternative epistemology — an approach of relational autonomy and of refusing to see land as a commodity. Acting from a position of relational autonomy that values connection instead of opposition, and relations of justice instead of formal law, the Onondaga presented their complex epistemologies of land and relationships in a respectful yet challenging manner within a U.S. Supreme Court courtroom. Their approach demonstrates how it is possible to respond in a strategic manner that is not directly oppositional. Although the court finally made the decision in 2012 to reject the Onondaga's argument in the hearing I describe above,[7] the strategies used by the Onondaga in the courtroom itself show how their treaty philosophy might look in action. They gently, yet firmly, worked to conceptually turn the Doctrine of Discovery on its head.

As we saw, however, although the nuanced and strategic treatying within the courtroom has great potential, it is still at this stage quite one-sided. For the most part it is the Onondaga who actually do the work of treatying between the rows, while the sedimented laws of the nation, and the Western epistemologies that inform them, allow the authoritative Court (representing the settler nation) the power to refuse (or accept) the key assumptions of relationality and autonomy in treaty relationships that have been proposed by the Onondaga. In the courtroom, the power of the settler state and its assumed supremacy is visceral and raw, even if partially hidden, and the settler jurisdictional and juridical imaginary is paramount. The adversarial system in some ways defines such terms. Nevertheless, the story I have told about the Onondaga in court raises the important question of what form treatying as a verb might take if it were more reciprocal. What might "treatying together" look like if it also reflected *settler* desires for decolonization and treaty practice? It is to this question that I turn in the next and final chapter.

Notes

1   There are similarities here with Whaley and Bresette's book regarding the activism around spear fishing in Wisconsin in the late 80s and early 90s. The Anishnaabe, they say, engaged in collaborative politics with non-Aboriginal people (who acted as "witnesses" amongst other actions). They argue that the non-violent alliances they made, in order to continue traditional activities despite violent protests from angry locals, was ultimately concerned with "healing, not winning" and that protecting the environment is what brought people together (Whaley and Bresette 1994).

2   Indian country is defined as "all land within the limits of any Indian reservation under the jurisdiction of the United States Government" (Berkey 2005-6, 374).

3   The Court Opinion stated: "The properties here involved have greatly increased in value since the Oneidas sold them 200 years ago. The longstanding assumption of jurisdiction by the State over an area that is predominantly non-Indian in population and land use creates '*justifiable expectations.*'... Similar justifiable expectations, grounded in two centuries of New York's exercise of regulatory jurisdiction, until recently uncontested by OIN, merit heavy weight here....The distance from 1805 to the present day, the Oneidas' long delay in seeking equitable relief against New York or its local units, and developments in Sherrill spanning several generations, evoke the doctrines of laches, acquiescence, and impossibility, and render inequitable the piecemeal shift in governance this suit seeks unilaterally to initiate. When a party belatedly asserts a right to present and future sovereign control over territory, *longstanding observances and settled expectations are prime considerations.* (Supreme Court of the United States 2005, emphasis mine)

4   Here, Fort cites: Sarah Krakoff (2005), *City of Sherrill v. Oneida Indian Nation of New*

York: A Regretful Postscript to the Taxation Chapter in Cohen's Handbook of Federal Indian Law, 41 TULSA L. REV. 5; Joseph Singer (2006), *Nine-Tenths of the Law: Title, Possession & Sacred Obligations*, 38 CONN. L. REV. 605.

5   I thank Samah Sabra for her suggestions about the concepts of reciprocal and retrospective empathy in this context.

6   Fee title is basically the same as "fee simple or full ownership": the right to do anything with the land; to hold all the "sticks in the bundle" or property rights.

7   The Auburn *Citizen* (October 20, 2012) reported that "A three-judge panel of the appeals court" said that Kahn, the 2010 judge, was right because "so much time had passed since the 'historical injustice' and because the long-delayed claims would be disruptive to the 'justifiable expectations' of people and entities far removed from the taking of the lands." Defense lawyers called it a finding that would have disrupted "settled expectations based on 200 years of non-Indian sovereignty, ownership and development."

Chapter Six

CREATIVE UNCERTAINTY AND DECOLONIZING RELATIONS

The only way you can take yourself seriously is if you can throw yourself into the next period beyond your little meager human-body-mouth-talking all the time.… You must believe that believing in human beings in balance with the environment and the universe is a good thing. (Johnson Reagon 1983, 365–66)

In this chapter I discuss two alliances between Indigenous and settler people that offer provocative ways to imagine decolonizing relationships. I describe how members of the organization SHARE and their allies, the Cayuga Nation of New York, work together. I also explore aspects of how the Onondaga Nation and their allies, NOON (Neighbors of the Onondaga Nation), practice and describe their actions. I argue that the activities and developing relationships between the Onondaga and NOON, and the Cayuga and SHARE, potentially nurture epistemological shifts that may allow people to enact the kinds of decolonizing relational ontologies I discussed in the previous chapter in their day-to-day lives. They do this by demonstrating how it may be possible to practice "treaty as a verb," by creatively enacting reciprocal "treatying" in the present. They demonstrate a way to understand the possibility of simultaneous relations of distinction and interdependence. They go beyond colonial relations of treaty modelled on hierarchical relationships, usually meaning entitled colonizers and subordinate Indigenous peoples, in favour of a respectful one of connected yet autonomous equals. I describe how people practice "treating together" through these alliances.

In Robin Wall Kimmerer's article about the Onondaga land rights action, "The Rights of the Land," she describes it as

> an invitation for the people of this watershed to engage in *becoming indigenous to place*. No *newcomer can ever match the Onondaga's* identity with these hills, but what does it mean for an immigrant culture to start thinking like a native one? Not to appropriate the culture of Indigenous peoples, not to take what is theirs, but to *throw off the mindset of the frontier*, the mindset that allows people to bury sacred sites under industrial waste, to fill a lake with mercury. Being *indigenous to place* means to live as if we'll be here for the *long haul*, to take care of the land as if our lives, both spiritual and material, depended on it. Because they do. (Kimmerer 2008, emphasis mine)

Kimmerer's view of Indigenous–non-Indigenous relationships to "place" is deeply compelling. I want to use her image of settlers *"becoming indigenous* to place" as a starting point to tease out some of my thoughts about settler roles and responsibilities of reciprocity if we are living treaty relationships with Indigenous peoples. Kimmerer defines "indigenous to place" as "to live as if we'll be here for the long haul, to take care of the land as if our lives, both spiritual and material, depended on it." She makes it clear that she does not mean to "appropriate the culture of Indigenous peoples, not to take what is theirs." Her sense of becoming Indigenous is thoughtful and respectful, in part because it includes the need to *"throw off the mindset of the frontier."* Thus it also includes epistemological shifts, moving from the epistemologies of domination discussed in previous chapters.

However, when I hear the phrase "becoming Indigenous" I have a sense of deep discomfort. This is because colonial and national narratives in settler nation-states often appropriate Indigenous symbols and relationships to land for their own purposes of claiming indigeneity, often without a corresponding respect for Indigenous lifeways and land rights. Using a strange combination of the simultaneous erasure of Indigenous authority and the appropriation of Indigenous authenticity, nationalist narratives that represent Indigenous people as linked to the land *and* as members of the nation may provide a nationalist "link between the settlers and the land ... that helps make Canada a 'Native land' to settlers and immigrants" (Mackey 2002; see also Marcus 1997), without changing social relations. As I have argued elsewhere, "Giving to the land," an image also present in Kimmerer's narrative, may, in a different context, become part of an inauthentic process of national "reconciliation" in which Indigenous people are seen to naturally forgive the settlers and yet are still an "absented presence" in the national imaginary (Mackey 1998, 2002). These images can produce a fantasy of "settler innocence regarding the colonial encounter" (Mackey 2002), or may represent what Tuck and Yang (2012, 1) call "settler moves to innocence." My main point here is not to disagree with Kimmerer, but to argue, as I will below, that we as settlers must have a very careful approach to relationships and alliances with Indigenous peoples, to be sure we don't, with all the best intentions, reproduce colonial patterns. If we wish, as settler peoples, to "treaty" (as a verb) with the Onondaga, it is necessary to undertake the sometimes difficult and uncomfortable work of unsettling ourselves. Doing so requires particular forms of reflection and restraint on our part.

I have been arguing that one constant in the Indigenous–non-Indigenous relations I have discussed so far in this book is that to create certainty for the settler project, Indigenous peoples have been constructed as inferior and subordinate to settlers, and settlers have been painted as entitled to their privileged, secure and certain positions. Thus decolonizing, for settlers, includes developing the ability to live more comfortably with *uncertainty* about how relationships between Indigenous and non-Indigenous people emerge and change. Significantly, it entails learning that developing relational autonomies, as symbolized by the lines between the two rows of the wampum, may mean that power relationships are not defined, fixed and apparently "certain."

When approached through relational autonomy, knowing how to think and relate may at times seem frightening and uncomfortable, because expected practices no longer work in the same way. Expectations are unsettled. Yet, at the same time, if relationships are released from repetitive and limiting epistemologies of mastery discussed so far, we see that such moments of uncertainty and discomfort may indeed be productive and potentially decolonizing. Uncertainty, almost always seen as a negative and threatening phenomenon, can also (indeed, must also) be embraced as a key to creativity and imaginative visions that depend on unsettling "settled expectations" and self-evident "settler states of feeling."

Allison Jones (with Jenkins 2008), a Pakeha (settler) scholar in Aotearoa/New Zealand, discussing her collaboration with Kuni Jenkins, a Maori scholar, develops a complex explanation of how they "work the hyphen" when they collaborate. Her description of "working the hyphen" is evocative, for me, of the kind of relational autonomy theorized in the Guswentha. This is because, although they work at the relationship between them, they do not try to "become" the other or become the same. They do not, we might say, attempt to cross the parallel rows of autonomy pictured in the Guswentha. I see the hyphen as a "contact zone" (Pratt 1992, 6), and similar to the spaces in-between the rows of the Guswentha. No contact zone (or space between autonomous peoples and cultures) exists without the tensions of power, history, dominance, privilege, injustice and in this case, the theft of both land and cultures. Jones' point is that the tension is necessary. One must learn from it and respect it. The hyphen, Jones says, "ideally demands a posture of alert vulnerability to or recognition of difference, rather than a pose of empathetic understanding that tends to reduce difference to the same. This is not a moral injunction, but one in the interests of knowledge. It is openness to difference that can provoke meaning beyond our own culture's prescriptions — and lead to new thought" (Jones 2008, 480).[1] This makes sense since, after all, "when one can control things, one is limited to one's own vision" (Smith cited in Perina 2008).

"Working the hyphen" in this way can also produce anxiety because, like the spaces between the rows, the result is never certain, there is "*perpetual lack of clarity and certainty*" (Jones 2008, 482, emphasis mine). Jones (2008, 482) argues that "it is 'a strategic act of interruption of the methodological will to certainty and clarity of vision' (Stronach and MacLure 1997, 4–5)" and the "colonizing impulses that attend it." Confronting difference without certainty may entail "a kind of trauma in encountering what is outside the subject" (Jones 2008, 481). This is because it "threatens the stability of the ego," it "disrupts its coherency," and "the subject tumbles into uncertainty, its past strategies for living challenged" (Todd 2003, 11, cited in Jones 2008, 481). It is the "strangeness of difference — the unfamiliar space of not knowing — that is so hard for the colonizer whose benevolent imperialism assumes both herself and himself as the center of knowing and that everything can be known" (Jones 2008, 481).

This certainty of knowledge in a larger sense (of nature, of "the Other," of time and the future) is integral to modernity and to the settler epistemological project of "mapping the world, rendering it visible and understood" (Jones 2008, 482). It emerges from a "Western Enlightenment desire for coherence, authorization and control," the kind of control and authority that have been central to settler colonial epistemologies and settler states of feeling. These impulses for coherence, singularity and certainty are also "central to liberal White desire for racial harmony, collaboration, and understanding" (Jones 2008, 482) and the desire for finding a dependable and right path, with fixed and clear-cut rules for how to relate to each other, and even for how to decolonize.

Such uncertainty and the resulting anxiety could result in paralysis: the inability to act "in relation" because of the hugeness of the problem — a retreat to separate worlds. For those who wish to engage, what it requires, instead, is the "hard work ... of coming to know our own location" within the relationship, and accepting, even embracing, "the difference marked by the hyphen" (Jones 2008, 482), or the in-between rows of the wampum. Jones argues that the "desire for engagement" must lead settlers to a deeper understanding of our own settler culture, society, and history as deeply embedded in a relationship with the culture, society, and history of Indigenous people. Such an orientation to the hyphen invites colonizer people to seek to know ourselves in the relationship with Others, to locate ourselves in the "between" — to develop a stronger sense of how our Selves are and have been formed in the troubled engagement with Indigenous peoples and their lands and spaces. (Jones 2008, 482)

I argue, based on the alliances that I discuss below, that such careful (and often restrained) settler movement into the uncertainty (and hard work) necessary to build relationships of autonomy and connection — whether seen as "contact zones," "hyphens," or the in-between rows of the Guswentha — is essential to the decolonization of settler-Indigenous alliances. Such uncertainty can also, as we see, be invigorating and creative. After all, the hyphen, as the rows of the Guswentha, "*joins* as well as separates" (Jones 2008, 475). It brings us "*into* relation" in new ways.

After I introduce the case studies I will move on to briefly discuss pivotal frameworks emerging from Indigenous peoples that influence these alliances. Finally, I focus on the actions of SHARE and NOON, in order to explore how settler subjects might engage with moving beyond epistemologies of mastery and into relations of autonomy and interconnection with Indigenous peoples, learning how share the land.

ENCOUNTERS IN SHARED HOMELANDS

The SHARE organization and SHARE farm emerged from the activism of a group of people, including academics, hairdressers, carpenters, government workers, students, etc. who live around the shores of Cayuga Lake in New York State, including the towns of Seneca Falls, Union Springs and Ithaca. In 1999, Julie and Jim Uticone, life-long residents of the area, began the organization SHARE to "promote friendship and mutual respect locally between non-Native and Native people" (Hansen and Rossen 2007, 133). The Uticones formed the group because they were deeply perturbed by the intensity of the hostile resistance to the Cayuga land claim that had been in the courts since 1980. As the Cayuga land claim case seemed to be coming to a climax, the hostilities increased, propelled in great part by the kind of UCE activism discussed in earlier chapters. The Uticones eventually aligned with cultural anthropologists Ernie Olsen and Brooke Hansen, and archaeologist Jack Rossen, who all worked in local colleges. For Rossen and Hansen, the motivation was more than academic: "We were not just working with Haudenosaunee people and learning about their history and culture, we also lived in and around the land claim, in essence, we were both local community members and anthropologists ... As an anthropologist, community member, and parent to a young child, it became clear that … ignorance about Native American treaties and law, coupled with widespread stereotypes about Indians as savages and drunks, were rampant" (Hansen and Rossen 2007, 129).

SHARE began to put out quarterly newsletters, hold gatherings, organize Native American festivals and visit local schools. In 2001, SHARE members decided to buy a 70-acre organic farm within the Cayuga homeland, located in a place of deep significance to the Cayuga, beside Great Gully and adjacent to Cayuga Castle, which had been the largest Cayuga settlement site before it was destroyed during the Sullivan Campaign.

They pooled their money, took out a large mortgage and purchased the property. The SHARE farm was born. Their ultimate goal was to repatriate the land to the Cayuga Nation, the only landless nation of the Haudenosaunee, an event which finally occurred in 2005 (Hansen and Rossen 2007). Because of the very volatile land claim protests in the area, they wished to help create a space in the Cayuga homeland for Cayuga people to come to, generate positive Indigenous and non-Indigenous relationships and build a site that might help educate non-Indigenous people in the area about local and national Indigenous issues.

For five years, SHARE operated the farm as an educational centre a location from which to advocate for Indigenous peoples, and as a place for diverse people to reconnect with each other and the land. They organised educational events and festivals, planted and sold organic crops including the "three sisters,"[2] cared for the land and the buildings, invited, interacted with and often fed the people who came from all over, including the Cayuga and other Haudenosaunee people. At the same time they created a place for non-Indigenous people to learn about and from the Haudenosaunee. They created a meeting space and a starting place for learning to build different kinds of relationships, that I suggest here work towards decolonization.

Through the farm, SHARE ultimately formed many alliances with Cayuga and Haudenosaunee people from the area and beyond. The SHARE farm collaborative projects included Indigenous crop plantings, herb gardens, medicinal workshops, wild plant collecting, a seed saving program and various public outreach initiatives, including many in which students at local colleges lived and worked at the farm.

I spent as much time as possible at the SHARE farm from 2001 until 2005. During that time I weeded the garden, staked tomatoes, shovelled manure, picked apples, helped cook food for the festivals and myriad of visitors, cleaned cobwebs, washed floors and dishes, helped decorate the yard for festivals and floats for parades, took photos and talked with many Indigenous and non-Indigenous people from the local area and beyond, including Cayuga and Onondaga people. At the same time, I was interviewing members of UCE. It was through my linkage with SHARE that I met several Onondaga members, began to learn about their community, and eventually learned about their land rights action. They introduced me to members of NOON (Neighbors of the Onondaga Nation), a "grassroots organization of Central New Yorkers which recognizes and supports the sovereignty of the traditional government of the Onondaga Nation. A program of the Syracuse Peace Council, NOON supports the right of Indigenous peoples to reclaim land, and advocates for fair settlement of any claims which are filed" (NOON 2010).

NOON has been very involved in developing complex and interconnecting relationships of alliance with the Onondaga, including co-sponsoring two year-long collaborative Educational Series intended to "bring together the Central New York community": the Onondaga Land Rights & Our Common Future, Part I in 2006 and Part II in 2009–10. Members attended the court hearing that I discussed in the previous chapter. During the course of my fieldwork, I attended as many of their events as possible and interviewed members of NOON and the Onondaga Nation.

Both SHARE and NOON work to engage in relations that aim to recognize both the distinctness and interconnectedness of Indigenous and non-Indigenous Americans. They work to develop relationships based on the recognition that Indigenous people and settlers are all treaty peoples, and that settler people have responsibilities to build relationships of respect with Indigenous peoples and to the land they share. They try to create alternative frameworks that might allow settlers to be reflexive about their own entitlement and privilege, in part by learning how to listen, hear and act differently. Before moving on to a detailed discussion of SHARE and NOON activities, I want to briefly discuss Haudenosaunee conceptualizations of the importance of stories and concepts of relational responsibility.

LISTENING OTHERWISE:
NEW STORIES, HISTORIES AND RELATIONAL RESPONSIBILITIES

The first key concept that emerges from Haudenosaunee philosophy, and is highlighted in the work of NOON and SHARE, concerns the role of previously silenced stories and histories. They provide people the opportunity to listen to stories that have not often been heard, as well as opportunities to learn *how* to hear openly, in a manner that does not simply place the stories into pre-conceived frameworks.

When I interviewed Onondaga Clan Mother Frieda Jacques, she spoke compellingly about the reasons for the Onondaga land rights action and the need for people to hear different kinds of stories and truths.

> People need to know. And this is one of the things that I said was the trade-off with our land rights action ... People would hear stories they had never heard. People — the government and ... the education system have been secretive on purpose. There are stories that they have never

heard…. [The lands rights action means that people] get to understand their history in a whole new way, a different way, but also recognize … that something has happened over time, and that things could be different [now and in the future].

Thus, a key part of the land rights action is that silenced stories — stories which may allow people to imagine different ways of relating to Indigenous peoples and understanding history — will finally be heard, as a way to imagine a different way of being.

Frieda's approach also challenges the foundational frameworks of state of nature and *terra nullius* that inform settler origin myths, because she works against preconceptions that Indigenous people are now assimilated, disappeared, or the mythical primitives often imagined. This is because, according to Frieda, one of the reasons the stories are important is that they allow for the recognition that Indigenous people still *exist*.

What I see as one of the goals [of the land rights action] is to recognize that *we can be here.* And it is *alright for us to be here. We can exist*…. Just getting to that point where the general public recognizes that we as Indigenous peoples exist. *Instead of thinking … that someday we'll go away.* Because people are often surprised that we're still here…. and their foreheads squinch up and they ask a question and you know that the reason they are asking … is because … we were *supposed to vanish and go away.* So we live in an atmosphere of people wishing us gone.

The sense Frieda expresses, of living with constant reminders that settler people expect and wish that you did not exist, is significant because such settler expectations are consequences of frameworks and goals integral to the past and present of ongoing settler colonialism. Frieda's sense that it is important or necessary simply to assert the *continued existence* of Indigenous peoples indicates that the ideology of *terra nullius* has in many ways been brutally successful. Frieda's versions of history, and the reality that Indigenous peoples exist and vibrantly claim justice, therefore challenge deep-seated settler epistemologies.

Frieda also frames her hope for *how* Indigenous peoples are "here" in a manner that proposes specific kinds of interrelationships. She said if people recognize these new stories and silent histories, then the long history of settlers assuming Indian people are gone might then be "switched to" one wherein they recognize that Indigenous peoples "*are* here," one in which non-Indigenous peoples might say, "Let's look at what they can share with us that's valuable. This is one of the reasons why it is ok for them to be here, because they have this seven generations look into the future … I think that that's a value that we can share."

Frieda continues to explain why rethinking history and hearing stories is necessary. It is important to point out that her approach is not simply about recognizing Indigenous *culture*, but also about particular versions of healing and justice realized through re-thinking relationships and recognizing Indigenous entitlement to land. This is the basis of what she, below, finally calls "reasonable reconciliation."

> We understand that the knowledge about what happened over time needs to come out. The general public needs to hear about it, to be recognized. The idea about [people someday] saying, "Yes, you are entitled to this land because you've been here from day one and we recognize your value here, and that you will be here forever." You know, that's the kind of title we want: "Yes, you've been here; yes, you're going to be here and we want to listen to what you have to say." That's the kind of thing we want to have so that we can encourage and help make the changes happen so it would be a healthy place to live. So we know those steps of hearing what happened, and knowing that you know what happened, are big steps in the healing process. And then we can say, "Well, where can we go from here?" It wouldn't be like, "Let's hide this and make believe it never happened." Those kinds of things do not encourage healing; do not encourage reasonable reconciliation between peoples.

"Reasonable reconciliation," then, is based on critical approaches to history, learning to hear different versions of the world, and thus learning new ways to develop relationships (what I have been calling "treaty as a verb") between Indigenous and settler peoples, relationships that maintain autonomy but do not settle on oppositional and binary separation.

RISKING RESPONSIBLE RELATIONALITY

The Onondaga land rights action explicitly works through relational concepts of treaty and responsibility that emerge from the stories and traditions of the Haudenosaunee. One community member and author, Robin Kimmerer, wrote:

> When they finally got their day in court … members of the Onondaga Nation argued that the land title they're seeking is not for possession, not to exclude, but for the right to *participate in the well-being of the land.* Against the backdrop of Euro-American thinking, which treats land as a bundle of property rights, the Onondaga are asking for *freedom to exercise their responsibility to the land.* This is unheard of in American property law. (Kimmerer 2008 my emphasis)

What Kimmerer and Frieda both describe is the challenge of what I call "relational ontologies in action." The anti-colonial epistemology of the Onondaga land rights action entails a radical reshaping of relationships as citizen-subjects around conceptions of relational responsibility, in this case based on the *Kaienerekowa*, the Haudenosaunee Great Law of Peace, the constitution of the Haudenosaunee. It is a sophisticated plan for governance that established and has maintained what is perhaps the oldest participatory democracy on earth (Manno and Powless 2008, 151; see also Horn-Miller 2005). Under the Great Law,

> every human being who is a member of a family, clan, and nation, has certain responsibilities and rights. Everyone has a responsibility to help and to preserve the Earth, our Mother, for the benefit of her children seven generations to come. Everyone has the right to come and to go, free to live in harmony with the laws of nature, free to enjoy liberty, to live in a natural way, as long as one continues to give thanks for all land and life. (Swamp 2004, 66, in Manno and Powless 2008, 151)

Central to the Haudenosaunee philosophy, and many other Indigenous belief systems, is a particular epistemology of responsibility and relationship to each other and to the world around them. Such notions of responsibility are based on maintaining complementarities, reciprocities, commitments and interconnectedness, without losing autonomy or respect. This model is quite different from liberal or neoliberal ideas of individual responsibility. This kind of approach to responsibility is evoked in testimony given by Leroy Little Bear at an Indigenous Knowledge workshop.

> I would just like you to try to imagine what it feels like. And for those Native people in the room, you know what it feels like whether you own land or not in your community. But you know what it feels like to travel through a place that you know you have a responsibility for it.
>
> Because it's not about land rights. We use that word because it's what works in the court system. But it's about responsibility and we know that we are born onto this earth with a set of responsibilities and when we're inhibited from being able to fulfil our responsibilities, there's a huge disconnection that goes on ... Most of us are not ready to give up that responsibility. (cited in Indigenous Knowledge Forum 2004, 84)

Frieda emphasized that the concept of responsibility, for the Haudenosaunee, is not based on Western concepts of power. When I asked her about her role as Clan Mother[3] she said:

> A clan mother's main job is to watch over the chief in her clan, the one

that's hers … She watches him to make sure that he does his job and his duties … to encourage him and be supportive to him and also share her opinions and the people's opinions … so that communication's good. And she is also — if it is ever needed, and it's rarely ever needed — if the chief needs a warning, in terms of him not doing his duties, then she would make that happen. People like to say that the Haudenosaunee women have power but actually we just have the same amount of responsibility as men have, it's just that they're from different vantage points.

E: So in a sense it's power but it's not direct power? It's more like authority?

F: Responsible.

E: Responsible.

F: Yeah, the word is responsible. Because it's not power; it's responsibility.

E: People call it power in a sense because in most patriarchal societies they can only think of things in terms of power…

F: That's why *we* have to give *you* a new word to use; so that *you* don't go there!

It is notable, within the framework of relational autonomy and responsibility that I have been discussing, that Frieda places herself in a pedagogical role here. She has a responsibility to explain and teach, yet not by making her epistemology of responsibility *the same as* or *completely translatable into* Western concepts of power or authority. She does not hesitate to assert the distinctiveness of these as Haudenosaunee ways of thinking and clarifies who is "we" and who is "you." She made it clear that although I thought I understood, I did not, and it was up to her to provide that knowledge. Thus, she ultimately gives a lesson in the meaning of responsibility as distinct from power, but also in how to "treaty." Frieda illustrated, in other words, that while alliances and understanding (between the rows in the wampum belt) are important, we are not the same and do not know or understand in the same way. These differences (the two separate rows) are important and should not be sacrificed in the name of a false unity or equality.

Directly linked to the Haudenosaunee concept of responsibility is the way in which the land rights action of the Onondaga and the work of NOON intersected with environmental responsibility. A key motivation was taking collective care of — responsibility for — the land, as I discuss below. What do "settler peoples" need to do to participate responsibly in such alliances? How can they be involved without unconsciously reproducing settled expectations of mastery? What processes and approaches are necessary? As I stated earlier, I am not proposing a general model. By briefly exploring the specificities of the relationships encouraged by SHARE,

NOON and the Onondaga and Cayuga Nations, I merely gesture towards some possibilities of how settlers, including myself, might go about this task.

UNSETTLING SUBJECTS: RISK, UNCERTAINTY AND DECENTERING

> [The crux of the matter] lies in the problematic connection between learning *about* difference and learning to *become* different; and, as in all learning, that connection is fraught with questions of power and authority. (Asad 1993, 262)

Kimmerer's challenge — to "throw off the mindset of the frontier" — is a compelling starting point to explore how, if settlers are to engage in living treaty as a verb with Indigenous peoples, we might think about settler roles and responsibilities of reciprocity. Throwing off the mindset of the frontier, I suggest, necessitates deep epistemological shifts, informed by notions of relationality, respect and responsibility. These shifts require mindfulness, to avoid reproducing contemporary versions of coloniality, despite what may be very good intentions. It may be necessary to seriously unsettle and decentre deep and pervasive patterns and epistemologies of entitlement, of always knowing and controlling. Doing so will require active reflexivity, engagement and the uncertainty of not knowing.

CREATIVE UNCERTAINTY AND RISKING CONNECTION

Although "risk" for UCE and CKCN had been seen as necessarily negative, synonymous with danger and loss of property, privilege and ontological certainty, SHARE members took risks and embraced uncertainty in order to find new ways of connecting. How they do so also shows the potential pleasures and creative energy that can come from embracing uncertainty. The initial contact with the Cayuga Nation that inspired the formation of SHARE was in 1999. SHARE founder Julie Uticone lived in Seneca Falls, the centre of UCE activity in the area. The area was littered with signs bearing slogans such as "Who will win, the farmer's heartbeat or the Indian's drumbeat?" "Scalp the land claim, NRA Forever," and "We fought four wars for this land."

Signs such as these — based on "state of nature" and *terra nullius* frameworks — communicate anger, entitlement, superiority and fear of uncertainty. For Julie, and then Brooke and Jack, also founders of SHARE, the signs elicited a different kind of fear. They were frightened of living with the defensive and violent epistemologies of mastery that the signs represented. Their fear mobilized them to cross historical boundaries and take risks to create the organization in an effort to provide a peaceful alternative to reactions such as those of UCE members.

It was Julie who took the first risky step out of her comfort zone. She began to persistently call the office of the Cayuga Nation to try to talk to "a Cayuga person" to find out what the Cayuga thought that she, as a non-Indigenous woman from the area, could and should do: she took the risk to reach out to cross the historically binary boundaries and distance that often exists between Indigenous and non-Indigenous people. Brooke and Jack (interrupting each other and finishing each others' sentences) tell the story this way:

> Julie started calling up the Cayuga Nation office trying to find somebody…and Judy answered the phone. She was like, "Who is this crazy white lady?" She basically put her off. But Julie was so persistent and called and called. Judy finally asked Birdie [Cayuga Clan Mother], "Will you talk to this woman and get her out of my hair?"
>
> And that's how [it happened] — as soon as they spoke, they connected. That's when Birdie agreed to come to Julie's house. So Birdie came to Julie's house and met her, and that's when Julie started getting this idea that, OK, we need to form some kind of organization.

A connection occurred because Julie was willing to risk being seen as "crazy" by the Cayuga and, later, by others in her community. The connection also occurred because Julie did not feel entitled, as a settler, to authoritatively decide on the right course of action *for the* Cayuga, or to assume that she would automatically know the right way for her as a settler to support them. Knowing the history of how non-Indigenous people have tried to "help" Indigenous peoples, and how often "help" has been paternalistic and ethnocentric, she was willing to embrace not knowing. On the other hand, she *acted*: she did not retreat and freeze action because it was "not her problem" to deal with, or because of her fears. Thus, her action came from alliance-building, based on terms defined by Cayuga, and not settler, frameworks and knowledge.

When Julie herself tells the story, it becomes a powerful narrative about the dangers and risks involved in rethinking her home as a contested "contact zone" (Pratt 1992). Julie talks about her simultaneous understanding of, and alienation from, her own community regarding its response to the Cayuga land claim. Other family members had joined UCE and everywhere she went she heard people talking about how the Indians were coming to invade people's property and how it would ruin the area. She said people were "angry and they didn't even know why." They felt "they had no voice," and "I understand their anger. They think I don't understand their anger, but I do." Here, precisely at the moment that Julie is questioning common-sense expectations of settler entitlement, she is also placing herself in a space in-between, in which she can also sympathize with the pain and anger of loss. She is, in my view, enacting treaty as a verb because acknowledging the possibly irreconcilable differences between the groups, she works between the rows, and in doing so takes the risk of unsettling her own entitlement.

It was through Julie's painful and conflicted leap of connection that SHARE was born. Julie explained later how difficult it was to be pegged a traitor in her own community. Yet, rather than retreating, Julie kept going, implicitly understanding herself as a treaty partner and beneficiary, and thus as responsible for building relationships between the Cayuga and settlers. She persisted and engaged with Birdie, creating a space for encounter: SHARE.

Stories also had a pivotal role in starting the SHARE farm. Stories told by Cayuga Clan Mother Birdie were the inspiration for the idea of returning land to the Cayuga. Birdie had grown up on the ancestral lands and reservations of other Haudenosaunee nations because the Cayuga had been expelled from their territory on Cayuga Lake. The story below, although it inspired the creation of SHARE, also shows that exclusionary notions of private property are not only used by settlers, but can also be mobilized cruelly by Indigenous peoples. Brooke explained the importance of the story, saying how in the early days of SHARE, before they bought the farm,

> Birdie was pretty involved mentoring us and Julie would ask … "what is it we can do? We hear your story Birdie, your people have been dispossessed and you want to come home." That's when Birdie told those other stories about when she was growing up, her mother used to be abused by the Seneca neighbor. The Seneca neighbor would taunt her and say, "Cayuga, what are you doing here, you don't belong here, why don't you go home?" And Birdie said that her mother was told, "You can't pick medicines here. You can't grow food here. This is not your place." And so Birdie would ask her mother, "Why aren't we home?" And her mother would explain that, "We've been trying to go home for a long time and maybe some time we'll get there." And Birdie had really beautiful discourses of her mother's description of the ancestral homeland and the crystal clear waters filled with fish and the corn that was twelve, fifteen feet high. So Birdie's stories were so powerful, that's what solidified us together and pushed us forward: saying "Birdie, how can we help you?" And clearly she wanted to come home and help to bring her people home.

Birdie's is a powerful story of exile from an idyllic homeland to a cruel and foreign place (in which even other Haunosaunce people do not welcome them)[4] and the longing for a safe home. It resonated with Julie and the other SHARE farm members and inspired them to move. When they researched the possibility of the Cayuga being able to return as a result of the land claim, it had already been in the court for 20 years and seemed it would be there "for another 20." It was Julie, Brooke said, who had the idea of making sure the Cayuga could "come home" by going "around, over and under the courts in a people-to-people solution." Buying the SHARE farm, then, Brooke said, "just seemed a no-brainer." In this way, the SHARE farm emerged from a relational and decolonial model of risk-taking, in which storytelling was a powerful instigator.

The SHARE farm was also based on another kind of risk: financial risk. The purchase of the SHARE farm was possible only because SHARE members went beyond good intentions about land rights and reconciliation, and took the risk to "put their money where their mouth is" as settler people. They therefore risked their own financial health in order to make a space for decolonizing alliances. Struggling every month to pay the mortgage, they sponsored festivals, sold organic vegetables that they grew on the farm, and constantly worked to find people willing to donate even a small amount. In this, it is clear that decolonization is much more "than a metaphor" (Tuck and Yang 2012), but is a risky material practice. They were creating a space of relational autonomy within which "the risk of connection is understood to be worth the struggle" (Weir 2008).

INVIGORATING UNCERTAINTY

Most significantly, Brooke and Jack talked about the incredible energy they had at the time, inspired as they were by Birdie's stories. Although there is a sense of risk, danger and even fear here, it was, more importantly, a matter of excitement.

> Adrenaline. Adrenaline and enthusiasm. Being moved by Birdie's stories. I mean her stories — she could bring down the house … telling her stories about her mother and the abuse and this desire to go home and bring her people home — just really incredible. And that's when the next part of the story happens. But it's good to understand the emotional context, of why a bunch of people would try to buy a quarter million dollar farm when you have no money, you know. There needs to be some explanation for that … It was a charged atmosphere, and charged atmospheres are catalysts, where sparks ignite into flames.

Thus, response-ability, as the *ability to respond* to Birdie's stories in the ways that they did, created a sense of risk and uncertainty but also of exhilaration. This exhilaration suggests that finding new ways to relate can mean that a sense of uncertainty may also feel pleasurable. Birdie's stories of her desire for home, no matter how mythic they may have been, lit sparks of relationality in this group of people. Here, it is possible to see how hearing and responding to stories was an important element in SHARE members' ability to develop epistemologies of relationality and to take the risk of connection, working to decolonize Indigenous–non-Indigenous relationships.

NOON: PEDAGOGIES OF RELATIONALITY

The Neighbours of the Onondaga Nation (NOON) is an organization that deftly and energetically promotes unsettling expectations as part of their educational activities. One example of this approach was their ambitious series of events entitled, "Onondaga Land Rights and Our Common Future," organised in 2006–7 and again in 2010. NOON collaborated with the Onondaga Nation and other community and university sponsors to present the year-long events. Topics for discussion included "Why Native American Sovereignty Makes Sense for All of Us," and "Environmental Stewardship: Finding Common Ground Between Traditional Environmental Knowledge and 'Modern' Environmental Science." Kimmerer describes the series in this way:

> Most evenings, there were two spot-lit chairs on the dark stage, chairs filled by some combination of Indigenous scholars, university professors, clan mothers, grassroots leaders, politicians, scientists, lawyers, all come to think collectively about what the land rights action could mean. (Kimmerer 2008)

One evening in particular illustrates the complex ways in which Haudenosaunee and others who lived in the area became connected through relationships that can help us to imagine allied futures. Not coincidentally, the Two Row Wampum, or Guswentha, plays a role. Kimmerer tells the story:

> One night, Chief Powless addressed the crowd, framing the land rights action in a historical context. "Sharing our ancient teachings is not just for understanding the past, but for a vision of what the future can hold," he said. Fumbling with something in his lap for a moment, he drew from its deerskin wrap a wide belt intricately woven of shell beads: the historic Two Row Wampum.

As he draped it between his outstretched hands he explained the meaning of the two paths of purple wampum and the white ground, representing "the river of life down which we all travel." The purple wampum represents

> "Two boats on the same river," he said, [it] is "an agreement to live side by side. But we're both on the same river. We need the same water. We're going to the same place. This belt," he continued, gently putting it back

into its wrapping, "reminds us that our futures are linked. The only way we have is forward, into the future, together." (Kimmerer 2008)

In this way, the wampum belt brings Indigenous and settler people together as distinct but interconnected treaty peoples, who must find new ways of interpreting the past and present in order to create more just futures together, moments of "polishing the Covenant Chain."

For non-Haudenosaunee participants, many of the events did not simply mean *hearing about* a different version of events, but about learning to *hear* differently and thus to *experience* how alternative versions of their own histories might shift frameworks of thinking. Instead of simply *learning about* difference as a detached observer, these moments may allow people to learn how to *be different*, to understand and relate in new ways that unsettle patterns of mastery. An example of how the Onondaga and NOON facilitate this experiential learning took place at the third event in the Onondaga Land Rights and Our Common Future series in 2007. Ellen Edgerton describes it on her blog:

> This one was about the history of relations between the Haudenosaunee and European settlers and featured Chief Irving Powless of the Onondaga Nation, and Cornell lecturer Bob Venables. Immediately after Richard Loder, head of Native American studies at SU, wrapped up the presentation (or so he thought), Powless started speaking again. You could sense the audience's tension/quizzicalness at the "normal" flow of an event being disrupted in such a way, but people mostly settled back into their seats and listened patiently and respectfully as he continued…One of the stories he told was about how, during some meeting with the state at Colgate, he spied an empty room and wondered if he should get permission from the Onondaga leadership to claim it for Onondaga, much in the manner that various "empty" locales in New York had been claimed in the 18th century by citizens given New York's blessing.
>
> This story and others like it went on for a good half hour, totally breaking all European-American rules of time and decorum. Then Powless got around to inviting any and all Haudenosaunee people in the audience to come up on stage and stand behind him. From up on stage where he was looking down at the non-Haudenosaunee in the audience…He informed us that the Onondaga were now claiming this auditorium. He then asked us to all squeeze into the first four rows of the auditorium, which many attempted to do. "This will be your reservation" [he said]. (Edgerton 2006)

Here people were invited to experience something outside of their expectations

— a different way of organizing time and space — in a manner that implicates but does not blame them. This moment is deeply pedagogical in an experiential way, offering an opportunity through which one's body may live within — experience — a different kind of epistemology, along with the uncertainty that may accompany it. Chief Powless and NOON created a space in which settlers could experience how it feels when someone else is entitled to define time and space, someone who also determines their occupation of, movement within, and senses of selves within that space.

Such experiences of uncertainty can be unsettling, but may also be part of a deeply political and transformative process, as Edgerton's description attests:

> Now if 100 people in an auditorium cannot listen respectfully to one Onondaga leader for "longer" than the "allotted time," and mold themselves for an extra half hour to his way of communicating, and to accept Onondaga authority over a theatre space ... well, there isn't much hope for whatever it is we're supposed to be doing ... [with land rights]
>
> Because it's going to involve a lot of central New Yorkers listening to a lot of Onondagas for a lot longer than a half hour ... and it's going to be concerning a lot bigger space than an auditorium. Because the land rights action is abou t... land rights (and authority over it), not just about conversation. (Edgerton 2006)

This transformation is not only about *thinking* differently but about the experience of learning to share, and *sometimes give over*, power and authority to those who have been historically constructed as shadow citizens and outsiders to Western frameworks of property, personhood and "civilization."

DECENTRING: NEGOTIATING RELATIONAL AUTONOMY

Such discomfort and uncertainty are central to settler decolonization. Here, I draw on concepts of discomfort and uncertainty to explore how complex power relationships concerning difference and autonomy were negotiated between SHARE and the Cayuga Nation. Such renegotiations entail a conscious "decentering" of settler epistemologies and a recentring of Indigenous ways of knowing and Indigenous authority. For Avril Bell (2008, 852), decentring is part of the necessary and "significant shift" required in settler societies. For Bell, the "center works as a metaphor for politics/power." As we have seen, settlers have "historically centered themselves through myriad institutional arrangements, discourses and practices of domination and marginalization of Indigenous peoples," all to legitimate their settled expectations of authority and sovereignty. She says the "challenge now is to modify our modes of relating to make way for, or give way to, the Indigenous project of recentering" (Bell 2008, 852), such as Linda Tuhiwai Smith's (1999, 97) view that the project of Indigenous survival and recovery is also one of "recentering Indigenous identities." Bell argues that an important part of this project is to "abandon 'the universality of the Western project,' the Enlightenment belief in Western universalism being a primary block to our ability to co-exist with Indigenous difference" (Bell 2008, 853). A major part of Western universalism concerns who can be the knower and who is the known. Decolonizing relationships entails asking questions about who has the authority to define the key terms and issues of the debate.

This process of decentering/unsettling requires rethinking some of our patterns as authoritative subjects. As settlers, we like to know. We feel entitled to know. We want to solve problems and define solutions. Such knowing, however, can also be a form of "epistemological domination" (Bell 2008, 855). One of the keys here is to embrace not knowing, to embrace uncertainty. We must be vigilant of our own urges to jump in and solve — to define problems and solutions — to "save" others. To think we know.

Sullivan, for example, argues that "One of the predominant unconscious habits of white privilege is that of ontological expansiveness."

> As ontologically expansive, white people tend to think and act as if all spaces — whether geographical, psychical, linguistic, economic, spiritual, bodily or otherwise — are or should be available for them to move in and out of as they wish. Ontological expansiveness is a particular co-constitutive relationship between self and environment in which the self assumes that it can and should have total mastery over its environment. (Sullivan 2006, 10)

"Ontological expansiveness" is not only a characteristic of settler or white individuals. The model of "ontological expansiveness" has been philosophical basis for the epistemological legacies we have inherited, such as the axiomatic assumptions that underpin "state of nature" and *terra nullius* arguments. Ultimately, the entitlement to be ontologically expansive — to assume the right and responsibility to know, control and master others — underpins both the strategy and the rationale for the self-ascribed entitlement to conquer the world.

From the outset, SHARE members engaged in alliances of relationality within which they decentred and unsettled themselves. One way of doing so was their constant attention to listening to what the Cayuga elders wanted. For settler subjects, to *not* be able to act as autonomous agents in control, especially when it comes to land and money, is not necessarily an easy task. SHARE members therefore worked hard to negotiate such relationships, constantly making sure they discussed and consulted with the Cayuga and the Haudenosaunee, following appropriate protocols of respect. For example, they ensured that they took the time to engage in appropriate formal protocol before they purchased the farm. If we use the wampum metaphor, SHARE members constantly worked to respectfully occupy the beads in the rows in between. But this sometimes meant giving over to uncertainty and loss of control.

Indeed, following the lead of Elders required learning to change ingrained Western habits, one of which is a binary and oppositional approach to conflict. Brooke says, "As soon as SHARE became solidified and Birdie came on board as our mentor, Birdie made it very clear that we were never to engage in...negative discourses. That we were to use a good mind." This meant never talking negatively about others, even one's supposed enemies. They did not want to reproduce the oppositional dualisms we have seen in UCE and CKCN discourses. Nevertheless, as Jack narrates in a story about the early days of SHARE, he had some difficulty learning this new way of relating.

> I was at one of these Voices of the Land Claim sessions, and there was an academic on stage. They had members of UCE on stage, they had Native people on stage ... and the academic was talking about how important UCE was as an organization, how they were asking all kinds of really important questions that needed to be asked, how they were providing this really important function in the community. I got really upset. And sometimes I have outbursts when I get upset in public settings, and I went up there and I said, "Can't you see that this is just a racist organization? All you have to do is read their literature to know they're a bunch of racists!"
>
> Then I felt really bad.... Connie Talcott from UCE said, "This is why we can't have a decent dialogue on this issue because of people like that." I felt really bad; I felt kinda stupid that I had had this outburst. And I said [to myself], "Oh Jack, why can't you just keep your mouth shut sometimes? You just kind of go bursting off at the seams."

Here, it is possible to see the difficult process of trying to decenter and follow Birdie's direction not to be oppositional and negative — to use the "good mind."

However, opposition is still enticing, and not only for Jack. He said that afterwards, when he was still feeling bad about blowing up,

> a whole bunch of Onondagas came over to me and gave this big group hug. And they said, "Thank you, thank you. We were sitting there thinking, who's going to speak up for us? And you did, you came right out." And I thought, alright. For me that was really important to see ... Now these people, nobody is really defending them against this stuff. There really needs to be people learning about what is really going on here.

The urges to use binary oppositions and heroically defend the Onondaga, while at the same time wanting to use the "good mind," were contradictory and not comfortable. Such discomfort nevertheless engendered a learning process for Jack and for SHARE. Jack continued:

> So I've really changed — I think we've changed our discourse a lot on UCE in general: To start to talk about them as people who are trying to make ends meet in a really depressed economy, and they can't and they're frustrated and they don't know who to be angry at — and there are politicians pointing them to native people as a convenient scapegoat. And that's not the discourse I started out with — I started out with, "These people are overt racists," and I had to develop and come around to this softer discourse about people, which I think is closer to the truth.

When I was talking about this with Jack and Brooke, I could still feel the tensions between Jack himself wanting to heroically defend the Onondaga by attacking UCE as "racists," and both of them committing to using the "good mind" as members of SHARE. One irony is that SHARE's long connection with the Onondaga began at that meeting in which Jack had his outburst. Jack said that they told him that they had been wondering about SHARE because they didn't know where we were "coming from." Jack felt that it was his outburst that let them know. Jack concluded, "Sometimes it takes a little outburst to know where you really stand." In this way we can see that such processes of learning are filled with ironies and contradictions. There can be no absolute certainty about the singular right way.

I also experienced moments of discomfort and learning that have made me confront how my own common-sense thinking and behaviour could unintentionally reproduce settler epistemologies. Indeed, sometimes "giving over" to learning new epistemologies requires being reminded that we are different, that we cannot "become Indigenous" or even understand other epistemologies simply by being curious and empathetic. Often such messages were communicated in subtle yet firm ways that reminded me, uncomfortably, of the differences between us. Frieda, for example, laughed when, at the beginning of an interview with her, I casually asked *how many acres* the Onondaga have. She responded:

> Don't ask "how many"! "How many" is one of those [ideas] ... from *your* culture. So I never have "how many" answers. Sorry about that ... We say this is what we *occupy*.

As I reflected on my seemingly "polite" question, she told a story about measuring borders that explained something important about different epistemologies. She said,

> Every year the state calls up our secretary's office and says, "Would you tell me where your borders are?" We refuse. Because if we said "these nine square miles of land that we are occupying at the moment was *it*," then they'd say, "On this date in 2000-and whatever, you said that this is what your land *is*." They'd just throw it back in our faces, so we know not to do that. Every year they ask … hoping that somebody will make a boo-boo. (Laughter)

Frieda here gently draws a line between us, not as individuals *per se*, but as members of cultures with different epistemologies. She reminds me that even such a casual question can embody epistemologies of measurement, boundaries and property ownership that were so central to colonialism, and that still frame the everyday life of the Doctrine of Discovery with which the Onondaga are forced to contend. Had I not realized that the Onondaga were in court, arguing for the idea of title as responsibility of occupation instead of bounded and certain ownership? The land rights case proposes that they have title to and responsibility for — but not ownership or possession of — a vast territory. My casual question took for granted the frameworks of the Doctrine of Discovery in terms of measurement, illustrating that fixed boundaries of ownership are part of my everyday life too. They are part of the settler jurisdictional imaginary I had unconsciously take on. My question, for Frieda, replicated the tricky jurisdictional move that New York State enacted yearly to try to fix and limit Onondaga territory. The epistemology of "how many" underpins both of those moves. Therefore, asking and expecting particular forms of certainty can be an unconscious and unintended, yet still oppressive, move. Such moments in which unconscious yet powerful frameworks are revealed as culturally specific (and not in a good way) are integral to making space for learning a complex and nuanced approach to difference, autonomy *and* interconnection. Frieda's comments about not counting the acres, and the importance of keeping the numbers uncertain, also mirrors the BC Indian Chiefs' statement about certainty that I cited at the end of Chapter 2.

We cannot know in the long run whether or not the Onondaga Nation's approach to working through Indigenous–non-Indigenous relations concerning land will be successful, legally, politically or culturally. This also, of course, depends on one's definition of "successful." One day when Clan Mother Frieda Jacques and I were talking about what she hopes might happen in terms of relationships between peoples through the land rights action, she showed me a poem by Robin Kimmerer, and asked me to put it in my book. It is now the epilogue to this study.

Already the local response to the Onondaga land rights action has been significantly different than local reaction to other land claims in upper New York State. Their events are very well attended and there has been virtually no significant resistance from groups who oppose land rights such as the UCE. Perhaps it is a result of the Onondaga framing their autonomy, their territory and their relationships with their neighbours in a non-oppositional manner that denies neither histories of injustice nor their autonomy or culture. Their autonomy is relational, defined in a manner that goes beyond embedded ideas about territory and human relationships that emerge within Western property regimes. This is a fragile and courageous step towards building shared responsibility for decolonizing spaces and frameworks and for unsettling expectations of mastery.

Opponents consistently argue that land rights are dangerous because they destroy communities and turn neighbours against each other. For instance, the state of New York, in the case of the Onondaga, argued that the land rights action was inherently "disruptive." However, the Onondaga land rights action has, according to Kimmerer (2008), been "profoundly creative of community." More than anything, it has helped generate new relationships between people that also challenge colonial ontologies. The Onondaga commitment to the environment and their neighbours has helped to develop a sense of shared responsibility and transformative dialogue. Unintentionally, this land rights action has also meant that land is returning to the Onondaga. Kimmerer (2008) writes that although the Onondaga "didn't take this action with the intent of acquiring other people's lands, lands are coming to them nonetheless."

> A local businessman is calling upon the county legislature to return lakeshore lands to the Nation. Others are willingly selling lands adjacent to the reserve to protect them from suburban development. Another extraordinary example, miles from the reservation, is a beautiful old dairy farm of green meadows and maple woods. It has been in one family for generations, bestowed by New York State for services rendered in the Revolutionary War. Those well-loved acres have been passed down again and again. But the deed carries a clause written by that long-ago forebear that one day the land must be returned to "the Indians from whom it was taken." A few years ago, the last heir, now elderly, contacted the Nation to give back what was rightfully theirs. (Kimmerer 2008)

Having individuals return pieces of land is extraordinary, and is indicative of a powerful change. So much of settler and class privilege and identity centres on passing down property to family members — passing on the inheritances of settler land entitlement. To break this pattern is to unsettle powerful epistemologies of mastery. The problem is that, at the same time, it still depends on the goodwill and charity of individual others. Rights should not be dependent upon individual charity.

It is also likely that for the Onondaga it is important that they someday receive official acknowledgement by state and federal governments of past and present injustices, and thus recognition of Onondaga nationhood and autonomy: from nation to nation, as it should be. They continue to work on all aspects of their relations, collaborating locally with others around Syracuse to clean Onondaga Lake, running the land rights series, and also working to have their land rights case acknowledged more broadly. In late February 2012, the leaders of the Onondaga Nation travelled to Washington to file a petition for a writ of certiorari with the Supreme Court — seeking review of the dismissal — and hold a news conference at the National Press Club. They brought with them the original Two Row Wampum belt commissioned by George Washington to mark the 1794 Treaty of Canandaigua, a treaty which guaranteed the Six Nations of the Iroquois "the free use and enjoyment" of their land. Onondaga Faithkeeper Oren Lyons said that all Americans should be outraged by the 2010 decision of a U.S. District Court judge to reject the Onondaga Nation land rights claim filed in March 2005 (Weiner 2012).[5] That appeal was rejected on October 15, 2013, on the same grounds, on the basis of the Sherrill decision. Tadodaho Sydney Hill said that "The federal courts' inherently discriminatory ruling refused to consider the merits of our case." The "court ruled that our actions are too old and 'inherently disruptive' and, therefore, cannot be considered. We believe that the actions of New York State continue to be disruptive to the people of the Onondaga Nation" (Onondaga Nation 2014).

More recently, since the response from the U.S. courts bars the Onondaga Nation from any domestic remedy for these treaty violations, on April 15, 2014, they filed a Petition against the United States with the Inter-American Commission on Human Rights (IACHR) (Onondaga Nation 2014). Onondaga Nation General Counsel, Joe Heath, said: "We have recognized for years, that no justice would come to the Nation in U.S. courts. The struggle for healing and justice will continue; and this is no longer a land rights case — it is a land rights movement. It is time to admit these historic harms; and it is time for justice, time for healing" (Onondaga Nation 2013). The "ultimate purpose," for the assertion of its land rights, says the Onondaga Nation, "is to enable the Nation to maintain its culture and way of life, and to protect the earth and its environment for all inhabitants of central New York" (Onondaga Nation 2014).[6]

The Onondaga Nation and NOON have continued to work for healing, to organize pressure to clean up Onondaga Lake, and many other actions and events. One example is the Two Row Wampum Renewal Campaign, which NOON initiated with Onondaga Nation support in 2013, to promote the covenants of the 1613 treaty. In the campaign, people paddled from Albany, New York, to New York City, "bringing to life the principles of the Two Row," said Andy Mager of NOON, as a row of "Haudenosaunee and other native paddlers ... travel side-by-side with a row of allies" (Onondaga Nation 2013). En route they made stops at which people could learn about the Haudenosaunee people and the Two Row Wampum. This is another example of "treaty as a verb" in action, when settlers take responsibility for keeping it alive.

For me, one of the small yet poignant examples of how settler-Indigenous relationships may change slowly, yet profoundly, is the indication of a shift in perspective of one of the close neighbours of the SHARE farm. In all the years I went to visit the SHARE farm, his cornfield abutting their organic fields sported a large UCE sign declaring "NO SOVEREIGN NATION – NO RESERVATION." When I first went to visit SHARE, Jack and Brooke told me about how a few weeks earlier he had agreed, as a neighbour and despite his opposing views on land rights, to plough the vegetable garden for them. Over the years when I visited, he also often made appearances around SHAREFEST and other events. One favourite memory is how at one SHAREFEST he brought out his beautifully painted antique tractor, latched it to a hay wagon, put a straw hat on his head and proceeded to give SHAREFEST celebrants hayrides around the farm all afternoon, despite the UCE sign in his field.

Another, more recent, memory is from one of the last times I went to the SHARE farm to celebrate that it had been finally passed on to the Cayuga Nation, who finally, after 200 years, now would own (in the Western sense) territory in their homeland. On that visit I noticed that his UCE sign, which had been a permanent fixture for at least six years, had been taken off his fencepost. As I looked around, I realized that he was there, attending the celebration. This time he wasn't driving the hay wagon or standing on the sidelines. He stood chatting comfortably with a group of Cayuga men around the fire. The whole group were tanned, had calloused hands, and were wearing work clothes and work boots. It looked, from the distance, like a synchronized dance, as they gestured around them at the fences, gardens, fields, trees, birds and sky. He had always been a good neighbour.

CONCLUDING THOUGHTS

In this book I have shared my experiences of developing a more critical and nuanced approach to the often contradictory, and sometimes painful, "spectacular life" (Simpson 2011, 211) of Canadian and U.S. settler colonialism and those who challenge it, based on ethnographic study of specific local contexts. Examining relationships between Indigenous people and settler people through the lens of an ethnography of conflict about land rights resulted in my approach, which juxtaposed the material structures of settler colonialism with the emotions and subjectivities of settler-citizens. Pivotal to this approach is the concept of "settler structures of feeling." My contribution to understanding settler colonialism revolves around how I have demonstrated and theorized the roles of certainty and uncertainty (in land, territory, sovereignty, futures, boundaries) in the building and the defense of settler colonialism, and in how it may be challenged.

In *Unsettled Expectations* (especially Part One and Part Two), I worked to understand a powerful contradiction at the core of Indigenous-settler relationships, and in Part Three, I worked at untangling how to move beyond it: The contradiction lies in the tension between the repeated assertions of settler certainty — "somewhat akin to an obsessive-compulsive disorder" (Smith 2011, 111) — that I documented, and the deep anxiety that often underpins them. On one hand, the settler state and settlers (as we have seen) constantly reproduce and attempt to naturalize the idea that settlement is settled, that colonization is over, that what exists now is right and inevitable, and that the settler state and settlers are entitled to the land and their authority over its jurisdiction in the past, present and future. Yet such claims to completion, wholeness, oneness, rightness and possession of the land emerge from an ideal — a desire , a fantasy — that has not and never will be fulfilled. Macoun and Strakosch suggest that

> Settler colonialism operates as a fantasy, in the sense that it endlessly merges together its desires and reality. For example, settlers simultaneously assert colonialism to be finished while seeking to finish it, and proclaim the land to be empty in the same moment they confront an Aboriginal person. Such fantasies are animated by the intensity of our political desires and emotions, and these desires belong to individuals even as they circulate throughout society. (Macoun and Strakosch 2013, 433–4)

As I have shown, centuries of attempts to produce certainty in the naturalization and inevitability of "settledness" on another's territory reveal it as a claim and not a reality. The work needed to secure certainty, as well as the repetition and shifting flexibility of the claims, reveals the anxiety that resides at the core of those claims. Indigenous peoples refuse to go away. Their vibrant collective and individual presence will not be encompassed or extinguished. If the "post" of the "post-colonial" requires such extinguishment, it will never happen. However, the repetitive assertions of settler certainty and entitlement are, as Jo Smith (2013, 103) says, "much like an ongoing DIY project" in which the settler subject constantly works to make themselves "unstrange" (ordinary, the unmarked norm) "by scrubbing away, weeding out or transforming Indigenous presences and visibilities into recognizable conduits for the sake of the settler nation" (Jo Smith 2013, 103) and its project of attaining certain entitlement.

Fantasies of ontological and epistemological certainty, based on supposedly universal Western ideas, have been integral to the Western project of modernity since before Descartes (Bauman 1997). Perhaps, I wonder as I complete this book, the fantasies of settler certainty that I have examined here are grounded in broader fantasies of certainty that are characteristic of modernity? Perhaps the modern fantasy of ontological certainty — linked to the "certainty" of private property emerging from agrarian cultures with their exchange-based systems, leading to its certainty about the superiority of private property and Western forms of "civilization" and capitalism, and the repetitious desire for singular fixed truths and boundaries — underpins the "settled expectations" I have explored in this book. Such certainty, however, will never be more than a fantasy, a fantastic but unrealizable desire. As we know, life is not certain, and cannot be made to be. The anxiety underpinning the search for settler and modern ontological certainty, then, will also not disappear, unless we can somehow shift our (modern settler) desires so that we resist pursuing such unrealizable fantasies of certainty.

I have argued that, for settlers, embracing particular kinds of uncertainty is likely required, even necessary for decolonization. For how can we take part in receptive and respectful relationships with our Indigenous partners/neighbours if we are trapped in our obsessive-compulsive search for certainty — to alleviate and deny the anxiety at its core? Settler colonialism is not settled, and never has been, because it is untenable, will be constantly resisted, and would only continue to produce more anxiety in any case.

So perhaps somehow learning to let go of the desire for certainty might allow us (as modern settlers) to begin to find ways to develop new kinds of relationships based on actually trying to see the "other" and not enfold them within our own project of relieving anxiety, which is not only a settler problem but also a much grander problem of modernity. It is possible that facing up to such anxiety and uncertainty could open a space for hope in transforming relations — with ourselves, as well with the Indigenous people who, engaged in "an act of sharing almost unimaginable in its generosity" (Tully 2008, 244) are still willing to treaty with us.

How we might decolonize is not pre-scripted, as discussed in Part Three, and must be worked out in specific contexts. There is no tried and tested path that we can follow. Nevertheless, as I have argued, it will likely require creativity, respect, alert vulnerability, restraint and learning from each other about how to "treaty as a verb." It will also require the hard work of learning how to paddle a metaphorical canoe without crashing into our neighbours' paths and taking over their canoes. To be able to even take a step into the treaty canoe, we settlers might first have to unsettle our expectations of certainty about the origin, the route and the destination, and learn to embrace the uncertainty of the voyage. Decolonization will take shape in ways "which we cannot now know" (Jo Smith 2013) but must entail creating a world in which we all want to live. If this is the case, the only certainty is knowing that, in order to continue to live here together on this planet, we must find ways to have good relationships with the land and with each other.

Notes

1   Jones (2008, 480) writes: "A desire to learn from otherness is in tension with the more common desire to make room for the voices of the other. The liberal injunction to listen to the Other can turn out to be *access for dominant groups* to the thoughts, cultures and lives of others," and the "imperialist resonances are uncomfortably apt." On this issue also see Simpson on "ethnographic refusal" (2007, 2014).

2   "Corn, beans and squash are commonly referred to by the Onondaga as well as all of the Haudenosaunee as the three sisters. These foods were the three foods first given to us from our mother earth" (Onondaga Nation 2007d). The three sisters are thus important both nutritionally and symbolically.

3   Regarding Haudenosaunee women's roles and *otiyaner* (Clan Mother) roles, see Horn-Miller (2005).

4   Such lateral violence within communities is not unusual, especially after centuries of colonialism (Lawrence 2004).

5   The Onondaga Nation said: "Paddling to New York City is an important facet of the Two Row Wampum Renewal. When the Haudenosaunee and Dutch met, there were significant differences between the two peoples. Despite these challenges of language, worship, governance, and culture, these two peoples forged an agreement of Peace and Friendship that would last as long as the waters run downhill, the grass grows green, and the sun rises in the east and sets in the west. Each people would carry their ways with them; one in a ship, one in a canoe as they travel down the river of life side-by-side." (Onondaga Nation 2013)

6   At the same time, the Onondaga Nation continues to assert its sovereignty: In 2015 it — as well as the Tonawanda Band of Seneca Indians of New York, and the Tuscarora Nation of New York — turned down more than $150,000 worth of federal grants intended for low-income housing. They did so "because it is viewed as inconsistent with their sovereignty," Joe Heath, general counsel for the Onondaga Nation, said. "The problem they have with any federal funding is that it comes with control and laws from another government" and would be inconsistent with the 1794 Treaty of Canandaigua (Weiner 2015).

EPILOGUE

"Even after Everything"
By Robin Kimmerer

Even after everything
You know, the history they won't tell you
The blankets
The scorched earth
The soldiers
The treaties
All broken
Even after everything

Our neighbors are still here
Still here and speaking for peace
Even after everything
The missions
The agents
The preachers
The boarding schools
That reach for the soul.

Even after everything
Our neighbors are still here
Still here and overflowing with spirit
Even after everything
The many gifts of Mother Earth still bless us

The sun, the moon
The stars, the water
The trees, the birds
The fish, the deer
Even after everything
Our neighbors are still here
Still here and living in gratitude

Even after everything
The wastebeds
The mercury
The DDT the PCBs
The salmon, the chestnut
The passenger pigeon
The lake
The creek
Witness to the wounds
Hands tied by law
Our neighbors are still here
Still here and healing the land

Let us not speak of all that was taken
But rather all that is given
The many gifts from our neighbors
Who shared with us
The roots of democracy
The rights of women and men
The three sisters who feed us
Medicines that heal us
The culture of Thanksgiving
The four white roots of peace
Self determination
Seven generations
Tonight we honor our good neighbors
Who stand among us as teachers
Even after everything.
Even after everything

Our neighbors are still here
Still here and reaching for justice
Not just for themselves
But in Audrey Shenandoah's words
Justice for the people
Justice for the land
Justice for all of creation

As our neighbors stand for justice
Let it be known that they do not stand alone
But are joined by friends
Who share these good green hills
Who breathe this air
Who grieve for the Lake
Who share their hopes
Who honor justice
And who believe that promises should be kept
And to each other
Even after everything.

— Robin Kimmerer

REFERENCES

AANDC (Aboriginal Affairs and Northern Development Canada). 2014. "Renewing the Comprehensive Land Claims Policy: Towards a Framework for Addressing Section 35 Aboriginal Rights." <aadnc-aandc.gc.ca/eng/1408631807053/1408631881247>.

____. 2010a. "Acts, Agreements, Treaties and Land Claims." <aadnc-aandc.gc.ca/eng/110 0100028568/1100100028572>.

____. 2010b. "Minister Strahl Announces Engagement Process on Renovation of Aboriginal Economic Development Programs." <aadnc-aandc.gc.ca/eng/1100100015816>.

Adams, Jim. 2006. "Supreme Court Drops Cayuga Land Claim Case: Decision Jeopardizes Historic Claims Suits." *Indian Country Today* 5/24. <indiancountrytodaymedianetwork. com/2006/05/24/supreme-court-drops-cayuga-land-claim-case-decision-jeopardizes-historic-claims-suits>

Adese, Jennifer. 2012a. "Colluding with the Enemy? Nationalism and Depictions of 'Aboriginality' in Canadian Olympic Moments." *The American Indian Quarterly*, 36 (4): 479–502.

____. 2012b. "Anxious States and the Co-Optation of Metisness." *No More Potlucks* <nomorepotlucks.org/site/anxious-states-and-the-co-optation-of-metisness-jennifer-adese/>.

Alfred, Taiaiake. 2010. "What is Radical Imagination? Indigenous Struggles in Canada." *Affinities: A Journal of Radical Theory, Culture, and Action*, 4 (2): 5–8.

____. 2009a. "Restitution Is the Real Pathway to Justice for Indigenous Peoples." In G. Younging, J. Dewar, and M. DeGagné (eds.), *Response, Responsibility, and Renewal*, 179–187. Ottawa: Aboriginal Healing Foundation.

____. 2009b. "Colonialism and State Dependency." *Journal of Aboriginal Health*, 5 (2): 42–60.

____. 2001. "From Sovereignty to Freedom: Towards an Indigenous Political Discourse." *Indigenous Affairs*, 3: 22–34.

____. 1999. *Peace, Power and Righteousness: An Indigenous Manifesto*, second edition. Don Mills: Oxford University Press.

____. 1993. "The People." In Haudenosaunee Environmental Task Force (eds.), *Words That Come Before All Else: Environmental Philosophies of the Haudenosaunee*, 8–14. New York: Native North American Travelling College.

Alfred, Taiaiake, and Jeff Corntassel. 2005. "Being Indigenous: Resurgences Against Contemporary Colonialism." *Government and Opposition*, 40 (4): 597–614.

Âpihtawikosisân. 2014. "Don't Worry, Modern Democracy Will Be Just Fine after Tsilhqot'in Decision." <rabble.ca/blogs/bloggers/apihtawikosisan/2014/07/dont-worry-modern-democracy-will-be-just-fine-after-tsilhqoti>.

Arat-Koc, Sedef. 1999. "Gender and Race in 'Non-Discriminatory' Immigration Policies in Canada: 1960s to the Present." In Enakshi Dua and Angela Robertson (eds.), *Scratching the Surface: Canadian, Anti-Racist, Feminist Thought*, 207–36. Toronto: Women's Press.

Arneil, Barbara. 1996. *John Locke and America: The Defence of English Colonialism*. Gloucestershire: Clarendon Press.

Asad, Talal. 2003. "Redeeming the 'Human' Through Human Rights." In *Formations of the Secular: Christianity, Islam, Modernity*. Stanford: Stanford University Press.

____. 1993. *Genealogies of Religion: Discipline and Reasons of Power in Christianity and Islam*. Baltimore: Johns Hopkins University Press.

Asch, Michael. 2014. *On Being Here to Stay*. Toronto: University of Toronto Press.

____. 2007. "Calder and the Representation of Indigenous Society in Canadian Jurisprudence." In Hamar Foster, Heather Raven, and Jeremy Webber (eds.), *Let Right Be Done: Aboriginal Title, the Calder Case, and the Future of Indigenous Rights*, 101–10. Vancouver: University of British Columbia Press.

____. 2002. "From Terra Nullius to Affirmation: Reconciling Aboriginal Rights with the Canadian Constitution." *Canadian Journal of Law and Society*, 17 (2): 23–39.

____. 1997. *Aboriginal and Treaty Rights in Canada: Essays on Law, Equality, and Respect for Difference*. Vancouver: University of British Columbia Press.

____ 1992a. "Errors in the Delgamuukw: An Anthropological Perspective." In Frank Cassidy (ed.), *Aboriginal Title in British Columbia: Delmuukw vs. the Queen*, 221–243. Vancouver and Montreal: Oolinchan Books and the Institute for Research on Policy.

____. 1992b. "Aboriginal Self-Government and the Construction of Canadian Constitutional Identity." *Alberta Law Review* (Constitution Series), XXX (2): 465–491.

____. 1984. *Home and Native Land: Aboriginal Rights and the Canadian Constitution*. Toronto: Methuen of Canada, Assembly of First Nations.

Asch, Michael, and Patrick Macklem. 1991. "Aboriginal Rights and Canadian Sovereignty: An Essay on R. v. Sparrow." *Alberta Law Review* XXIX (2): 498–517.

Baloy, Natalie J.K. 2015. "Spectacles and Spectres: Settler Colonial Spaces in Vancouver." *Settler Colonial Studies*, 1–26. doi: 10.1080/2201473X.2015.1018101.

Bannerji, Himani. 2000. *The Dark Side of the Nation: Essays on Multiculturalism, Nationalism and Gender*. Toronto: Canadian Scholars' Press.

Barclay, Linda. 2000. "Autonomy of the Social Self." In Catriona Mackenzie and Natalie Stoljar (eds.), *Relational Autonomy: Feminist Perspectives on Autonomy, Agency and the Social Self*, 52–71. New York: Oxford University Press.

Barker, Adam J. 2013. "An Open Letter to My Settler People." *Cultivating Alternatives*. <cultivatingalternatives.com/2013/03/04/an-open-letter-to-my-settler-people-adam-barker/>.

____. 2009. "The Contemporary Reality of Canadian Imperialism, Settler Colonialism, and the Hybrid Colonial State." *The American Indian Quarterly*, 33 (3): 325–351.

Basset, William. 1986. "The Myth of the Nomad in Property Law." *Journal of Law and*

Religion, 4 (1): 133–152.

Battiste, Marie, and James Youngblood Henderson. 2009. "Naturalizing Indigenous Knowledge in Eurocentric Education." *Canadian Journal of Native Education,* 32 (1): 5–18.

Bauman, Zygmunt. 1997. *Postmodernity and its Discontents.* New York: New York University Press.

____. 1991. *Modernity and Ambivalence.* Ithaca: Cornell University Press.

Beck, Ulrich. 2000. "Risk Society Revisited: Theory, Politics and Research Programs." In Barbara Adam, Ulrich Beck, and Joost Van Loon (eds.), *The Risk Society and Beyond: Critical Issues for Social Theory,* 211–29. London: Sage.

____. 1992. "From Industrial Society to the Risk Society." *Theory, Culture & Society,* 9 (1): 97–123.

Beck, Ulrich, Anthony Giddens and Scott Lash. 1994. *Reflexive Modernization: Politics, Tradition and Aesthetics in the Modern Social Order.* Stanford, CA: Stanford University Press.

Bell, Avril. 2008. "Recognition or Ethics?" *Cultural Studies,* 22 (6): 850–69.

Bell, Catherine, and Michael Asch. 1997. "Challenging Assumptions: The Impact of Precedent in Aboriginal Rights Litigation." In Michael Asch (ed.), *Aboriginal and Treaty Rights in Canada: Essays on Law, Equality, and Respect for Difference,* 38–74. Vancouver: University of British Columbia Press.

Benda-Beckmann, Franz Von, Keebet Von Benda-Beckmann and Melanie Wiber. 2009. "The Properties of Property." In Keebet Von Benda-Beckman, Franz Von Benda-Beckmann, and Melanie G. Wiber (eds.), *Changing Properties of Property,* 1–39. New York: Berghan Books.

Bentham, Jeremy. 1978a. "Property." In Crawford B. Macpherson (ed.), *Property: Mainstream and Critical Positions.* Toronto: University of Toronto Press.

____. 1978b. "Security and Equality of Property." In Crawford B. Macherson (ed.), *Property: Mainstream and Critical Positions,* 39-58. Toronto: University of Toronto Press.

____. 1931 [1802]. *The Theory of Legislation.* London: Routledge.

Berger, L. 1985. "An Analysis of the Doctrine that First in Time Is First in Right." *Nebraska Law Review,* 64: 349–88.

Berkey, Curtis. 2005-6. "City of Sherrill v. Oneida Indian Nation." *American Indian Law Review,* 30 (2): 373–384.

Berman, M. 1988. *All That Is Solid Melts into Air: The Experience of Modernity.* New York: Penguin Books.

Bhandar, Brenna. 2015a. "Possession, Occupation and Registration: Recombinant Ownership in the Settler Colony." *Settler Colonial Studies,* 1–14. doi:10.1080/22014 73X.2015.1024366.

____. 2015b. "Title by Registration: Instituting Modern Property Law and Creating Racial Value in the Settler Colony." *Journal of Law and Society,* 42 (2): 253–82.

____. 2011. "Plasticity and Post-Colonial Recognition: 'Owning, Knowing and Being.'" *Law Critique,* 22: 227–249.

Bhandar, Davina, Doreen Fumia and Zoe Newman (eds.). 2008. "Decolonizing Spaces/ Espaces Decolonisants." *Resources for Feminist Research (Special Issue),* 2 (1).

Biermann, Soenke. 2011. "Knowledge, Power and Decolonization: Implication for

Non-Indigenous Scholars, Researchers and Educators." In George J. Sefa Dei (ed.), *Indigenous Philosophies and Critical Education: A Reader*, 386–98. New York: Peter Lang Publishing.

Biolsi, Thomas. 2007 [2001]. *Deadliest Enemies: Law and Race Making on and off the Rosebud Reservation*. Minnesota: University of Minnesota Press.

Black, Kelly. 2015. "Extracting Northern Knowledge: Tracing the History of Post-Secondary Education in the Northwest Territories and Nunavut." *Northern Review,* (40): 35–61. <journals.sfu.ca/nr/index.php/nr/article/view/462>.

Black, Kelly, and Amanda Murphao. 2015. "Unsettling Settler Belonging: (Re)naming and Territory-Making in the Pacific Northwest." *American Review of Canadian Studies,* 45 (3). <tandfonline.com/doi/pdf/10.1080/02722011.2015.1063523>.

Blackburn, Carole. 2005. "Searching for Guarantees in the Midst of Uncertainty: Negotiating Aboriginal Rights and Title in British Columbia." *American Anthropologist,* 107 (4): 586–96.

Blomley, Nicholas. 2008. "Simplification Is Complicated: Property, Nature, and the Rivers of Law." *Environment and Planning,* A, 40: 1825–1840.

____. 2004. *Unsettling the City: Urban Land and the Politics of Property*. New York and London: Routledge.

Boler, Megan. 1999. *Feeling Power: Emotions and Education*, 175–195. New York: Routledge.

Borrows, John. 2010. *Canada's Indigenous Constitution*. Toronto: University of Toronto.

____. 2008. "Seven Generations, Seven Teachings: Ending the Indian Act." Research Paper for the National Centre for First Nations Governance. <fngovernance.org/research/index.htm>.

____. 2002. *Recovering Canada: The Resurgence of Indigenous Law*. Toronto: University of Toronto Press.

____. 1999. "Sovereignty's Alchemy: An Analysis of Delgamuukw v. British Columbia." *Osgoode Hall Law Journal,* 37 (3): 538–96.

____. 1997. "Wampum at Niagara." In Michael Asch (ed.), *Aboriginal and Treaty Rights in Canada: Essays on Law, Equity, and Respect*, 154–72. Vancouver, BC: University of British Columbia Press.

Brace, Laura. 2004. *The Politics of Property: Labour, Freedom and Belonging*. New York and Basingstoke: Palgrave MacMillan.

Brandão, José António. 2010. "Covenant Chain." *The Encyclopedia of New York State.* <syracuseuniversitypress.syr.edu/encyclopedia/entries/convenant-chain.html>.

Brodie, Janine. 1998. "Restructuring and the Politics of Marginalization." In Caroline Andrew and Manon Tremblay (eds.), *Women and Political Representation in Canada,* 19–37. Ottawa: University of Ottawa Press.

Bruyneel, Kevin. 2007. *The Third Space of Sovereignty: The Postcolonial Politics of U.S.-Indigenous Relations*. Minneapolis: University of Minnesota Press.

Brydon, Diana. 2006, "Is There a Politics of Postcoloniality?" *Postcolonial Text* 2 (1). N.p. <postcolonial.org/index.php/pct/article/viewArticle/508/852>.

Byrd, Jodi A. 2011. *The Transit of Empire: Indigenous Critiques of Colonialism*. University of Minnesota Press.

Cairns, Allan. 2000. *Citizens Plus: Aboriginal Peoples and the Canadian State*. Vancouver and Toronto: University of British Columbia Press.

Caldwell, Lynn, Carianne Leung and Darryl Leroux. 2013. *Critical Inquiries: A Reader in Studies of Canada.* Halifax and Winnipeg: Fernwood Publishing.

Calhoun, Craig. 2006. "The Privatization of Risk." *Public Culture,* 18 (2): 257–263.

Cameron, Emilie. 2015. *Far Off Metal River: Inuit Lands, Settler Stories, and the Making of the Contemporary Arctic.* Vancouver: University of British Columbia Press.

____. 2011. "Reconciliation with Indigenous Ghosts: On the Politics of Postcolonial Ghost Stories." In May Chazan et al. (eds.), Unsettling Multiculturalism: Lands, Labours, Bodies, 142–154. Toronto: Between the Lines Press.

____. 2008. "Cultural Geography Essay: Indigenous Spectrality and the Politics of Post-Colonial Ghost Stories." *Cultural Geographies,* 15 (3): 383–393.

Cattelino, Jessica. 2008. *High Stakes: Florida Seminole Gaming and Sovereignty.* Durham, NC: Duke University Press.

Cayuga Nation of New York. 2009. "Cayuga Nation: The People of the Great Swamp, Tribal History." <cayuganation-nsn.gov/About/TribalHistory>.

____. 2014. "Cayuga Nation." <cayuganation-nsn.gov>.

Christie, Gordon. 2007a. "Aboriginal Nationhood and the Inherent Right to Self Government." *Research Paper for the National Centre for First Nations Governance,* Ottawa. <fngovernance.org/ncfng_research/gordon_christie.pdf>.

____. 2007b. "Culture, Self-Determination and Colonialism: Issues Around the Revitalization of Indigenous Legal Traditions." *Indigenous Law Journal,* 6 (1): 13–30.

____. 2005. "A Colonial Reading of Recent Jurisprudence: Sparrow, Delgamuukw and Haida Nation, 23." *Windsor Yearbook of Access to Justice.*

Chunn, Dorothy E., and Shelley A.M. Gavigan. 2004. "Welfare Law, Welfare Fraud, and the Moral Regulation of the 'Never Deserving' Poor." *Social Legal Studies,* 13 (2): 219–43.

Churchill, Ward. 2002. "The Law Stood Squarely on Its Head: U.S. Legal Doctrine, Indigenous Self-Determination and the Question of World Order." *Oregon Law Review,* 81: 663–706.

The Citizen. 2012. "Court Rejects Onondaga Nation's Land Claim." October 20. <auburnpub. com/news/local/court-rejects-onondaga-nation-s-land-claim/article_47a855f0-3b27-5d7b-a4c4-c107c02560a4.html>.

CKCN (Chatham-Kent Community Network). 1999a. "Open Letter to All Citizens of the Municipality of Chatham Kent." <blenheim.webgate.net/~ckcn/pressrelease12.html>.

____. 1999b. Submission to Jane Stewart, from CKCN. In author's possession.

Code, Lorraine. 2006. *Ecological Thinking: The Politics of Epistemic Location.* Oxford, New York: Oxford University Press.

____. 2000. "The Perversion of Autonomy and the Subjection of Women: Discourses of Social Advocacy at Century's End." In Catriona Mackenzie and Natalie Stoljar (eds.), *Relational Autonomy: Feminist Perspectives on Autonomy, Agency and the Social Self,* 181–209. New York: Oxford University Press.

____. 1991. "Chapter Three: Second Persons." In *What Can She Know? Feminist Theory and the Construction of Knowledge,* 7–109. Ithaca, NY: Cornell University Press.

Coleman, Daniel. 2006. *White Civility: The Literary Project of English Canada.* Toronto: University of Toronto Press.

Colloredo-Mansfeld, Rudi. 2002. "Autonomy and Interdependence in Native Movements: Towards a Pragmatic Politics in the Ecuadorian Andes." *Identities,* 9: 173–95.

Cook, Frederick (ed.). 2000 [1887]. *Journal of the Military Expedition of Major General John Sullivan Against the Six Nations of Indians in 1779 with Records of the Centennial Celebrations*. New York: Heritage Books.

Corntassel, Jeff. 2012. "Re-Envisioning Resurgence: Indigenous Pathways to Decolonization and Sustainable Self-Determination." *Decolonization: Indigeneity, Education & Society*, 1 (1): 86–101.

Corntassel, Jeff, Richard C. Witmer II and Lindsay Robertson. 2008. *Forced Federalism: Contemporary Challenges to Indigenous Nationhood*. Norman: University of Oklahoma Press.

Coulthard, Glen. 2014. *Red Skin, White Masks: Rejecting the Colonial Politics of Recognition*. Minneapolis: University of Minnesota Press.

____. 2010. "Place Against Empire: Understanding Indigenous Anti-Colonialism." *Affinities: A Journal of Radical Theory, Culture, and Action*, 4 (2): 79–83.

____. 2007. "Subjects of Empire: Indigenous Peoples and the 'Politics of Recognition' in Canada." *Contemporary Political Theory*, 6: 437–460.

Cowlishaw, Gillian. 2004. *Blackfellas, Whitefellas and the Hidden Injuries of Race*. Oxford: Blackwell Publishing.

____. 1999. *Rednecks, Eggheads and Blackfellas: Racial Power and Intimacy in North Australia*. Sydney and Ann Arbor: Allen and Unwin with Michigan University Press.

Cowlishaw, Gillian, and Barry Morris (eds.). 1997. *Race Matters: Indigenous Australians and 'Our' Society*. Canberra: Aboriginal Studies Press.

Crouch, Simon. 1998. "Native Reserve Plan Divides Neighbours." *London Free Press*, Dec 22.

Culhane, Dara. 1998. *The Pleasure of the Crown: Anthropology, Law and First Nations*. Burnaby: Talon Books.

Davies, Margaret. 1999. "Queer Property, Queer Persons: Self-Ownership and Beyond." *Social and Legal Studies*, 8 (3): 327–52.

Davis, Lynne. 2010. *Alliances: Re/Envisioning Indigenous-Non-Indigenous Relationships*. Toronto: University of Toronto Press.

Dean, Jodi. 2013. "Collective Desire and the Pathology of the Individual." In Atne De Boever and Walren Neidic (eds.), *The Psychopathologies of Cognitive Capitalism, Part One*, 69–88. Berlin: Archive Books.

Debo, Angie. 1984 [1940]. *And Still the Waters Run: The Betrayal of the Five Civilized Tribes*. Norman: University of Oklahoma Press.

Dei, George J. Sefa. 2002. "Situating Spirituality in the Agenda for Transformative Learning." In Edmund V. O'Sullivan, Amish Morrell and Mary Ann O'Connor (eds.), *Expanding the Boundaries of Transformative Learning: Essays on Theory and Praxis*, 121–33. New York: Palgrave.

Diabo, Russell. 2015. "The Tsilhqot'in Decision and Canada's First Nations Termination Policies." *New Socialist Webzine*. <newsocialist.org/782-the-tsilhqot-in-decision-and-canada-s-first-nations-termination-policies>.

____. 2012. "Harper Launches Major First Nations Termination Plan: As Negotiating Tables Legitimize Canada's Colonialism." *Intercontinental Cry*. <intercontinentalcry.org/harper-launches-major-first-nations-termination-plan-as-negotiating-tables-legitimize-canadas-colonialism/>.

Diabo, Russell, and Shiri Pasternak. 2015. "Canada Responds to Tsilhqot'in

Decision: Extinguishment or Nothing!" *New Socialist Webzine.* <newsocialist. org/787-canada-responds-to-tsilhqot-in-decision-extinguishment-or-nothing>.

____. 2011. "Canada Has Had First Nations Under Surveillance: Harper Government Has Prepared for First Nations 'Unrest.'" *First Nations Strategic Bulletin* 9 (1–5): 1–23. <scribd.com/doc/57561401/First-Nations-Strategic-Bulletin-Jan-May-2011>.

Donnelly, Jack. 1990. "Human Rights and Western Liberalism." In Abdullah Ahmed An-Nacim and Francis M. Deng (ed.), *Human Rights in Africa: Cross-Cultural Perspectives,* 31–55. Washington, DC: The Brookings Institute.

Douglas, Mary. 1992. *Risk and Blame: Essays in Cultural Theory.* London: Routledge.

____. 1990. "Risk as a Forensic Resource." *Daedalus,* 119 (4): 1–16.

Edgerton, Ellen. 2006. "NYCO's blog." <silent-edge.org/wp/?p=232>.

Emberley, Julia. 2007. *Defamiliarizing the Aboriginal: Cultural Practices and Decolonization in Canada.* Toronto: University of Toronto Press.

Epp, Roger. 2003. "We Are all Treaty People: History, Reconciliation and the 'Settler Problem.'" In Carol A.L. Prager and Trudy Govier (eds.), *Dilemmas of Reconciliation: Cases and Concepts,* 223–244. Waterloo: Wilfred Laurier University Press.

Epstein, Richard A. 1979. "Possession as the Root of Title." *Georgia Law Review,* 13: 1221–43.

Eyford, Douglas R. 2015. "A New Direction: Advancing Aboriginal and Treaty Rights." Report of the Ministerial Special Representative on Renewing the Comprehensive Land Claims Policy to AAND Minister Valcourt. <aadnc-aandc.gc.ca/eng/142616919 9009/1426169236218>

Faux, Jeff. 1999. "Lost on the Third Way." *Dissent* (Spring): 67–76.

Feit, Harvey. 2004a. "James Bay Crees' Life Projects and Politics: Histories of Place, Animal Partners and Enduring Relationships." In Mario Blaser, Harvey A. Feit and Glenn McRae (eds.), *In the Way of Development: Indigenous peoples, Life Projects and Globalization,* 92–110. London and New York: Zed Press.

____. 2004b. "Contested Identities of 'Indians' and 'Whitemen' at James Bay, or the Power of Reason, Hybridity and Agency." *Senri Ethnological Studies* (Osaka; Special Issue on Circumpolar Ethnicity and Identity), 66: 109–26.

Fitzmaurice, Andrew. 2006. "The Great Australian History Wars." <usyd.edu.au/news/84. html?newsstoryid=948>.

Fletcher, Matthew L.M., Kathryn E. Fort and Nicholas J. Reo. 2014. "Tribal Disruption and Indian Claims." MSU Legal Studies Research Paper No. 11-26, *Michigan Law Review,* 112: 65–72. <papers.ssrn.com/sol3/papers.cfm?abstract_id=2388342-%23>.

Fort, Kathryn. 2011. "Disruption and Possibility: The New Laches and the Unfortunate Resolution of the Modern Iroquois Land Claims." *Wyoming Law Review,* 11 (2): 375–405.

____. 2008–9. "The New Laches: Creating Title Where None Existed." MSU Legal Studies Research Paper No. 06–15; 16: 1–55. <digitalcommons.law.msu.edu/cgi/viewcontent. cgi?article=1372&context=facpubs>.

Francis, Margot. 2011. *Creative Subversions: Whiteness, Indigeneity, and the National Imaginary.* Vancouver: UBC Press.

Frank, Steven. 2000. "Getting Angry Over Native Rights." *Time Magazine* (Canada) 155 (20): 16–24.

Frankenberg, Ruth. 1993. *White Women, Race Matters: The Social Construction of Whiteness.* Minnesota: University of Minnesota Press.

Friends of Ganondagan. 2010. "Wampum." Ganondagan. <ganondagan.org/wampum.html>.

Furniss, Elizabeth. 1999. *The Burden of History: Colonialism and the Frontier Myth in a Rural Canadian Community.* Vancouver: University of British Columbia Press.

Giddens, Anthony. 1990. *The Consequences of Modernity.* Cambridge: Polity Press.

Gilmour, R.J., Davina Bhandar, Jeet Heer and Michael C.K. Ma (eds.). 2012. *"Too Asian?" Racism, Privilege, and Post-Secondary Education.* Toronto: Between the Lines.

Goldstein, Alyosha. 2008. "Where the Nation Takes Place: Proprietary Regimes, Antistatism, and U.S. Settler Colonialism." *South Atlantic Quarterly,* 107 (4) (Fall): 834–861.

Government of Canada. 2008. "Final Agreement and Background Information about Nisga'a Agreement: Certainty." Department of Aboriginal Affairs and Northern Development. Vancouver, November 10. <ainc-inac.gc.ca/al/ldc/ccl/fagr/nsga/nfa/cty-eng.asp>.

____ 2006. "Caldwell First Nation and the Government of Canada Move Ahead with Claim Settlement Process." Department of Aboriginal Affairs and Northern Development. Press Release, Ottawa, October 6. <aadnc-aandc.gc.ca/aiarch/mr/nr/s-d2006/2-02788-eng.asp>.

____. 2005. "Canada's Responses to the List of Issues: Presentation of the Fifth Report on the International Covenant on Civil and Political Rights." Human Rights Committee. <pch.gc.ca/ddp-hrd/docs/reponses-responses/index-eng.cfm>.

____. 1998. "Nisga'a Final Agreement: Nisga'a Nation, Federal Crown and Provincial Crown." Aboriginal Affairs and Northern Development. <aadnc-aandc.gc.ca/eng/1100100031252>.

Hahn, C. M. 1998. "Introduction: The Embeddedness of Property." In C.M. Hahn (ed.), *Property Relations: Renewing the Anthropological Tradition,* 1–47. Cambridge, UK: Cambridge University Press.

Handler, Richard. 1988. *Nationalism and the Politics of Culture in Quebec.* Madison: University of Wisconsin Press.

Hansen, Brooke, and Jack Rossen. 2007. "Building Bridges Through Public Anthropology in the Haudenosaunee Homeland." In John H. Jameson and Sherene Baugher (eds.), *Past Meets Present: Archeologists Partnering with Museum Curators, Teachers, and Community Groups,* 127–48. New York: Springer.

Harris, Cheryl I. 1992–3. "Whiteness as Property." *Harvard Law Review,* 106 (8): 1707–91.

Harris, Cole. 2004. "How Did Colonialism Dispossess? Comments from an Edge of Empire." *Annals of the Association of American Geographers,* 94 (1): 165–82.

——. 2002. *Making Native Space: Colonialism, Resistance, and Reserves in British Columbia.* Vancouver and Toronto: University of British Columbia Press.

Henderson, James Sákéj Youngblood. 2002a. "Postcolonial Indigenous Legal Consciousness." *Indigenous Law Journal,* 1: 1–56.

____. 2000b. "The Context of the State of Nature." In Marie Battiste (ed.), *Reclaiming Indigenous Voice and Vision,* 11–38. Vancouver: UBC Press.

____. 2000c. "Postcolonial Ghost Dancing: Diagnosing European Colonialism." In Marie Battiste (ed.), *Reclaiming Indigenous Voice and Vision,* 57–76. Vancouver: UBC Press.

Henderson, Jennifer. 2015. "Settler Sense and Indigenous Resurgence." Keynote address at the ACQL and CACLALS conference, June. Ottawa.

____. 2013. "The Camp, the School, and the Child: Discursive Exchanges and (Neo) Liberal Axioms in the Culture of Redress." In Jennifer Henderson and Pauline Wakeham (eds.), *Reconciling Canada: Critical Perspectives on the Culture of Redress*, 63–83. Toronto: University of Toronto Press.

____. 2003. *Settler Feminism and Race Making in Canada*. Toronto: University of Toronto Press.

Henderson, Jennifer, and Pauline Wakeham (eds.). 2013. *Reconciling Canada: Critical Perspectives on the Culture of Redress*. Toronto: University of Toronto Press.

____. 2009. "Colonial Reckoning, National Reconciliation? First Peoples and the Culture of Redress in Canada." *English Studies in Canada*, 35 (1), Special Issue on Aboriginal Redress: 1–26.

Hill, Sidney. 2006a. "A Time to Heal." *The Post-Standard*, March 20.

____. 2006b. "Declaration of Tadodaho Sydney Hill, Onondaga Nation." United States District Court. Northern District of New York. The Onondaga Nation v. The State of New York, et al., Civil Action No. 05-CV-314.

Hill, Susan M. 2008. "Traveling Down the River of Life Together in Peace and Friendship, Forever: Haudenosaunee Land Ethics and Treaty Agreements as the Basis for Restructuring the Relationship with the British Crown." In Leanne Simpson (ed.), *Lighting the Eighth Fire: The Liberation, Resurgence and Protection of Indigenous Nations*, 23–45. Winnipeg: Arbiter Ring Publishing.

Hobbes, Thomas. 1651. *Of Man, Being the First Part of Leviathan* (e-Book). Hoboken, NJ: BiblioBytes.

Holmes, Joan, and Associates. 1994. "Caldwell First Nation Report." Prepared for the Indian Commission of Ontario. November 1994. Author received hand-marked copy from Pickard's office.

Horn-Miller, Kahente. 2010. "From Paintings to Power: The Meaning of the Warrior Flag Twenty Years after Oka." *Socialist Studies*, 6 (1): 96–124.

____. 2005. "Otiyaner: The 'Women's Path' Through Colonialism." *Atlantis: Critical Studies in Gender, Culture* 29 (2): 57–68.

Hugill, David, and Owen Toews. 2014. "Born Again Urbanism: New Missionary Incursions, Aboriginal Resistance and Barriers to Rebuilding Relationships in Winnipeg's North End." Human Geography, 7 (1): 69–84.

INAC (Indigenous and Northern Affairs Canada). 2010. "Land Claims." <aadnc-aandc. gc.ca/eng/1100100030285/1100100030289>.

Indian Law Resource Center. 2010. "Projects: Onondaga." Indian Law Centre Website. <indianlaw.org/en/projects/landrights/Onondaga>.

Indigenous Knowledge Forum. 2004. "Ipperwash Public Inquiry." Transcript (draft version only held at Forest, Ontario).

Innisfil Public Library. 2009. "Chapter 9: The Iroquois." The Native Peoples of Simcoe County. <innisfil.library.on.ca/natives/natives/chp9.htm>.

Irlbacher-Fox, Stephanie 2012. "#IdleNoMore: Settler Responsibility for Relationship." Blog associated with the journal *Decolonization: Indigeneity, Education & Society*. <decolonization. wordpress.com/2012/12/27/idlenomore-settler-responsibility-for-relationship/>.

Iseke-Barnes, Judy. 2008. "Pedagogies for Decolonizing." *Canadian Journal of Native Education,* 31 (1): 123–48.

Jacobs, Margaret D. 2009. *White Mother to a Dark Race: Settler Colonialism, Maternalism, and the Removal of Indigenous Children in the American West and Australia, 1880–1940.* Lincoln: University of Nebraska Press.

Jemison, Peter G., and Anna M. Schein (eds.). 2000. *Treaty of Canadaigua 1794: 200 Years of Treaty Relations Between the Iroquois Confederacy and the United States.* New York: Clear Light Publishers.

Jenkins, Christopher D. 2001. "John Marshall's Aboriginal Rights Theory and Its Treatment in Canadian Jurisprudence." *The University of British Columbia Law Review* 35: 1–42.

Johnson, Larry. 1999. "Letter to the Municipality." *Ridgetown Independent.*

Johnson Reagon, Bernice. 1983. "Coalition Politics: Turning the Century." In Barbara Smith (ed.), *Home Girls: A Black Feminist Anthology,* 356–368. New York: Kitchen Table—Women of Color Press.

Jones, Allison, with Kuni Jenkins. 2008. "Rethinking Collaboration: Working the Indigenous-Colonizer Hyphen." In Norman K. Denzin, Yvonna S. Lincoln and Linda Tuhiwai Smith (eds.), *Handbook of Critical Indigenous Methodologies,* 471–486. New York: Sage Publications.

Kimmerer, Robin. 2008. "The Rights of the Land: The Onondaga Nation of Central New York Proposes a Radical New Vision of Property Rights." *Orion Magazine* (November/ December). Great Barrington, MA.

Krakoff, Sarah. 2005. "City of Sherrill vs. Oneida Indian Nation of New York: A Regretful Postscript to the Taxation Chapter in *Cohen's Handbook of Federal Indian Law.*" *Tulsa Law Review,* 41 (1): 5–20.

Kuokkanen, Rauna. 2010. "The Responsibility of the Academy: A Call for Doing Homework." *Journal of Curriculum Theorizing* 26 (3): 61–74.

Laforme, Harry S. 1991. "Indian Sovereignty: What Does it Mean?" *The Canadian Journal of Native Studies,* 11 (2): 254–66.

Lalonde, Theresa, and Dick Gordon. 1999. "Ontario Report." CBC's *This Morning.* January 21. Transcript by Media Reach.

Landsman, Gail. 1988. *Sovereignty and Symbol: Indian-White Conflict at Ganienkeh.* Albuquerque: University of New Mexico Press.

Larner, Wendy. 2000. "Neo-Liberalism: Policy, Ideology, Governmentality." *Studies in Political Economy,* 63: 5–25.

Lawrence, Bonita. 2004. *"Real" Indians and Others: Mixed-Blood Urban Native Peoples and Indigenous Nationhood.* Vancouver: University of British Columbia Press.

Lawrence, Bonita, and Dua Enakshi. 2011. "Decolonizing Anti-Racism." In Ashok Mathur, Jonathan Dewar, and Mike DeGagne (eds.), *Cultivating Canada: Reconciliation Through the Lens of Cultural Diversity,* 233–262. Ottawa: Aboriginal Healing Foundation. <ahf. ca/downloads/cultivating-canada-pdf.pdf>.

Lindberg, Tracy. 2010. "The Doctrine of Discovery in Canada." In Robert J. Miller, Jacinta Ruru, Larissa Behrendt and Tracey Lindberg (eds.), *Discovering Indigenous Lands: The Doctrine of Discovery in the English Colonies,* 89–125. Oxford: Oxford University Press.

Lloyd, Genevieve. 2000. "Responsibility and the Philosophical Imagination." In Catriona Mackenzie and Natalie Stoljar (eds.), *Relational Autonomy: Feminist Perspectives on*

Autonomy, Agency and the Social Self, 112–28. New York: Oxford University Press.

Locke, John. 1690. *Second Treatise on Government* (e-Book). Raleigh, N.C.

Lowman, Emma Battall, and Adam J. Barker. 2015. *Settler: Identity and Colonialism in 21st Century Canada.* Halifax: Fernwood Publishing.

Lueck, Dean. 1998. "First Possession." *The New Palgrave Dictionary of Economics and the Law.* Palgrave Macmillan.

Lupton, Deborah. 1999. *Risk.* London & New York: Sage Publishers.

Mackenzie, Catriona, and Natalie Stoljar. 2000. "Introduction: Autonomy Refigured." In Catriona Mackenzie and Natalie Stoljar (eds.), *Relational Autonomy: Feminist Perspectives on Autonomy, Agency and the Social Self,* 3–31. New York: Oxford University Press.

Mackey, Eva. 2014. "Unsettling Expectations: (Un)certainty, Settler States of Feeling, Law, and Decolonization." *Canadian Journal of Law and Society / Revue Canadienne Droit et Société,* 29: 235–252.

____. 2013. "The Apologizers' Apology." In Jennifer Henderson and Pauline Wakeham (eds.), *Reconciling Canada: Historical Injustices and the Contemporary Culture of Redress,* 47–62. Toronto: University of Toronto Press.

____. 2005. "'Universal' Rights in National and Local Conflicts: 'Backlash' and 'Benevolent Resistance' to Indigenous Land Rights." *Anthropology Today,* 21 (2): 14–20.

____. 2002. *The House of Difference: Cultural Politics and National Identity in Canada.* Toronto: University of Toronto Press.

____. 1999a. "Constructing an Endangered Nation: Risk, Race and Rationality in Australia's Native Title Debate." In Deborah Lupton (ed.), *Risk and Sociocultural Theory: New Directions and Perspectives.* Cambridge University Press.

____. 1999b. "As Good as It Gets? Apology, Colonialism and White Innocence." *Olive Pink Society Bulletin,* 11 (1): 34–40.

____. 1998. "Becoming Indigenous: Land, Belonging, and the Appropriation of Aboriginality in Canadian Nationalist Narratives." *Social Analysis,* 42 (2): 149–78.

Macklem, Patrick. 2001. *Indigenous Difference and the Constitution of Canada.* Toronto: University of Toronto Press.

MacMillan, Ken. 2006. *Sovereignty and Possession in the English New World: The Legal Foundations of Empire, 1576–1640.* Cambridge: Cambridge University Press.

Macoun, Alissa, and Elizabeth Strakosch. 2013. "The Ethical Demands of Settler Colonial Theory." *Settler Colonial Studies,* 3 (3–4): 426–443.

Macpherson, Crawford B. 1978. "The Meaning of Property." In Crawford B. Macpherson (ed.), *Property: Mainstream and Critical Positions,* 1–14. Toronto: University of Toronto Press.

Manno, Jack, and Irving Powless Jr. 2008. "Brightening the Covenant Chain: The Onondaga Land Rights Action and Neighbors of the Onondaga Nation." In Klaus Bosselman, Ron Engel and Prue Taylor (eds.), *Governance for Sustainability: Issues, Challenges, Successes,* 149–58. Gland, Switzerland: IUCN.

Manuel, Arthur, and Ronald M. Derrickson. 2015. *Unsettling Canada: A National Wake-Up Call.* Toronto: Between the Lines Press.

Manuel, George, and Michael Posluns. 1974. *The Fourth World: an Indian Reality.* Foreword by Vine Deloria Jr. New York: The Free Press.

Marcus, Julie. 1999. *A Dark Smudge Upon the Sand: Essays on Race, Guilt and the National*

Consciousness. Sydney: LHR Press.

____. 1997. "The Journey Out to the Centre: The Cultural Appropriation of Ayers Rock." In Gillian Cowlishaw and Barry Morris (eds.), *Race Matters: Indigenous Australians and 'Our' Society*, 29–51. Canberra: Aboriginal Studies Press.

Marris, Peter. 1996. *The Politics of Uncertainty: Attachment in Private and Public Life*. London and New York: Routledge.

____. 1993. "The Social Construction of Uncertainty." In Colin Murray Parkes, Joan Stevenson-Hinde, and Peter Marris (eds.), *Attachment Across the Life Cycle*, pp. 77-90. London and New York: Routledge.

Marx, Karl, and Frederick Engels. 1848. *The Communist Manifesto*. <marxists.org/archive/marx/works/download/pdf/Manifesto.pdf>.

Mawani, Renisa. 2012. "Law's Archive." *Annual Review of Law and Social Science* 8: 337–65.

____. 2009. *Colonial Proximities: Cross-Racial Encounters and Juridical Truths in British Columbia 1871-1921*. Vancouver: University of British Columbia Press.

____. 2007. "Legalities of Nature: Law, Empire, and Wilderness Landscapes in Canada." *Social Identities*, 13 (6): 715–734.

____. 2005. "Genealogies of the Land: Aboriginality, Law, and Territory in Vancouver's Stanley Park." *Social and Legal Studies*, 14 (3): 315–40.

McIvor, Bruce. 2014. "Legal Review of Canada's Interim Comprehensive Land Claims Policy for the Union of B.C. Indian Chiefs." First Peoples Law, Barristers and Solicitors. <firstpeopleslaw.com>.

McLaren, John, A.R. Buck and Nancy E. Wright (eds.). 2004. *Despotic Dominion: Property Rights in British Settler Societies*. Vancouver: University of British Columbia Press.

Merrill, Thomas W., and Henry E. Smith. 2001. "What Happened to Property in Law and Economics?" *The Yale Law Journal*, 111 (2): 357–98.

Mill, John Stuart. 1977 (1836). "Civilization." In *The Collected Works of John Stuart Mill, Vol. XVIII: Essays on Politics and Society*, 118–47. Toronto: University of Toronto Press.

Miller, James. 2000. *Skyscrapers Hide the Heavens: A History of Indian-White Relations in Canada*. Toronto: University of Toronto Press.

____. 1991. *Sweet Promises: A Reader on Indian-White Relations in Canada*. Toronto: University of Toronto Press.

Miller, Robert J. 2005. "The Doctrine of Discovery in American Indian Law." *Idaho Law Review*, 42 (1): 21–75.

Miller, Robert J., Jacinta Ruru, Larissa Behrendt and Tracey Lindberg. 2010. *Discovering Indigenous Lands: The Doctrine of Discovery in the English Colonies*. Oxford: Oxford University Press.

Mills, Aaron (Wapshkaa Ma'iingan). 2010. "Aki, Anishinaabek, kaye tahsh Crown." *Indigenous Law Journal*, 9 (1): 107–166.

Mills, Charles W. 1997. *The Racial Contract*. Ithaca and London: Cornell University Press.

Minister of Indian Affairs and Northern Development. 1999. Caldwell First Nation Claim: Canada's response to Report of Jerry Pickard, MP., including letter from Robert D. Nault to Mr. Jerry Pickard. Report in author's possession.

Mohanty, Chandra Talpade. 2003. "'Under Western Eyes' Revisited: Feminist Solidarity Through Anti-Capitalist Struggle." *Signs: Journal of Women in Culture and Society*, 28 (2): 499–535.

Mohawk, John C. 2000. "The Iroquois Land Claims: A Promise of Fairness." *Native Americas,* 17 (1): 20–23.

Monaghan, Jeffrey. 2013. "Settler Governmentality and Racializing Surveillance in Canada's North-West." *Canadian Journal of Sociology,* 38 (4): 2013.

Monaghan, Jeffrey, and Kevin Walby. 2012. "Making Up 'Terror Identities': Security Intelligence, Canada's Integrated Threat Assessment Centre and Social Movement Suppression." *Policing and Society: An International Journal of Research and Policy,* 22 (2): 133–134.

Monture-Angus, Patricia. 1998. *Journeying Forward: Dreaming First Nations Independence.* Halifax, NS: Fernwood Publishing.

Moreton-Robinson, Aileen (ed.). 2007. *Sovereign Subjects: Indigenous Sovereignty Matters.* Sydney: Allan and Unwin.

____. 2003. "I still Call Australia Home: Indigenous Belonging and Place in a White Postcolonizing Society." In Sara S. Ahmed, Claudia Castañeda, Anne-Marie Fortier and Mimi Sheller (eds.), *Uprootings/Regroundings: Questions of Home and Migration,* 33–40. Oxford: Berg.

____. 2000. *Talkin' Up to the White Woman: Indigenous Women and Feminism.* Queensland: University of Queensland Press.

Morgensen, Scott. 2012. Theorising Gender, Sexuality and Settler Colonialism: An Introduction, *Settler Colonial Studie* 2 (2): 2–22.

____. 2011. "Un-Settling Settler Desires." *Unsettling America: Decolonization in Theory & Practice.* <unsettlingamerica.wordpress.com/2011/09/08/un-settling-settler-desires/>.

Morse, Bradford W. 2002. "An Overview of Canadian Aboriginal Law." *Native North American Almanac,* first edition, 510–16. Detroit: Gale Research Inc.

Nadasdy, Paul. 2003. *Hunters and Bureaucrats: Power, Knowledge, and the Restructuring of Aboriginal-State Relations in the Southwest Yukon, Canada.* Vancouver, BC: University of British Columbia Press.

Nader, Laura. 1997. "Controlling Processes: Tracing the Dynamic Components of Power." *Current Anthropology,* 38 (5): 187–213.

Native Languages of the Americas. 2009. "Native American Tribes of New York." Native Languages of the Americas website. <native-languages.org/york.htm>.

Nault, Robert, D. 1999. "Letter to Jerry Pickard Re: Caldwell Nation Land Claim" and attached report "Caldwell First Nation Land Claim: Canada's Response to Report of Jerry Pickard, M.P." Author received copy from Pickard's office.

Nedelsky, Jennifer. 1994. "The Puzzle and Demands of Modern Constitutionalism." *Ethics,* 104 (3): 500–15.

____. 1990. "Laws, Boundaries and the Bounded Self." *Representations* 30: 162–89.

____. 1989. "Reconceiving Autonomy: Sources, Thoughts and Possibilities." *Yale Journal of Law and Feminism* 1 (1): 7–16.

Newcomb, Steven T. 2008. *Pagans in the Promised Land: Decoding the Doctrine of Christian Discovery.* Golden, CO: Fulcrum Publishing.

Nicoll, Fiona. 2004a. "'Are You Calling Me a Racist?': Teaching Critical Whiteness Theory in Indigenous Sovereignty." *Borderlands* ejournal 3 (2). <borderlands.net.au/vol3no2_2004/nicoll_teaching.htm>.

____. 2004b. "Reconciliation In and Out of Perspective: White Knowing, Seeing, Curating, and Being at Home In and Against Indigenous Sovereignty." In Aileen Moreton-Robinson (ed.), *Whitening Race: Essays in Social and Cultural Criticism,* 19–29. Canberra: Aboriginal Studies Press.

NOON. 2010. "Neighbors of the Onondaga Nation: Working in Solidarity with the Onondaga Nation." Neighbors of the Onondaga Nation. <peacecouncil.net/NOON/index.html>.

O'Malley, Pat. 2004. *Risk, Uncertainty and Government.* London: Glasshouse Press.

Onondaga v. New York. 2007. Transcript of Proceedings. The Onondaga Nation, Plaintiffs, versus 05-CV-0314 the State of New York and Onondaga County, Defendants.

Onondaga Nation. 2014. "Onondaga Nation Files Second Historic Land Rights Case." Onondaga Nation press release. <onondaganation.org/news/2014/onondaga-nation-files-second-historic-land-rights-case/>.

_____. 2013. "Final Denial of Justice to the Onondaga Nation: United States Supreme Court Denies Certiorari." Onondaga Nation press release. <onondaganation.org/news/2013/final-denial-of-justice-to-the-onondaga-nation-united-states-supreme-court-denies-certiorari/>.

_____. 2007a. "Court Cases." Onondaga Nation. <onondaganation.org/gov/court.html>.

_____. 2007b. "History—Timeline." Onondaga Nation. <onondaganation.org/aboutus/timeline.html>.

_____. 2007c. "Land Claim FAQ." Onondaga Nation. <onondaganation.org/land/faq.html#aa>.

_____. 2007d. "Culture: Food." Onondaga Nation. <onondaganation.org/culture/food.html>.

_____. 2006. Plaintiff's Memorandum of Law in Opposition to Defendants' Motions to Dismiss United States District Court Northern District Court of New York. The Onondaga Nation, Onondaga Nation, Plaintiff, v. Civil Action No. 05-CV-314 (LEK/DRH). The State of New York, et al., Defendants. November 16.

_____. 2005a. "Onondaga Nation Announces Land Rights Action Promising No Evictions and No Casinos." Onondaga Nation. <onondaganation.org/news.press31005.html>.

_____. 2005b. First Amended Complaint for Declaratory Judgment. United States District Court Northern District of New York. Civil Action 05-CV-314 (LEK/DRH). Onondaga Nation vs. State of New York et al. August 1. <onondaganation.org/landclaims.briefs.html>.

_____. 2005c. "Onondaga Presses Forward with Land Rights Action Targeting Corporate Polluters." Onondaga Nation. <onondaganation.org/news.complaint2.html>.

Pagden, Anthony. 1995. *Lords of All the World: Ideologies of Empire in Spain, Britain, and France, c.150–c. 1800.* New Haven and London: Yale University Press.

Parekh, Bhiku. 1995. "Liberalism and Colonialism in Locke and Mill." In Jan Nederveen Pieterse and Bhiku Parekh (eds.), *Decolonization of Imagination: Culture, Knowledge and Power,* 81–98. London, UK: Zed Books.

Pasternak, Shiri. 2014. "Jurisdiction and Settler Colonialism: Where Do Laws Meet?" *Canadian Journal of Law and Society / Revue Canadienne Droit et Société,* 29: 145–161.

Pateman, Carol. 2007a. *The Settler Contract: Contract and Domination,* Carole Pateman and Charles Mills (eds.), 35–78. Cambridge: Polity Press.

Pearcey, Mark. 2013. "Civilization and the Expansion of International Society: An Inter-Societal Perspective." PhD thesis, Political Science, Carleton University, available

through Carleton University website. <carleton.ca/system/files/etd/add637a4-
1b4e-468e-9676-74faaae5fca1/etd_pdf/3705956e6365d757926510cb4db038f1/
pearcey-indigenouspeoplescivilizationandtheexpansion.pdf>.

Perina, Kaja. 2008. "Final Analysis: Kiki Smith on Creative Struggle." *Psychology Today.*
<psychologytoday.com/articles/200807/final-analysis-kiki-smith-creative-struggle>.

Phung, Melissa. 2011. "Are People of Colour Settlers, Too?" In Ashok Mathur, Mike
DeGagné and Jonathan Dewar (eds.), *Cultivating Canada: Reconciliation Through the
Lens of Cultural Diversity,* 289–99. Ottawa: Aboriginal Healing Foundation.

Povinelli, Elizabeth, A. 1993. *Labor's Lot: The Power, History, and Culture of Aboriginal Action.*
Chicago and London: University of Chicago Press.

Pratt, Anna, and Mariana Valverde. 2002. "From Deserving Victims to 'Masters of
Confusion': Redefining Refugees in the 1990s." *The Canadian Journal of Sociology* 27
(2): 135–61.

Pratt, Mary Louise. 1992. *Imperial Eyes: Travel Writing and Transculturation.* London and
NY: Routledge.

Razack, Sherene (ed.). 2002. *Race, Space and the Law: Unmapping a White Settler Society.*
Toronto: Between the Lines.

RCAP (Royal Commission on Aboriginal Peoples). 1996. *Report of the Royal Commission on
Aboriginal Peoples.* Minister of Supply and Services Canada. <aadnc-aandc.gc.ca/eng/
1100100014597/1100100014637?utm_source=sgmm_e.html&utm_medium=url>.

Reddy, Sanjay. 1996. "Claims to Expert Knowledge and the Subversion of Democracy: The
Triumph of Risk over Uncertainty." *Economy and Society,* 25 (2): 222–54.

Regan, Paulette. 2010. *Unsettling the Settler Within: Indian Residential Schools, Truth Telling,
and Reconciliation in Canada.* Vancouver: UBC Press.

____. 2005. "A Transformative Framework for Decolonizing Canada: A Non-
Indigenous Approach." <web.uvic.ca/igov/research/pdfs/A%20Transformative%20
Framework%20for%20Decolonizing%20Canada.pdf>.

Reyes Cruz, Mariolga. 2012. "Ni Con Dios ni con el Diablo: Tales of Survival, Resistance,
and Rebellion from a Reluctant Academic." *Decolonization: Indigeneity, Education
&Society,* 1 (1): 141–157.

Ridgetown Independent. 1999. Letter to the Editor. Author unidentified. March 11.

Rifkin, Mark. 2014. *Settler Common Sense: Queerness and Everyday Colonialism in the
American Renaissance.* Minneapolis and London: University of Minnesota Press.

____. 2013. "Settler Common Sense." *Settler Colonial Studies,* 3: 3–4.

____. 2011. "Settler States of Feeling: National Belonging and the Erasure of Native
American Presence." In Caroline F. Levander and Robert S. Levine (eds.), *A Companion
to American Literary Studies,* 342–355. Hoboken: Wiley-Blackwell.

____. 2009. *Manifesting America: The Imperial Construction of U.S. National Space.* Oxford:
Oxford University Press.

Ritskes, Eric. 2013. "The Terms of Engagement with Indigenous Nationhood." Blog associated
with the journal *Decolonization: Indigeneity, Education & Society.*.

Roehr, Sally, and Robert Roehr. 1999. Letter to editor. *Syracuse Post-Standard.*

Rose, Carol M. 2004. "Economic Claims and the Challenges of New Property." In Katherine
Verdery and Caroline Humphrey (eds.), *Property in Question: Value Transformations in*

the Global Economy, 275–96. Oxford and New York: Berg.

———. 1994. *Property and Persuasion: Essays on the History, Theory and Rhetoric of Ownership.* Boulder, CO: Westview.

Rossen, Jack. 2008. "Field School Archeology, Activism, and Politics in the Cayuga Homeland of Central New York." In Stephen W. Silliman (ed.), *Collaborating at the Trowel's Edge: Teaching and Learning in Indigenous Archeology*, 103–19. Tuscon, AZ: University of Arizona Press.

Said, Edward. 1994. *Culture and Imperialism*. Toronto: Random House of Canada.

Schwenger, Kathryn. 1999. "The Caldwell First Nation Land Claim in Historical Perspective." Report prepared for Jerry Pickard, M.P. Chatham-Kent—Essex, Sept 18.

Seed, Patricia. 2006 [1995]. *Ceremonies of Possession in Europe's Conquest of the New World, 1492–1640*. New York: Cambridge University Press.

Sehdev, Robinder Kaur. 2011. "People of Colour in Treaty." In Ashok Mathur, Jonathan Dewar and Mike DeGagne (eds.), *Cultivating Canada: Reconciliation Through the Lens of Cultural Diversity*. Ottawa: Aboriginal Healing Foundation.

Shore, Cris, and Susan Wright (eds.). 1997. *Anthropology of Policy: Critical Perspectives on Governance and Power.* NY: Routledge.

Silbey, Susan. 2005. "After Legal Consciousness." *Annual Review of Law and Social Science* 1: 323–68.

Silverstone, Roger. 1995. *Television and Everyday Life*. London: Routledge.

Simon, Roger I., Sharon Rosenberg and Claudia Eppert (eds.). 2000. *Between Hope and Despair: Pedagogy and the Remembrance of Historical Trauma*. Lanham: Rowman and Littlefield Publishers.

Simpson, Audra. 2014. *Mohawk Interruptus: Political Life Across the Borders of Settler States.* Durham: Duke University Press.

———. 2011. "Settlement's Secret." *Cultural Anthropology*, 26 (2): 205–217.

———. 2007. "On Ethnographic Refusal: Indigeneity, 'Voice,' and Colonial Citizenship." *Junctures*, 9: 67–80.

Simpson, Leanne. 2011. *Dancing on Our Turtle's Back: Stories of Nishnaabeg Re-creation, Resurgence and a New Emergence*. Winnipeg: Arbiter Ring Publishing.

——— (ed.). 2008. *Lighting the Eighth Fire: The Liberation, Resurgence and Protection of Indigenous Nations*. Winnipeg: Arbiter Ring Publishing.

Singer, Joseph. 2006. "Nine-Tenths of the Law: Title, Possession & Sacred Obligations." *Connecticut Law Review*, 38: 605–629.

Sium, Aman, Chandni Desai and Eric Ritskes. 2012. "Towards the 'Tangible Unknown': Decolonization and the Indigenous Future." *Decolonization: Indigeneity, Education & Society*, 1 (1): i–xiii (open access).

Smith, Andrea. 2013. "The Problem with 'Privilege.'" *Andrea366: The 18-Year Plan to End Global Oppression*. <andrea366.wordpress.com/2013/08/14/the-problem-with-privilege-by-andrea-smith/>.

———. 2012. "Indigeneity, Settler Colonialism, White Supremacy." In Daniel Martinez HoSang et al. (eds.), *Racial Formation in the Twenty-First Century*, 66–90. Berkley: University of California Press.

———. 2010. "Queer Theory and Native Studies: The Heteronormativity of Settler Colonialism." GLQ: *A Journal of Lesbian and Gay Studies*, 16 (1–2): 41–68.

Smith, Jo. 2013. "Maori Television's Indigenous Insistence." *Studies in Australasian Cinema*, 7 (2 & 3): 101–10.

_____. 2011. "Aotearoa/New Zealand: An Unsettled State in a Sea of Islands." *Settler Colonial Studies*, 1 (1): 111–131.

Smith, Linda Tuhiwai. 1999. *Decolonising Methodologies: Research and Indigenous Peoples.* London and New York: Zed Books.

Snelgrove, Corey, Rita Dhamoon and Jeff Corntassel. 2014. "Unsettling Settler Colonialism: The Discourse and Politics of Settlers, and Solidarity with Indigenous Nations." *Decolonization: Indigeneity, Education & Society,* 3 (2): 1–32 (open access).

St. Catherines Milling and Lumber Company v The Queen [1888] UKPC 70, [1888] 14 AC 46 (12 December).

Stasiulis, Daiva K., and Nira Yuval-Davis. 1995. *Unsettling Settler Societies: Articulations of Gender, Race, Ethnicity and Class.* London, U.K. and Thousand Oaks, CA: Sage.

Stogre, Michael, 2001. "Doctrine of Discovery and Terra Nullius. Presentation to General Synod." *Anglican Church of Canada and Evangelical Lutheran Church in Canada.* <www2. anglican.ca/gs2001/rr/presentations/terranullius.html>.

Street, Brian. 1993. "Culture Is a Verb." In David Graddol, Linda Thompson and Mike Byram (eds.), *Language and Culture,* 23–43. Clevedon, Avon: British Association for Applied Linguistics and Multilingual Matters.

Stremlau, Rose. 2005. "To Domesticate and Civilize Wild Indians: Allotment and the Campaign to Reform Indian Families, 1875–1887." *Journal of Family History,* 30 (3): 265–86.

Sugars, Cynthia (ed.). 2004. *Unhomely States: Theorizing English-Canadian Postcolonialism.* Peterborough, ON: Broadview Press.

Sugars, Cynthia, and Gerry Turcotte. 2009. *Unsettled Remains: Canadian Literature and the Postcolonial Gothic.* Kitchener-Waterloo: Wilfred Laurier University Press.

Sullivan, Shannon. 2006. *Revealing Whiteness: The Unconscious Habits of Racial Privilege.* Bloomington: Indiana University Press.

Supreme Court of the United States. 2005. Opinion of the Court, City of Sherrill, New York, Petitioner v. Oneida Indian Nation of New York et al. [544 U.S. 197]

Tejeda, Carlos. 2008. "Dancing with the Dilemmas of a Decolonizing Pedagogy." *Radical History Review,* 102: 27–31.

Thobani, Sunera. 2007. *Exalted Subjects: Studies in the Making of Race and Nation in Canada.* Toronto: University of Toronto Press.

Tomlins, C. 2007. "Review of Sovereignty and Possession in the English New World: The Legal Foundations of Empire, 1576–1640 by Ken MacMillan." *Reviews in History.* <history.ac.uk/reviews/ paper/tomlins.html>.

Truth and Reconciliation Commission of Canada (TRC). 2015. *Honouring the Truth, Reconciling for the Future. Summary of the Final Report of the Truth and Reconciliation Commission of Canada.* Truth and Reconciliation Commission of Canada.

Tsilhqot'in Nation v. British Columbia, 2014 Supreme Court of Canada SCC 44, [2014] 2 S.C.R. 256 Date: 20140626 Docket: 34986. <scc-csc.lexum.com/scc-csc/scc-csc/ en/14246/1/>.

Tuck, Eve, and K. Wayne Yang. 2012. "Decolonization Is Not a Metaphor." *Decolonization: Indigeneity, Education & Society* 1 (1): 2–40.

Tully, James. 2008. *Public Philosophy in a New Key: Volume 2, Imperialism and Civic Freedom.* Cambridge, UK: Cambridge University Press.

———. 2000a. "Reconsidering the BC Treaty Process." Paper Presented at Speaking Truth to Power: A Treaty Forum. Vancouver, BC.

———. 1995. *Strange Multiplicity: Constitutionalism in an Age of Diversity.* Cambridge: Cambridge University Press.

———. 1994. "Aboriginal Property and Western Theory: Recovering a Middle Ground." *Social Philosophy and Policy* 11: 153–80.

Turner, Dale. 2006. *This Is Not a Peace Pipe.* Toronto: University of Toronto Press.

Turner-Strong, Pauline, and Barrik Van Winkle. 1993. "Tribe and Nation: American Indians and American Nationalism." *Social Analysis: The International Journal of Social and Cultural Practice* 33, *Nations, Colonies and Metropoles:* 9–26.

UBCIC (Union of BC Indian Chiefs). 2014a. Resolution no. 2014-29 RE: Rejection of Federal Interim Policy "Renewing the Comprehensive Land Claims Policy: Towards a Framework for Addressing Section 35 Aboriginal Rights."

———. 2014b. October 3, Letter to Honourable Bernard Valcourt Minister, Aboriginal Affairs and Northern Development Canada RE: Rejection of Federal Interim Policy "Renewing the Comprehensive Land Claims Policy: Towards a Framework for Addressing Section 35 Aboriginal Rights."

———. 2012. "Certainty: Canada's Struggle to Extinguish Aboriginal Title." 13 March. Union of BC Indian Chiefs. <ubcic.bc.ca/Resources/certainty.htm#axzz1ownSFWKx>.

UCE (Upstate Citizens for Equality). 1999. "The Cayuga Indians and Their Land Claim." Upstate Citizens for Equality. <upstate-citizens.org/cayugaclaim.htm>.

Valaskakis, Gail Guthrie. 2005. *Indian Country: Essays on Contemporary Native Culture.* Waterloo: Wilfrid Laurier University Press.

Veracini, Lorenzo. 2011. "Introducing Settler Colonial Studies." *Settler Colonial Studies* 1 (1): 1–12.

———. 2007. "Settler Colonialism and Decolonisation." *Borderlands* 6 (2). <borderlands.net. au/vol6no2_2007/veracini_settler.htm>.

Verdery, Katherine, and Caroline Humphrey (eds.). 2004. *Property in Question: Value Transformations in the Global Economy.* Oxford and New York: Berg.

Wakeham, Pauline. 2012. "Reconciling 'Terror': Managing Indigenous Resistance in the Age of Apology." *American Indian Quarterly,* 36 (1): 1–33.

Waldron, Jeremy. 1990. *The Right to Private Property.* Oxford, UK: Clarendon Press.

Wandres, Patrick W. 2006–7. "Indian Land Claims: Sherrill and the Impending Legacy of the Doctrine of Laches." *American Indian Law Review* 31 (1): 131–42.

Watson, A. (ed.). 1985. *The Digest of Justinian,* Vol. 1 (with Latin text ed. T. Mommsen and P. Krüger). Philadelphia, PA: University of Pennsylvania Press.

Watson, Blake A. 2006. "John Marshall and Indian Land Rights: A Historical Rejoinder to the Claim of 'Universal Recognition' of the Doctrine of Discovery." *Seton Hall Law Review* 36 (2): 481–550.

Waziyatawin. 2012. "The Paradox of Indigenous Resurgence at the End of Empire." *Decolonization: Indigeneity, Education &Society,* 1 (1): 68–85.

Weaver, John C. 2003. *The Great Land Rush and the Making of the Modern World, 1650–1900.* Montreal: McGill Queen's University Press.

____. 1999. "Frontiers into Assets: The Social Construction of Property in New Zealand, 1840–65." *The Journal of Imperial and Commonwealth History* 27 (3): 17–54.

Weiner, Mark. 2012. "Onondaga Nation Leaders Visit D.C. with Historic Treasure, Wampum Belt from George Washington." *The Post-Standard*, February 28. <syracuse.com/news/index.ssf/2012/02/onondaga_nation_leaders_visit.html>.

____. 2015. "HUD Tries to Give Away Federal Money, but Onondaga Nation Says No Thanks." *The Post-Standard*, March 09. <syracuse.com/news/index.ssf/2015/03hud_tries_to_give_away_federal_money_but_onondaga_nation_says_no_thanks.html>.

Weir, Allison. 2008. "Home and Identity: In Memory of Iris Marion Young." *Hypatia*, 23 (3): 4–21.

Whaley, Rick, and Walter Bresette. 1994. *Walleye Warriors: An Effective Alliance Against Racism and for the Earth.* Philadelphia, PA and Gabriola Island, BC: New Society Publishers.

Wildcat, Matthew, Stephanie Irlbacher-Fox, Glen Coulthard and Mandee McDonald (eds.). 2014. "Learning From the Land: Indigenous Land Based Pedagogy and Decolonization." In Special Issue on Indigenous Land-Based Education: *Decolonization: Indigeneity, Education and Society,* 3 (3). <decolonization.org/index.php/des/issue/view/1584/showToc>.

Willman, Elaine Devary, and Kamie Christensen Biehl. 2005. *Going to Pieces: The Dismantling of the United States of America.* Toppenish, WA: Equilocus Press.

Wolfe, Patrick. 2013. "Recuperating Binarism: a Heretical Introduction." *Settler Colonial Studies,* 3 (3-4): 257–279.

____. 2006. "Settler Colonialism and the Elimination of the Native." *Journal of Genocide Research,* 8 (4): 387–409.

____. 1999. *Settler Colonialism and the Transformation of Anthropology: The Politics and Poetics of an Ethnographic Event.* London: Cassell.

Wright, Cynthia, and Nandita Sharma. 2008–9. "Response to Lawrence and Dua—Decolonizing Resistance." *Social Justice,* 35 (3): 120–138. <socialjusticejournal.org/archive/113_35_3/113_07Sharma.pdf>.

Wright, Susan. 1998. "The Politicisation of 'Culture.'" *Anthropology Today* 14 (1): 7–15.

Young, Iris Marion. 2002. "House and Home: Feminist Variations on a Theme." In Constance L. Mui and Julien S. Murphy (eds.), *Gender Struggles: Practical Approaches to Contemporary Feminism,* 314–46. Lanham, MD: Rowman and Littlefield.

____. 2001. "Two Concepts of Self-Determination." In Austin Sarat and Thomas R. Kearns (eds.), *Human Rights: Concepts, Contests and Contingencies,* 25–44. Michigan, MI: University of Michigan Press.

Yu, Henry. 2011. "Nurturing Dialogues Between First Nations, Urban Aboriginal, and Immigrant Communities in Vancouver." In Ashok Mathur, Jonathan Dewar and Mike DeGagne (eds.), *Cultivating Canada: Reconciliation Through the Lens of Cultural Diversity.* Ottawa: Aboriginal Healing Foundation.

Zemblyas, Michalinos, and Megan Boler. 2002. "On the Spirit of Patriotism: Challenges of a Pedagogy of Discomfort." *Teachers College Record,* 11007. <tcrecord.org/library>.

INDEX